STAFF RELATIONSHIPS IN THE PRIMARY S

Staff Relationships in the Primary School:

A Study of Organizational Cultures

Jennifer Nias
Geoff Southworth and
Robin Yeomans

CASSELL

Cassell Educational Limited
Villiers House
41/47 Strand
London WC2N 5JE

First published 1989
Reprinted 1993

British Library Cataloguing-in-Publication Data

Nias, Jennifer
  Staff relationships in the primary school: a study
  of organizational cultures.
  1. Primary schools. Teachers. Interpersonal
  relationships with colleagues
  I. Title II. Southworth, Geoff III. Yeomans, Robin
  372.11′04

ISBN 0–304–31693–8

Phototypeset by Input Typesetting Ltd, London
Printed in Great Britain at Redwood Books, Trowbridge

Contents

Acknowledgements

We gratefully acknowledge the financial assistance of the Economic and Social Research Council (Ref. No. C0925 0003) and the Cambridge Institute of Education which made possible the research (The Primary Schools Staff Relationships Project) on which this book is based. We could not, however, have undertaken it or carried it through without the cheerful co-operation and forbearance of the school staffs whose practice we have reported. We are very grateful to the headteachers, teachers and ancillary staff in the schools where we worked and wish that we could thank them under their real names rather than through the pseudonyms by which they are known in this book. We enjoyed working with them and learnt much from them.

We would also like to thank our colleagues at the Cambridge Institute of Education for discussing our ideas with us as they emerged and for the encouragement and formative comment we received from: Alan Blyth, Jim Campbell, Tricia David, Alan Fox and Andrew Pollard. Headteachers and members of staff from the project schools and advisers and inspectors from the local authorities also helped us extend and clarify our thinking, through their participation in seminars at the Cambridge Institute of Education. We are grateful to them for sharing in this endeavour.

This book would never have been published without the patience and unstinting help of Angie Ashton, Rita Harvey, Mavis Hulford and Fiona Wiedeking. We are deeply indebted to them and to all those other people who put so much painstaking work into transcribing, typing, editing and duplicating.

Our families put up with a great deal while we were writing first the case studies and then this book. Probably the best way in which we can thank them for all they have done, and refrained from doing, is to finish it as quickly as we can.

Finally, we would like to express our gratitude to each other. Neither multi-site case study nor multiple authorship is easy, but we are glad that we undertook them and that we have been able to work together and learn from each other. Our collaboration has been a source of strength and pleasure to us all.

Preface

In recent years school management has often been advanced as a panacea. As a result, management courses for headteachers, deputy heads and curriculum co-ordinators have burgeoned. Many of these courses are essentially practical, being designed and taught by advisers/inspectors, practising headteachers and in-service tutors. Whilst course planners have undoubtedly benefited from participants' knowledge of primary schools and of headship, such courses lack a sound basis of research into primary schools as organizations upon which to draw. We believe our project (Primary School Staff Relationships Project: Economic and Social Research Council, Ref. No. C0925 0003) goes some way towards filling this gap, by providing a set of insights into primary schools as organizations in which adults work with one another as well as with children. We hope course planners, heads, teachers and officers of the local education authorities will set these insights alongside their personal knowledge and experience of primary schools. We believe that they contain a number of implications for primary school organization and management which will be helpful in the in-service education of headteachers, teachers and ancillary staff.

We also feel that tutors of courses for, and students in, pre-service education will find useful the light that this book throws upon schools, as distinct from classrooms. It is our experience that many future teachers still· receive an education which prepares them to work in classrooms with children but not in schools with headteachers and their fellow staff, teaching and ancillary.

Our research demonstrates that although many primary schools are small, they are not simple. To understand them as organizations of adults one must be able to perceive their formal and informal structures and the ways in which these are maintained, to recognize the symbols in which they abound, to interpret and speak the language used by the staff, much of which has meanings intelligible only to an insider. In short, one must penetrate and make sense of their organizational cultures. Yet coming to perceive, to know, to understand and, finally, to participate in a school's culture is neither a swift nor a straightforward process. It requires an intimate knowledge of the school and its staff, based upon an awareness of the significance of many features: history; buildings; organizational arrangements; patterns of interaction; individual people; talk; humour; the distribution of authority and influence; the identity and behaviour of leaders. Over a period of time, familiarity with these features begins to reveal the shared meanings and norms of the staff and the beliefs and values which underlie them. One cannot understand a school from brief and infrequent visits to it. Primary schools are best comprehended through the personal knowledge which comes from living and working in them and which results from careful observation over time.

Yet there are few descriptions of primary schools as organizations which reveal this kind of intimate knowledge, and only one which uses the notion of culture to express it: Waller's (1932; 1961 edn) classic study of American schooling which still offers many contemporary insights to English primary teachers. To be sure, Handy (1984) and Handy and Aitken (1986) use the concept in discussing school management in both secondary and primary schools, and Goodchild and Holly (1989) describe a secondary school in terms of its culture. But none of these books helps one to understand the organizational cultures of particular primary schools. Nor can many inferences be drawn from published work on staff relationships. Jackson (1964) paints a vivid picture of some aspects of staffroom life in one primary school, as part of a wider account of the organization of children's learning. Many years on it still provides a rich and insightful picture of the complex interaction which exists in schools between beliefs, values and adult behaviour. More recent studies by Hartley (1985), Pollard (1985) and Nias (1989b) describe some of the divisive characteristics and effects of staff sub-groups. Other insights into schools as organizations of adults can be derived from Yeomans (1985), Pollard (1987) and Nias (1989b). In addition, Sharp and Green (1975), King (1978) and Berlak and Berlak (1981) paint pictures of teachers' classroom behaviour from which inferences about schools may be drawn. But apart from Waller (1932; 1961 edn) only Riches (1984) discusses the part played in primary schools by ancillary staff.

Not surprisingly, given the dearth of ethnographic evidence, the literature on the organization and management of primary schools tends, with the exception of Open University (1988), to be based on either secondary school studies or prescriptions designed originally for business and industry. Publications relating to the management of primary schools are concerned almost entirely with headteachers; very little attention is paid to the role of deputies or of curriculum co-ordinators (see Chapter 6 for references to work on leadership in primary schools). Virtually no suggestion is made in any published work on school management that staff relationships might be the responsibility not just of the headteacher but also of teachers.

This book therefore breaks new ground in three respects. It provides ethnographic descriptions of staff relationships in five medium-sized English primary schools. At the same time, it interprets these relationships in terms of organizational culture. Finally, it suggests ways in which courses in pre-service and in-service teacher education might be modified to take account of the insights we provide.

Chapter 1 describes the methods which were used to gather and analyse the evidence reported in this book and establishes our understanding of the term 'culture'. Chapter 2 describes the individual schools as we first encountered them, while Chapter 3 looks at those aspects of their life and organization which had most impact upon the development of cultures within them. Chapter 4 analyses the culture which was dominant in three of the schools and which, we suggest, made collaboration among the staff in those schools a taken-for-granted, unexceptional affair. Chapter 5 suggests how this culture was developed and maintained and Chapter 6 examines the key role played in all of this by leadership. Chapter 7 picks up and examines in detail the related notions of change and continuity. Chapter 8 returns to the idea, briefly noted in Chapters 3 and 4, that disagreement is endemic even within schools with strong cultures and examines how in these schools it was contained or resolved. Chapter 9 summarizes the implications of our work for an understanding of schools as organizations and for teacher education courses, with particular reference to the changes resulting from, or likely to result from, the Education Acts of 1986 and 1988.

For the families of us all and for all of our families

Chapter 1

Researching and Understanding the Schools

In this chapter we first describe and discuss the background to the research, the methods we used to gather and analyse evidence about primary schools as organizations of adults and about the staff's relationships with one another. We then give an account of the term 'culture' which, in the form of organizational culture, is the main concept that we have used throughout this book to interpret and organize our evidence.

RESEARCH AIMS AND METHODOLOGY

Background to the Research

During the 1980s teachers began to be under increasing pressure to move outside their classrooms and to become involved in school-wide curriculum planning, development and implementation. Educationalists such as Campbell (1985), Richards (1986), Tomlinson (1986) and Thomas (1987) advocated 'collegial' ways of working. HM Inspectorate, the Department of Education and Science, local government officers and politicians talked of 'co-ordination', 'collaboration', 'whole school plans' and the development within schools of combined teaching units (DES, 1985; ILEA, 1985; House of Commons Select Committee, 1986; DES, 1987). Further, when, in response to the Education Act 1981, greater numbers of children with special educational needs began to appear in ordinary classrooms, the hitherto largely unrecognized significance of teachers' relationships with ancillary and support staff increasingly became evident. Yet none of the advocates of collegiality, collaboration or whole-school development succeeded in showing what these phenomena looked like in practice, how headteachers, teachers and ancillaries behaved when they 'worked together', or what kinds of organizational structures or behaviour enabled them to do so. Furthermore, as we indicated in the Preface, there is no published work on staff relationships or on primary schools as organizations which throws any convincing light on any of these topics.

The authors of this book, all of whom have been primary teachers (two of us headteachers) and two of whom worked with teachers and headteachers on in-service courses, became increasingly aware of the gap which was opening up between the prescriptions of educationalists and the public knowledge available to teacher educators and administrators. Yet the research reported in this book was deliberately limited in scope. Our intention, put in everyday terms, was to document and interpret inter-adult relationships in a small number of schools in which the staff felt that they worked well together. In the absence of any other fine-grained analysis of staff relationships and of the structures which shape and support them we decided to limit our enquiries to schools where, in very loose terms, 'things were going well'. One does not, we felt, lay the foundations for a new body of professional knowledge by starting with its pathologies. Moreover, it was unlikely that any staff group conscious of personal or professional divisions would allow us access to sensitive areas of their institutional lives.

We deliberately left unresolved further questions of definition. In the first place we did not know, and wanted to discover, what staff themselves meant by 'working together'. To have used our own interpretations of that term would have been to place artificial restrictions upon the limits of our subsequent understanding. Similarly we wished to 'ground' (Glaser and Strauss, 1967) our insights into the meanings attributed by participants to 'good' staff relationships and the purposes they served, and not to impose our preconceptions upon them.

We did not set out to explore or report on classroom practice. We accept that the main business of schools is the education of children and that unless the behaviour of the staff towards one another results eventually in more effective teaching it could be said to be of peripheral importance. But we made the deliberate decision not to address the issue of the relationship between staffrooms and classrooms, believing that the time and personnel that we had available would be best employed in attempting to understand schools as settings in which adults work. We have however argued, especially in Chapters 4 and 6, that the ways in which headteachers and staff related to one another were often educational in intent. Although as organizations primary schools have some features in common with, for example, offices, restaurants, hospitals or garages, unlike any of these their main purpose is education, a fact reflected in many aspects of the ways in which they are structured and run.

Three other points need to be made clear. First, our account does less than justice to the density of the adult population of the schools in which we worked. We have omitted a number of key ancillary workers (principally cleaners, cooks and dinner supervisors), several regular visitors from the educational support services (e.g., mother-tongue language teachers, educational psychologists) or other social services (e.g., social workers, medical officers), volunteers (parent and non-parent), students, parents (and grandparents, even though these were a regular part of classroom and sometimes staffroom life), governors (also frequently to be seen in and around the schools) and intermittent visitors such as inspectors, education officers, health and welfare officers, policemen and representatives of publishing and equipment companies. The constant presence of these and other adults complicated the picture we have presented in two respects. It meant that staff had more people to interact with, more often than our evidence suggests, and it added to the amount and kind of change that characterized the schools (see Chapter 7).

Second, by omitting almost all mention of the schools' most important members, its pupils, and by virtually ignoring the impact of their parents, and of the schools' governors, we may have created the impression that these people had little or no influence upon the culture of the schools or upon the ways in which their staffs behaved. Once again, our impression was that this was not the case, but we have not attempted to document the ways in which the various participants influenced one another. To use a zoological analogy, we have chosen to put a specific slice of tissue from a largely unexamined organism under the research microscope, but this does not mean that we are or were unaware that this fragment is taken from a living institution all of whose parts are connected in complex, mutually interacting ways. Case studies of relationships between pupils, staff, headteachers, governors, parents and community members in and surrounding individual primary schools remain to be undertaken by ethnographic fieldworkers with a taste for complexity and the capacity to unravel and make sense of many intricate threads and patterns.

Finally, we decided to limit our enquiries to schools with between five and 12 teaching staff (including the headteacher), a caretaker, a secretary and at least one other ancillary. We were aware that size might affect the extent and nature of inter-adult interaction in both much larger and much smaller schools but since about half of all children of primary school age in England and Wales attend schools with this number of teaching staff (DES, 1985) it seemed the logical place in which to start.

Finding the Schools and Negotiating Entry

As a first step towards locating suitable schools, we approached seven local education authorities (that is, normally primary advisers or inspectors) and asked them to suggest up to four schools which offered a 'positive model of adult relationships'. We did not follow up certain of their suggestions since some schools faced unusual circumstances in the forthcoming year, such as a major building project or a change of headteacher. Others were too far away to make possible the observation of before- and after-school activities, given that although Robin Yeomans, as Research Fellow, worked full-time on the project, Geoff Southworth and Jennifer Nias were able to commit only a notional one day a week to the research (though in the event, it was considerably more than this). This left 12 schools, all of which we visited twice, once to make initial enquiries and again to explain our purposes to the staff in greater detail and to ask if we could work there.

We met all the staff, teaching and ancillary, told them that the local education authority had described their school as offering a 'positive model of adult relationships' and that we wanted to become members of staff, albeit temporary and part-time, for an academic year, in order to study the ways in which they worked together. We answered their questions as fully as we could and explained that they stood to benefit by having the use of an extra pair of free hands for a year. We then left them to reach a decision as to whether or not they would be willing to open themselves up, as a staff, to our enquiries. None refused, so we chose six schools which represented as broad a cross-section as possible of characteristics which from everyday experience we thought might turn out to be important. Apart from their size (one school was Group 3, one Group 5 and four were Group 4), the schools varied considerably in terms such as: local authority, catchment area, type of building, length of experience of heads and most staff members, numbers of men and women, numbers of part-time staff. Further details are given in Table 1 and fuller descriptions of the schools in Chapter 2. Overall, we were repeatedly struck not so much by the schools' similarities as by the differences between them. Despite the generalizations which we eventually felt able to make and which form the substance of this book, each school was unique and membership of its staff had to be both learned and earned.

Table 1.1. *School Details*

	SCHOOLS					
	Sedgemoor	Lowmeadow	Greenfields	Hutton	Lavender Way	School 6
1. Male head			√	√		√
2. Female head	√	√			√	
3. Head's time in school	10 yrs	18 yrs	18 yrs	5 yrs	1½ yrs	5 yrs
4. Head's experience	18 yrs	18 yrs	18 yrs	10 yrs	1½ yrs	11 yrs
5. School size group	4	4	3	5	4	4
6. Staff group size*	8.3(3)	7.5(6)	5.7(3)	9.8(3)	8(3)	9(3)
7. Gender	F 6.3(3) M 2 (0)	F 7.5(6) M 0 (0)	F 3.7(3) M 2	F 7.8(2) M 2 (1)	F 7(2) M 1(1)	F 6(2) M 3(1)
8. Most staff more than 15 years' experience		√	√			√
9. Most staff less than 15 years' experience	√			√	√	
10. Open Plan	√				√	
11. Cellular		√	√	√		√
12. Denominational				C. of E. (VA)		
13. Urban	√	√				√
14. Rural			√			
15. Surburban				√	√	
16. Infant School		√				
17. Junior School				√		√
18. 5–11 Primary	√		√			
19. 5–9 First school					√	
20. Special features		Multi-cultural population	Community primary			S.P.A.

* First figure = teachers including head.

Figure in brackets = ancillary, caretaking, secretarial expressed as 'workers', many part-time.

We committed ourselves to an ethical stance which would give each staff member, teaching and ancillary, the right to veto use of any interview material for which he/she was responsible and any particularly sensitive observations in which he/she was involved. This decision was made both because of our own commitment to overt research and because we felt headteachers and staff members would welcome the safeguards it offered. In the event, hardly anyone in five of the six schools in which we subsequently worked chose to exercise this option. However towards the end of the year's fieldwork we agreed not to use material from the sixth school, because we were unable to agree with the head and some of the staff a version of particular events which satisfied both the researcher and the participants.

This statement creates, of course, a Catch-22 situation for readers and for ourselves as authors: if we explain what happened, we breach our contract with the staff of that school, and if we do not, we leave readers free to imagine that we have chosen to report only 'good relationships'. We must therefore ask readers to accept two assurances: the particular circumstances that led to our withdrawal from the school were unusual but, in other respects, what we heard and observed over almost a full year there was consistent with the generalizations that we have made in the rest of this book.

Collecting, Analysing and Checking the Evidence

Each school deployed us in ways that suited the staff of that school. Between us we team-taught, acted as supply teachers and ancillaries, attended meetings, participated in school camps and journeys, helped with plays, assemblies and displays, joined in extra-curricular activities such as staff parties, cricket matches and summer fairs. Sometimes we worked for a day a week, at others we were in particular schools for one, two or three weeks at a time. Both patterns had advantages and disadvantages to the schools and to ourselves as researchers. On average, we spent about 60 days in each school. It could be argued that this was not a long enough time to allow us to become members of staff, that as would-be participant–observers, we could be the latter, but not the former (McCall and Simmons, 1969). This length of time is, however, the same as that worked by many supply teachers or, put another way, it represents almost a full term, equivalent to the span of many temporary contracts. Nor, given the fleeting nature of contact between staff in some schools, is it dissimilar to the experience of many permanent part-time teachers. Certainly, as we describe below, we all felt that we 'became' full staff members. Further, the fact that we spent an academic year in the schools meant that we saw the staff and shared their experience during periods characterized by different types of activity and levels of intensity.

The methods we used for the collection and recording of evidence were standard to ethnographic research (see e.g., Hammersley and Atkinson, 1983; Burgess, 1984; Walker, 1986). We studied documents (e.g., governors' reports; school brochures; curriculum guidelines). Throughout the year we made observations, using small unobtrusive notebooks for jottings of key words and incidents which were transformed every evening into long, reflective fieldnotes. Then towards the end of year (though before then in exceptional circumstances, e.g., when staff changes occurred) we interviewed all staff members. All but one of these interviews were tape-recorded (with participants' permission), transcripts (or in two cases summaries)were made and individuals had the opportunity to alter, add to or delete material from these before we made further use of what they had said. Almost all the interviews took place in school, many during school time. They were loosely structured round key questions specific to the circumstances of each school, but interviewees were encouraged to talk freely and for as long as they wished. They also had the right to turn off the tape-recorder. Interviews varied in length from 40 minutes to two hours.

Although it took varying lengths of time for us to be absorbed into different schools, and although it would be naive to claim that our presence did not affect staff interactions and relationships, we felt both that the staff in all the schools allowed us to be as unobtrusive as we individually wished and that we were accepted by them. For much of the academic year, for much of the time, the ancillary and teaching staff of an individual school appeared to forget that we were researchers — until the tape-recorders appeared. Indispensable as the interviews were in offering fresh perspectives and new information, they were sometimes more self-conscious and perhaps therefore more constrained than informal conversations held in the corridor, the staffroom or the teaching area. But this was not always the case; sometimes they were conducted in the spirit of, and experienced as, extended discussions between two colleagues, one of whom was seeking better to understand the other's perspective on particular topics. All in all, we frequently had to struggle against the temptation (often noted in the literature on qualitative research) to 'go native'. As we became members of staff, it was increasingly difficult not to identify so closely with the schools that the cutting edge of our observations and analysis was blunted. To become an insider is to risk losing the outsider's ability to record and comment with detachment, yet until we became insiders there were things that we failed to perceive and much that we did not understand. In this respect, our full-time researcher was at an advantage; he found that moving from school to school helped him to combine an outsider's perspective with an insider's understanding.

It will be clear that we rapidly began to accumulate what ended up as a formidable mass of evidence — school documents, our own handwritten or dictated fieldnotes, transcripts or validated summaries of interviews. To begin with we recorded a tremendous amount every day, being unsure what was or would prove to be relevant or significant. Soon however, using 'progressive focusing' (Parlett and Hamilton, 1977), we began to look more closely at specific phenomena which at different times and in different schools seemed particularly important.

So, in one sense analysis of the evidence began almost as soon as its collection. Our regular team meetings helped this dual process. Once a month we met for about three hours and talked to one another about our fieldwork and the ideas it had generated for us. In these meetings we supported each other through periods of uncertainty and difficulty and stimulated one another's interest and perception.

Yet the most difficult part of our analysis was undertaken independently and alone. At the end of the year's fieldwork we wrote individual case studies for each of the schools, and only after these were completed did we read what the others had written. Thus every one of the studies reflects, as accurately as its author could ensure, the circumstances of that school. The particular analytic categories which we used in each study were grounded in the evidence (Glaser and Strauss, 1967) and this in turn was unique to each school.

We all tended to use the same general method in analysing the evidence from 'our' schools. Broad themes were suggested by what we saw and heard in the course of our fieldwork, though an awareness of particular ideas was sharpened by our regular discussions. Having decided on a theme, we proceeded in a well-established fashion

(Schatzman and Strauss, 1973; Hammersley and Atkinson, 1983). We progressively re-sorted the evidence, refining the categories which appeared from it, looking for contradictions and negative instances and using these to help in the process of clarification. Only when categories were 'saturated' (that is, when new evidence contributed nothing further to our understanding of them) did we accept that they represented as nearly as we could contrive the realities which the staff of the school were experiencing. Our final check in this respect came when we took what we had written back to the schools for validation. We knew that, as qualitative researchers, we would often 'provide a language for speaking about that which is not normally spoken about' (Hargreaves, 1978, p. 19). But we had also agreed that if the staff did not recognize the phenomena we had 'named', it was more likely to be us than them who were wrong. We accepted Elliott's (1981) proposition that the most powerful validation for case studies comes from participants, and although we had been part of the schools in the previous year, at the time of writing we were not. This is not to suggest that we unquestioningly accepted the perspectives on particular events which were advanced by individuals or groups within the schools. The themes we used and the interpretations we made, though grounded in the evidence and discussed with staff, are ultimately ours.

When we took the draft case studies back to the schools for validation, we gave individuals the chance to check for accuracy substantial observations in which they were involved and to veto the use of material (e.g., from interviews) which they had contributed. We also invited them to comment upon our interpretations and the meanings we had attributed to words, events and behaviours. As with the transcripts, very few took advantage of these opportunities and it is, in our view, a tribute to the resilience of the staff individually and collectively that we were able to portray them substantially as we saw and understood them, warts and all.

During the final research stage, the fruits of which are presented in this book, the three of us compared and contrasted our validated case studies, looking for common themes and overarching concepts. We also discussed our emerging ideas with 'critical friends' from schools, local authorities and the academic community. Further details of our methodology, of the ethical problems that we encountered and of the ways in which we attempted to overcome them are available in Nias (1987c); Southworth (1987c); Yeomans (1987b). We also need to make it clear that we have had considerable difficulty in selecting for the purposes of this book from the mass of evidence which we accumulated during 12 months' study of five schools. We have restricted the number and quantity of illustrative examples and ask the reader to accept that many more remain unused. The case studies, produced by the Cambridge Institute of Education, are listed in the Bibliography as Nias (1986), Southworth (1986), Yeomans (1986c, 1987a, 1987c).

In one sense this methodological account is not only brief but misleading, for it gives an illusory picture of tidy thinking and precise analysis. In fact, as we worked out our plans for each case study and as we struggled, individually and together, to make sense of the accumulated evidence, we were muddled, frustrated, tortuous and repetitive, discarding as much material and almost as many ideas as we finally included. Moreover, the process of writing imposes a false order upon the evidence because it requires that one tries to represent a shifting, multi-dimensional reality in linear patterns of words. Hoyle (1986) reminds us that organizational theorists seeking to describe schools have tended to fall back on metaphors. We have added our own to those that already exist, finding in the visual image of a suspended mobile a more satisfactory way of describing the complexities, changes and delicate balances of primary schools than words alone appear to offer (see Chapter 9).

Typicality and Relevance

There was one sense in which our time in the schools was clearly atypical. During 1985–6, the teacher unions were in dispute with the government over a pay award and a review of conditions of service. The larger unions had instructed their members to withdraw 'good will' (e.g., teachers were advised not to attend after-school or lunchtime meetings, not to undertake additional duties during lunchtimes or in the evenings and not to attend extra-curricular events). In addition they had called a series of one-day strikes. These events affected our research in two ways. They limited it, because we were able to participate in fewer than normal staff meetings and saw very little formal activity on the part of curriculum co-ordinators (e.g., leading workshops after school). However, in other respects union action proved beneficial, since it threw into relief certain strains in relationships which might otherwise have remained beneath the surface of staffroom life and, in the process, highlighted the means that were used to disperse or deal with them.

In addition, the concepts and ideas that we present in the following chapters have been generated from the study of particular schools as cases and are necessarily tentative. It is left to our readers to compare the cameos and analyses that we present with their own knowledge and experience and to see whether our interpretations throw light on their own worlds. Yet although we make no claim for the typicality of the project schools or for our time in them, we feel it is important to stress that none was chosen because it was felt to be a 'show place' or because its staff was a community of saints. In the first place the project schools were not sheltered from the familiar pressures of institutional life. Leaving union action aside, in one school or another the staff encountered during the year: vandalism, theft, a break-in by an ex-pupil; over-large classes and cramped accommodation; absences, staff shortages or changes (including the return of one headteacher from a year's study leave and two changes of deputy); the potentially severe illness and subsequent absence of one head; disagreements with parents and, in one instance, a parent–governor; the start of disciplinary procedures against a caretaker; a local authority decision to terminate the contract of one teacher, and one school's decision not to renew the temporary contract of two others. As part-time teachers we experienced stress, illness and fatigue, but these states were as nothing in comparison with the exhaustion which we repeatedly observed among the full-time staff (especially towards the ends of terms). Secondly, that they behaved as they did in the face of these and similar pressures is, we suggest, a reflection not so much on any inherent qualities which they possessed as on the staffroom climates in which they worked. We agree with Sarason (1982, p. 211) that the 'characteristics of individuals are always, to some extent, a reflection of the setting in which these characteristics were manifested'.

Notwithstanding these disclaimers, we are aware that we may have given the impression in this book that the schools whose staff relationships we studied were archetypal representatives of the 'cosy' institutions portrayed by much of the progress-ive educational literature of the 1950s and 1960s and implicitly attacked by the work of academics such as Sharp and Green (1975) and King (1978). We have tried to make it clear that in our view this was not the case. Disagreements occurred among the staff but the latter had evolved ways of confronting and resolving these and of turning individual differences to constructive educational effect (see Chapter 8). One of the problems of trying to understand the practice of any occupational skill is that expert practitioners make their work seem easy. To us, as people who have been privileged to spend a good deal of time in many primary schools, it was clear that these staffs were exercising a wide range of interpersonal, pedagogic and political skills in purposeful and positive ways and were not myopically refusing to perceive and confront the disagreeable.

What this book does not seek to do therefore is to offer an *apologia* for a familiar 'ideal' type of primary school or, by implication, to offer prescriptions for inter-adult practice in other schools. It can, however, be seen to have contemporary relevance. In addressing an area of professional practice which has been virtually ignored by educational writers it translates what has hitherto been represented as intangible (being described, for instance, as 'atmosphere', 'ethos' or 'good relationships') into the details of day-to-day practice. Much of our evidence concerns the apparently trivial (e.g., coffee cups, greetings, staff notices). This, we would argue, is one of its strengths. By raising to the level of consciousness the details of daily living which many headteachers and staff take for granted and by examining the beliefs and values which underlie them, it enables an analysis of professional practice germane to current changes in education. As Finch (1986) makes clear, to be significant to policy decisions, ideas do not have to be of direct or immediate relevance to them. Rather, fresh conceptualizations of or new approaches to familiar topics may, by changing the terms of the debate, have an impact on public thinking. Financial and legislative developments since 1986 have sought to alter the conditions under which many teachers work and to call in question a variety of established classroom practices. Detailed knowledge of the institutional context in which teachers operate can enhance our subsequent understanding of the success or failure of these attempts, and may in consequence make a substantial contribution to the policy debates of the 1990s. Another way of putting this is to suggest that we have not, as might at first sight appear, described anachronistic practice in quiet educational backwaters. Rather, we have provided insights into the *milieux* in which new policies will in the future flourish, wither, or be transformed. Recent studies of change in schools (e.g., Fullan, 1985; Holly, 1986) stress the importance of such understandings to the successful implementation of educational innovations. Yet, as we established in the Preface, no other detailed descriptions exist of primary schools as organizations in which adults live and work together. There is little point in educationalists claiming that innovations fail unless they are 'institutionalized' if we do not know what that means in practice. We suggest that in this sense in particular this book has much to offer educational decision-makers at many levels.

ORGANIZATIONAL CULTURE

The main organizing concept employed in this book is that of organizational culture. Before we discuss this notion further, we need to make it plain that we use it not in the reified sense in which it sometimes appears, but to describe part of the multiple social realities that people construct for themselves. We take an active view of human beings, accepting that they structure their own view of the world in which they live and create order for themselves through interaction with one another. This interaction is both the product of and results in the acceptance of tacit, mutually binding rules. Viewed in this way, organizations are simply one of many places (or *milieux*) in which members actively construct their own meanings and forge for themselves an ordered rule-bound existence (Silverman, 1970). As part of this process they also construct its culture, that is a deeply internalized sense of 'the way we do it around here' or 'what keeps the herd moving west' (Deal and Kennedy, 1983, p. 14).

Yet the very fact that the culture which a group creates is taken for granted may give newcomers or outsiders a sense that it has an existence independent of those who participate in it, and that becoming acculturated is a passive process of accommodation to a 'given' situation. Indeed, some studies of socialization (e.g., Kelman, 1961; Coulter and Taft, 1973) suggest that this is the case, arguing that three broad stages of social influence appear to follow one another: people first comply with the behavioural norms of a group which they aspire to join; then they identify with its members and their ways of behaving; finally, they internalize the latter's values and perspectives.

Our own experience of discovering the culture of these schools in one sense confirms this view. We certainly found that understanding adult relationships in the project schools was a progressive process, requiring penetration through successive layers of human action and thought. Action, we could see, was governed by norms which were, in turn, an expression of values, in that they expressed staff members' views on the differential worth and utility of particular artefacts, opinions, activities, lifestyles and so on. But these values themselves appeared to be an expression of beliefs to which it was very hard for an outsider to gain access because, being shared and understood, they were seldom voiced.

Yeomans' (1986b) account of how he 'became' a member of staff at one school shows, however, that entering into and participating in a culture are active processes which do not deprive individuals of their capacity for independent action. First, he learnt, by watching and listening attentively, what were the acceptable ways for an adult to speak and act in that school. Then, as through appropriate behaviour he demonstrated his capacity to 'fit in', he gradually came to understand the reasons for the norms he was following. In turn this enabled him to apprehend the principles on which these norms were constructed and the silent agreements which underlay them. Acceptance of these gave access to the shared language in which they were expressed and to the realization that he was able to hear what he called the 'secret harmonies' of the school. He was able at last to experience from inside what the staff described as 'the Sedgemoor way' and to feel it in a manner that enabled him both to act in appropriate ways without first consciously selecting them and to influence, if he chose, the views and behaviour of others.

We suggest, then, that individuals actively construct the cultures of which they become part and in becoming members of them acquire the capacity to alter them. Unfortunately, the way in which the notion of organizational culture has been treated in the past makes it particularly easy to slip into a view of it as fixed and reified. Since Waller's (1932, 1961 edn) seminal account of the 'separate culture of the school', educational writers have made intermittent use of the term, usually to describe behavioural norms or shared assumptions (e.g., Sarason, 1971; Goodlad, 1975; Deal and Kennedy, 1983; Handy and Aitken, 1986; Hoyle, 1986; Heckman, 1987; Goodchild and Holly, 1989). Meanwhile, organizational theorists and students of management, especially in the USA, have employed the term in discussions of the human side of enterprise (see, e.g., Handy, 1981; Deal and Kennedy, 1982; Peters and Waterman, 1982; Schein, 1985). Yet all of these writers leave the concept relatively undefined. One recent educational work, for example, claims that 'effective school self-evaluation and school improvement requires a change in the culture of the school' (Reid, Hopkins and Holly, 1987, p. 136), but is content to equate culture with 'tone or ethos or climate' (*ibid*, p. 1). Such deliberate imprecision may perhaps be because, as Handy (1981, p. 185) argues, 'a culture cannot be precisely defined, for it is something perceived, something felt'. Indeed Handy, in common with other authors, makes a virtue of his inexactitude, claiming (*ibid.*, p. 435) that 'a rigorous definition might destroy the "flavour" [of the cultural approach to organizations]'.

Aspects of Culture

Yet, although we are much in agreement with the idea that some of the most important aspects of schools are felt and experienced (see Chapter 7), we also feel that the cultural perspective on organizations stands in need of clarification (Nias, 1989a). Accordingly, we have taken 'culture' to comprise a number of identifiable elements. Following Deal (1985) and Stenhouse (1983), these are: beliefs and values; understandings, attitudes, meanings and norms (arrived at by interaction); symbols, rituals and ceremonies. In addition, cultures have 'culture-bearers' who, in some special way, represent in their persons and by their speech and behaviour what it is that the members deem to be worthwhile (i.e., what it is they value) and of what they approve. We also argue that primary schools have 'culture-founders' (Schein, 1985), that is, people whose right, responsibility or distinctive contribution it is to change the culture of the staff group and to install in its place a new set of beliefs and values.

The beliefs that underlie a culture are the hardest part of it to discern or reveal. Because group members share and understand them, they have little need to articulate them. Many beliefs are indeed so deeply buried that individuals do not even know what they are. We found that headteachers, whom we saw to be the 'founders' of their school cultures (see Chapter 6), were able to state the beliefs which underpinned the cultures they had created (or were trying to create), and so too were their deputies. In general, however, staff members could identify the values (seen also as aims or 'socially approved ends', Stenhouse, 1983, p. 21) that their corporate ways of life embodied much more readily than the beliefs from which the former stemmed. So, for example, in Chapter 4 we have had to use inference from staff actions, as well as a few explicit statements by staff, to establish the beliefs underlying the 'culture of collaboration'. By contrast, in identifying its values we have often been able to use what individuals said as well as drawing on what they did. Even so, staff generally found it difficult to describe or discuss what they valued, for

> acculturation is directed to shaping a person's definition of reality, *not only what it is but what it should be*. To a very large extent we are passive participants in the process, beginning as it does from the day of birth. The carriers of culture (e.g., parents, teachers) ordinarily do a very effective job of inculcating in children that view of what is and what should be . . . so effective, in fact, that it takes very special, upsetting conditions to cause one to ask why one has thought and acted the way one has.
>
> (Sarason, 1982, p. 14) (author's italics)

It is often therefore easier, and possibly more accurate, to establish what teachers feel to be worthwhile and what they are therefore trying to achieve (in Sarason's words, what they believe 'should be') by observing what they do and say than by asking them. Aims, goals and purposes must often 'be inferred from behaviour' (Stenhouse, 1983, p. 23) because they are 'nearly implicit' (Woods, 1983, p. 8).

However inexplicit or concealed the beliefs and values of a group may be, they lie at the heart of its culture. Attention has repeatedly been paid to this fact in the industrial and business studies cited above. More recently, educational writers, particularly in the USA, have begun to rediscover the importance of values in 'effective schools' (e.g., Goodlad, 1975; Deal and Kennedy, 1983; Heckman, Oates and Sirotnik, 1983; Heckman, 1987). As Deal (1985, p. 608) puts it:

> In schools, where diverse expectations, political vulnerability and the lack of a tangible product make values, beliefs and faith crucial in determining success, the development of a solid culture is even more important than it might be in business.

We found values to be central to an understanding of the project schools (see Chapters 4, 5 and 6 in particular). Furthermore, our impression was that, as Deal (*ibid.*) suggests, the sharing of common values encouraged in headteachers, teachers and ancillaries 'high morale, confidence and commitment'.

Yet our research explicitly excluded enquiry into classroom practice, and Heckman (1987) has noted that schools exist which are 'renewing' at the organizational, but not the classroom, level. We explore in Chapter 4 the relationship between one type of school culture and the staffs' educational practice, but would accept that schools have cultures which affect their staffrooms more than their classrooms. Further research is needed in this area.

Though rooted in beliefs and values, culture develops through interaction, especially talk, between group members (Chapters 3 and 5). A cycle appears to exist: individuals who share the same beliefs and values have similar 'basic assumptions' (Abercrombie, 1969) about the world in which they live, that is, they unconsciously perceive it in similar ways, attending and reacting to certain stimuli but screening out others. In other words, they have similar perspectives ('a coordinated set of beliefs, ideas and actions a person uses for coping with a problematic situation', Delamont, 1976, p. 55), or, as Rosenholtz (1985, p. 367) puts it, a 'consensus about school life'. So members of the same culture will define situations in similar ways and endow them with agreed meanings. Because they therefore understand one another they can talk to one another: 'Groups which can interact without misunderstanding do so on the basis of a consensus of meanings manifested in linguistic usage and dependent upon a deeper consensus of values and understandings' (Stenhouse, 1985, p. 22).

Moreover, the process of sharing meaning gives meaning. With repeated usage, words, events, actions, images, metaphors come to stand for things other than what they seem to an outsider. They become symbols, and in that guise enable communication between members to be increasingly efficient and densely coded.

Interaction also results in established ways of behaving (i.e., norms) (see also Little, 1987; McLaughlin and Yee, 1988). Adherence to these in turn confirms both the existence of the culture and membership of it. As Stenhouse (1983, p. 23) argues, 'The group can only control and sustain its culture by reacting to the behaviour of individual members. These individuals act within the group and the group reacts, exerting pressures on the individual in an effort to shape his behaviour'. Distinctive ways of doing things result from group interaction (e.g., conventions, approved and outlawed topics of conversation, forms of talk, ways of dressing, speaking and behaving). These are affirmed as newcomers are socialized into conformity to them, becoming in turn the socializing agents for others.

This vague, ill-defined but, to a member, clearly understood set of beliefs, values, perspectives, meanings and norms adds up, in any group, to 'the way we do it around here' (Deal and Kennedy, 1984, p. 4). Parts of this are often symbolized by words, actions, pictures or objects in ways to which members respond both cognitively and affectively (Deal, 1985; Hoyle, 1986). The meanings which these symbols convey are socially constructed and usually rooted in the past. Often they are embodied in stories, the telling of which both reaffirms for members a common history with a shared meaning and helps to induct newcomers into an understanding of and emotional commitment to the culture (Clark, 1983; Deal, 1985). Symbolic meanings, however conveyed, can be understood as group members understand them only from within the culture. Similarly, the rituals and ceremonies through which the most important symbols are displayed are understood differently by those who are acculturated and those who are not. Symbolic and ritual artefacts and acts can be seen without being perceived, their significance can be noted but not understood. 'Membership' implies something deeper than physical attendance at an event or an encounter (Chapter 5).

Cultural leadership too has a symbolic as well as a practical function because leaders embody the beliefs and values of the culture which they found or inherit (Deal, 1985; Schein, 1985). In language carefully chosen, though apparently ill-matched to the world of business, Peters and Waterman (1982, p. 281) describe the founding of an organizational culture as establishing the 'mission' of the institution, for, they argue, 'excellent' companies are 'value-driven' (*ibid.*, p. 279). Quoting Selznick (1957) they argue that, 'the institutional leader is primarily an expert in the promotion and protection of values' and, they claim, 'leadership fails when it concentrates on sheer survival. Institutional survival, properly understood, is a matter of maintaining values and distinctive identity' (Peters and Waterman, 1982, pp. 85 and 281).

Moreover, the ways in which leadership is exercised must be consistent with the culture which has been, or is to be, established, for 'a failure to behave in a culturally appropriate manner will result in a breach of the psychological contract, in lack of trust' (Handy, 1981, p. 367). To be effective, leaders must lead from within their cultures. This in turn means that they must be in tune with them, must represent and exemplify the values from which the culture grows. At the same time they must be capable of infusing their followers' daily activities with meaning. Culturally sensitive leadership enables those who perform even the most mundane tasks within an institution to see the ways in which their work relates to and derives from the values for which the latter stands. Interestingly, studies of 'school effectiveness', particularly in the USA, undertaken without reference to the notion of culture, have identified the critical part played in 'effective leadership' by 'vision', 'mission', painstaking attention to value-commitment among all school members and a participatory style of management (Manasse, 1985; Rosenholtz, 1985; Holly, 1986).

There are five main ways in which leaders ensure that the beliefs and values that they embody permeate the entire institution (see Chapters 5, 6 and 7). The first two — personal example and quality-monitoring and enforcement — mean that the leaders must be visible and accessible (Peters and Waterman, 1982; Manasse, 1985). Third, they select staff who share their values (Peters and Waterman, 1982; Rosenholtz, 1985; Southworth, 1987b). Next they use language, both to symbolize particular institutional attributes (Smith and Keith, 1971) and to create shared meanings (Hoyle, 1986). Lastly they help the institution, as a reified structure, to achieve a sense of corporate identity. The means by which they achieve the latter are largely symbolic and involve the use of words, actions, artefacts and settings (Deal, 1985; Hoyle, 1986). Out of these materials they 'construct presentations, create myths and devise stories' (Hoyle, 1986, p. 156). We would also add that leaders preside over or participate in key institutional ceremonies and rituals.

Leaders are not however the only people who symbolize the culture of their institutions. Groups also have 'culture-bearers' (Deal and Kennedy, 1983, p. 15, portray them as 'priests and priestesses') who perform important ceremonial and practical functions for the institution as a whole. They are often, for example, the main custodians of its past, the repositories of its humour, the stage-managers of its presentations, they play a central but supporting role in its ceremonies, understand and attend to the detail which helps to ensure the smooth and efficient translation of values into action. In our study, deputy heads were the chief 'culture-bearers' (see Chapters 5 and 6), but the 'pastoral leaders' identified in Chapter 6 also played a significant role in keeping the schools' cultural values alive and intact.

Conflict and Change within School Cultures

So far we have written as if schools are homogeneous institutions and may have created the impression that a 'culture', once constructed, is unchanging and inert. Indeed, Heckman (1987, p. 77) argues that a school's culture does 'conspire to maintain the status quo'. But we would not wish to subscribe to this view. In the first place, we have already argued that order and stability depend in organizations, as they do in all other human groups, upon the interaction of members and upon their active participation in the creation of tacit but mutually binding rules. Viewed this way, even institutions with strong cultures seem 'complex and highly fragile social constructions of reality' (Day, 1977, p. 132). Secondly, as Day (*ibid.*) also suggests, 'conflict and change are just as much a part of organizational life as consensus and stability'. In all the project schools, individuals belonged to reference groups and sub-cultures outside school and brought into school with them the assumptions and beliefs that they shared with members of these. As people, they also had personal identities and other related interests which they were quick to defend (Woods, 1981; Pollard, 1985; Nias, 1989b). In addition, in two of the schools, sub-groups existed, each with its own culture, making it difficult for the heads of those schools to gain shared acceptance of their own beliefs and practices (see Chapters 3 and 5).

In reconciling these facts with the existence within all the schools of a unique and binding set of understandings about the 'way we do it here', we have found helpful Pollard's (1985, p. 116) notion of 'institutional bias', a term he selected in preference to 'ethos' or 'climate' because both the latter were too redolent of unexamined notions of cohesion and consensus. His argument can be summarized thus: individual staff members bring their own socially conditioned beliefs, values and perspectives into a school and they all therefore have views or, at the least, assumptions about, for example, the curriculum, discipline, pedagogy. But they do not all have the same capacity to enforce their views upon others or to persuade others to adopt them. Moreover, self-interest is involved, since some practices may serve the interests of particular individuals or groups but not of others. There are therefore direct and indirect incentives for staff to bargain or negotiate with one another (even though much of this activity may be implicit: Hoyle, 1986; see also Ball, 1986) and to form alliances which will assist them in this process. The product of this negotiation is a relatively stable set of understandings arrived at over time, 'a type of generally shared knowledge' (Pollard, 1985, p. 116) about school practices and the assumptions which underlie them. This institutional bias is 'the product of the creative activity and negotiation of people within a school, bearing in mind not only their degree of power, influence and interpersonal skills but also the effect of the various external constraints and pressures which bear on them' (*ibid.*). Staff, pupils and visitors most commonly experience this tacit settlement which reflects power differentials yet 'transcends structures' (Hoyle, 1986, p. 3) as feelings or impressions. Although imprecise and elusive, it deeply affects classroom and staffroom processes throughout the whole school.

Now Pollard's use of institutional bias is very similar to our use of culture. If we accept that the two are closely related, we must also recognize that a school's culture is not its only, but is its dominant one. As such, it will always contain within itself the capacity for conflict, modification and development, as personnel change and circumstances in the wider environment alter.

This is not to deny that some schools, especially small ones, can give the impression of being mono-cultural (see, e.g., Handy, 1984). There were three such schools among those which we studied (see Chapter 4). Yet strong and deeply penetrating as the culture of each was, it was neither unitary nor apolitical. Two factors in particular tend to mask these facts. First, the type of culture we found in these schools encouraged consideration for others and co-operation with them and it is therefore easy, though erroneous (see Chapter 8), to assume that the staff had no interpersonal or inter-professional differences. Second, this 'collaborative culture' was so strongly established and in consequence normative control was so pervasive that it is easy to lose sight of the fact that it too was the product of a power differential. Each school had a head with a strong 'mission' and well developed political skills who had been in post for at least ten years and to whom had accrued during that time a considerable amount of personal authority (see Chapter 6). Yet close study of adult interactions in these schools revealed that the stability of the 'institutional bias' in each of them owed much to the explicit and implicit negotiation continually taking place between staff members and between head and staff. The equilibrium which characterized these schools was dynamic rather than inert.

Two related points may be made. First, though the culture of these three schools was strong, the staff did not experience it as stifling. Second, the schools appeared to be more open to change generated from within than to influences perceived as coming from without.

The first of these points is especially clear when one looks at their formal structures. In none of them was there a tight bureaucracy. Instead, the expression of individual differences was encouraged and divergence of practice was culturally sanctioned. These schools allowed and rewarded 'autonomy, entrepreneurship and innovation from the rank and file' (Peters and Waterman, 1982, p. 318; also see Chapters 4 and 8).

Yet normative control limited individualism. Choice was exercised within the parameters set by the schools' central beliefs and values, as these were exemplified in its main policies. In turn, the latter originated from the headteachers. So although in many senses the schools were 'loosely coupled' (Hoyle, 1980, p. 169) and allowed teachers and ancillaries considerable scope to 'be themselves', their sense of collective purpose was established through co-ordination as well as through collaboration. Holly (1986, p. 350) suggests that in these circumstances it is misleading to use the word 'collaboration', because the staff are 'dancing to the head's tune'. They are working together on the means necessary to the fulfilment of someone else's ends rather than participating in the formulation of their own policies. This form of collaboration which is later (*ibid.*, p. 361) equated with 'thrusting "macho", managerialist leadership' is seen to be restrictive and 'instrumental'. What this analysis overlooks however is the possibility that heads can gather round them staff who willingly embrace the same ends that they do. This, we suggest, was the case in the three mono-cultural project schools. Their staffs shared common aims and enjoyed working together to implement them. At the same time they felt free to exercise initiative and to celebrate both their own individuality and that of others. Because they were all constrained by the same freely accepted normative controls, they did not feel manipulated or exploited.

There is an obvious link between this point and the second, that is the openness that these staff showed in relation to developments which they perceived as coming from within the culture and over which they therefore had some sense of control (see Chapter 9). In this sense our work complements that of writers such as Fullan (1982) who argue that in attempting to understand schools' apparent resistance to innovation researchers have paid insufficient attention to the meanings which teachers attach to projected changes in their work or working conditions. We suggest (Chapters 6 and 7) that change in schools occurs and is experienced at different levels, the deepest and most difficult to reach being that of beliefs and values. It is the likelihood that a new headteacher will arrive with a fresh 'mission', and will attempt to impose a different corporate identity upon a school, which causes staff to experience head-teacher succession as a traumatic rather than simply a disruptive affair. Similarly it is the fact that teachers' classroom practice is rooted in their beliefs about the ends of education and the nature of effective practice which makes them so tenacious in its defence. The evidence we offer, though limited in scope, suggests that modifications to teachers' practice and to the structures which support it can best be accomplished by culturally appropriate leadership from within schools rather than by outside forces (though this does not preclude the possibility that individuals may be stimulated into initiating change by experiences which they undergo outside their schools). In this sense the three project schools with a 'culture of collaboration' (Chapter 4) were not 'task cultures' (i.e. job or project-oriented cultures in which 'flexibility and sensitivity to the market or environment are important'; Handy, 1981, p. 182). But their combination of tight agreement over goals and loose, differentiated structures did make them, as Peters and Waterman argue, open to innovation on the part of their own staff. Moreover the culture was characterized by many of those attributes which Little (1982; 1988; 1989), Fullan (1985), Rosenholtz (1985), Holly (1986), Heckman (1987) and Lieberman (1988) suggest are essential to school development. In other words these were not static institutions even though they often vigorously defended themselves from outside intervention.

One final point needs to be made. Cultures, though created by and expressed through individuals and groups, are historically rooted, determined by economic and political forces, expressed in and through societal structures. Moreover, in the modern world, few national cultures are monolithic — rather, members of sub-cultures compete to enforce their definitions of value, even of reality, upon one another. Yet although we have acknowledged the force of history in the project schools (Chapter 3), have taken cognizance of the cultural variety which individuals represented (Chapters 4 and 8) and have acknowledged the existence and use of authority and influence within primary schools (Chapter 8), we have not attempted to show the connections which existed between individuals' past and present experiences and their values and beliefs on the one hand or between school cultures and macro-societal forces on the other. If we had had more time and money we would have done this, since we recognize that cultures are constructed by people who are themselves part of worlds beyond their work. The fact that we have apparently ignored the connections between the staff of these schools and their other contexts could be seen as an omission at any time. We would freely concede that in the present political and economic climate some readers may view it as a major weakness, vitiating the fresh understanding of primary schools that we have tried to offer. In Chapter 9 we have speculated about the effects of the Education Acts of 1986 and 1988 upon schools such as the ones we describe here. But more research is needed, both into the effects of these and other changes and into the biographies and life histories of individuals, and the histories and social contexts of particular schools, in attempts to link micro-studies with broader notions of societal power and control.

SUMMARY

In the first part of this chapter we described the background to the research which is reported in subsequent chapters, explaining what we did and did not set out to do, and why; how we found schools in which to work; the methods we used to collect and analyse evidence; and how we checked our interpretations and final accounts with the schools. We also confronted, and refuted, possible suggestions that the schools which we studied were 'cosy' and anachronistic backwaters.

In the second part we explained our understanding of the term 'culture', particularly as it relates to organizations. A vague, imprecise notion which is felt more readily than it is analysed, its main components, exemplified through and in the words and actions of its 'founders' and 'bearers', are: beliefs and values; understandings, attitudes, meanings and norms (arrived at by interaction); symbols, rituals and ceremonies. All these are actively constructed by members of the culture who also therefore have the power to change them. For the same reason, organizational cultures should be seen as dominant cultures, that is, as the product of negotiation between members who may have different beliefs and values and varying amounts of power and influence. They are not monolithic and may be altered, especially from within. Paradoxically, the deeper the agreement on the policies which express the organization's dominant culture, the freer its members feel to act with autonomy and initiative. The schools that we studied had strong cultures but, because these encouraged individualism and innovation, the schools were not, as institutions, stagnant or resistant to internally initiated change.

In the next chapter we describe the schools as they seemed to us in our early encounters with them and show how we became aware that a full understanding of staff relationships required us to move from an observation of behaviour to an appreciation of values and beliefs.

Chapter 2

The Schools: First Impressions

In Chapter 1 we suggested that becoming a member of a culture is a slow process, which normally starts with conformity to the observed speech and actions of those around oneself, and that a full understanding of the beliefs from which these norms are generated comes only after a long period of compliance to them. Certainly, in our final encounters with the project schools, we saw things (for example, particular pieces of non-verbal communication between the staff, ways of behaving at assembly) whose significance we felt to be greater than the actual behaviours which took place but which we did not at the time understand. Accordingly, the descriptions in this chapter are intended to serve two purposes. The first is to present outline pictures of the schools as they seemed to us during our early encounters with them, as a prelude to the illumination of meanings, values and beliefs. The second is to provide readers with background information about each school, which they may find helpful in interpreting the detailed evidence that we subsequently present.

THE FIVE SCHOOLS

Greenfields Community Primary School

Greenfields was one of the six designated community schools established by its LEA in 1972, although the head, who has been at the school for 21 years, has long believed in the importance of community education. The school is in an affluent village which is both a rural community and a dormitory settlement for professional workers in the nearby town. Children are also 'bussed-in' from a second village. The school is the smallest of the five, being a Group 3, 5-to-11 primary school, with five classes in cellular classrooms. Two classrooms are in the original nineteenth-century school building, with two further classes, library, toilets, office and staffroom in a later extension. A further separate block, built in the 1960s, houses the fifth classroom, hall and kitchen. The piecemeal growth of the building means that three classes have no sink, three rooms are small and two are large. The reception classroom is isolated from the rest of the classes, being situated in the separate block. The secretary works in the staffroom. Moving around the school sometimes means going outside or along a draughty corridor, though the school is otherwise warm. The staff consisted of a head (Graham), deputy (Jim), five full-time teachers (Victoria, Carol, Vera, Alexis and Julie), and a part-time teacher (Mary). Additionally there were an ancillary (Norma), a secretary (Natalie) and a caretaker (Violet, replaced by Mark). Graham had a 0.3 teaching commitment, and Jim a 0.5 commitment, to allow Jim to fulfil his duties as union representative on the Education Committee. In practice his class was taught full-time by a 'new' teacher (Julie) who was employed at the school on a temporary annual contract. This temporary contract served two purposes. First it allowed the school additional staffing to cover for Jim's absences when carrying out Education Committee duties. Second it allowed the LEA the opportunity to give Julie a different school placement since in her previous school she had been identified as having difficulties in the classroom. Two teachers held additional responsibilities. Victoria was responsible for maths, Vera for infants and language. Carol acted as special needs co-ordinator, and was paid an additional amount as community teacher. When Vera left the school at the end of the spring term 1986, Carol took on Vera's infant responsibility. Graham, the head, was the oldest member of staff. He was in his early fifties. All the other staff were in their forties or late thirties. Most of them had worked together for several years at Greenfields and were experienced teachers. When the reception teacher (Vera) left she was replaced by Alexis. Everyone calls everyone else by Christian name. Numerous parents helped in the school, and there was a steady stream of visitors, support workers and peripatetic teachers.

Table 2.1. *Greenfields Community Primary School*

School	Number on roll (Sept. 1985)	Group size	Number of teachers (excluding head)	Number of ancillaries	Head's tenure	Staff changes during year	Number of classes
Greenfields Community Primary School	155	3	6.2 (6f) (1m)	1 ancillary (f) 1 secretary (f) 1 caretaker (f) (m)	18 yrs (m)	caretaker head of infants	5

Hutton C of E (Aided) Junior School

Hutton serves a large village on the edge of a growing city. The village is chiefly a dormitory for the city, though reasonably priced new housing attracts commuters working in other towns. The village has expanded so rapidly during the last decade that it has a suburban feel to it, and it is a surprise to drive through the estates and find the meandering original village street at the edge of the countryside. The school is at the heart of the newer part of the village, flanked by the new library and a small shopping centre. The school was opened in September 1976 and is built on traditional lines. There are eight cellular classrooms, four on each of two parallel arms, linked at one end by the hall. Walking from one end of the school to the other involves walking through classrooms. The courtyard formed by the U-shaped buildings has seats and a small fishpond. There are a separate dining hall and kitchens beyond the main hall. The offices and staffroom are separated from the classrooms by an entrance lobby which opens on to the hall. The single mobile classroom at the back of the school is used for maths withdrawal groups. The inside of the school had been extensively improved in recent years using funds raised by the school. The entrance hall and several classrooms are carpeted, and the head and caretaker have modernized the appearance of the hall and entrance hall by adding display boards and pine panelling.

Though there is no formal PTA, the school had raised money to build a learner swimming pool on the edge of the spacious field. The head had started a school farm which has ducks, hens, goats and lambs. In this village, the animals are undisturbed by vandalism.

Most of the school's 262 children come from extensive estates of small private housing. The school is run as two-form entry, and parallel classes are housed in adjoining rooms. Mr Richard Handley (variously known as 'Mr Handley', 'Richard', 'Rich' or 'the boss') has been a head for 16 years in all, just over four of them at Hutton. His staff in September 1985 was eight full-time teachers, one part-time teacher (four days), a part-time secretary (June), part-time ancillary (Diane), and full-time caretaker (Bill). Four teachers (Rachel responsible for language, Maureen responsible for PE, Ellen responsible for the library, and Juliet) had been at the school when Richard was appointed. He subsequently made Rachel his deputy head. Of the five teachers Richard appointed, Alison had come as a probationer four years previously, Keith (Scale 3) was responsible for resources and maths, Lesley and Marion had arrived within the previous two years and held responsibility posts for art/drama and language/lower school co-ordination respectively. Jean had just been appointed to a one-year temporary part-time post. In practice she was a full-time class teacher, since throughout the year she covered for Juliet's weekly absence on a maths diploma course. Juliet herself took maths withdrawal groups from the exceptionally large third-year classes. Staff ages ranged from mid-twenties to mid-forties. The year was one of constant staff changes. Rachel, Marion and Maureen were promoted to posts outside the school. After Christmas Teresa came in as new deputy head and Jill on a two-term temporary contract basis. Then Keith, Jean and Jill moved to new posts at the end of the year.

Table 2.2. *Hutton C of E (aided) Junior School*

School	Number on roll (Sept. 1985)	Group size	Number of teachers (excluding head)	Number of ancillaries	Head's tenure	Staff changes during year	Number of classes
Hutton Junior School	262	5	8.8 (8f) (1m)	1 ancillary (f) 1 secretary (f) 1 caretaker (m)	4 yrs (m)	3 teachers left 2 arrived 0.8 became full-time further temporary part-time appointment	8

Lavender Way First School

Lavender Way stands on the top of a steep hill in a pleasant country town. It is on the edge of a private housing estate which it was built to serve ten years previously. Expensive new housing began to creep along one side of the school boundary during the year, evidence of the town's continuing growth and prosperity. The school is still growing. Parents tend to be concerned that their children should progress well, and are supportive rather than critical.

The building is attractive both inside and out. It is surrounded by extensive shrubs, which complement the low pebble-dashed exterior. Inside, the carpeted entrance hall flows without interruption into a library and L-shaped dining area. The offices and staffroom are immediately by the entrance. At the back of a small, carefully tended central court-yard are two open-plan areas, joined by a shared play space. Each area is shared by two 'infant' classes. To the right is a short, wide corridor, which leads to the 'junior' part of the school. This is one large, open area used by two classes, with a separate classroom used by a third 'junior' class. The school has its own kitchen and a large hall.

The four 'infant' classes are parallel vertical groups of children whose ages range from 4 to 7. Normally the children stay in the same class until they are seven, when they transfer to one of the three parallel 'junior' classes of children aged 7 to 9, before moving to middle schools in the town.

The staff consists of a head and 6.5 teachers, plus a part-time secretary, part-time ancillary helper, and caretaker. Though Catherine, in her first headship, has only been at the school for 13 months (since January 1984), she has appointed all but three teaching staff. Jayne, as head of infants (Scale 3), came to the school during its first year, followed after two years by Rita, an infant teacher responsible for language. Julie came as a probationer the year before Catherine. Of the other staff, Catherine had appointed Ben, her deputy, and Stella and Sandy, the other two infant teachers, during her first year. Amanda was appointed in September 1985 as part-time teacher in the juniors, though with her own class. This meant that for most of the year the junior curriculum was organized so that other staff, including Catherine, covered Amanda's class during afternoon sessions. Joanne, the secretary, Avril, the ancillary, and Charlie Rose, the caretaker, had all been at the school for most of its life. The staff's ages ranged from mid-twenties (Julie) to early fifties (Jayne) but most, including the head, were in their thirties.

There were some staff changes during the year. Avril was replaced as ancillary by Audrey, who already worked in the school as cleaner and lunchtime supervisor and,

Table 2.3. *Lavender Way First School*

School	Number on roll (Sept. 1985)	Group size	Number of teachers (excluding head)	Number of ancillaries	Head's tenure	Staff changes during year	Number of classes
Lavender Way First School	190	4	6.5 (6f) (1m)	1 ancillary (f) 1 secretary (f) 1 caretaker (m)	1 yr 2 terms (f)	change of ancillary 0.5 became full-time for summer term	7

as the school grew, Jayne became 0.7 and then full-time during the summer term. At the end of the year Jayne left and was replaced by Phyl on a Scale 1 temporary contract, whilst Stella became responsible for co-ordinating mathematics.

Lowmeadow Nursery and Infant School

Lowmeadow is a multi-cultural nursery/infant school in a medium-sized town with some light industry. One third of its pupils are from non-white groups (chiefly Asian) and the pupils come from a wide social background.

The 1920s building was originally a community centre, but it was modernized in 1982 and transformed into an attractive though idiosyncratic school building. Immediately by the entrance are a dining area and large hall, with a stage at one end. Offices and the large staffroom are close by. In most of the building, corridors have been opened up to make them an integral part of classroom spaces, but the two oldest classes are in self-contained classrooms, close to one another. There are short staircases in unexpected places, and corridors which turn at right angles to reveal corners with small displays of flowers and children's paintings. One such corridor leads through three semi-open-plan teaching areas to the nursery. The outside play areas are small, but well provided with play equipment.

The children are in five classes, loosely grouped by age, with two separate nursery classes in addition (one morning, one afternoon). Groups of children are withdrawn from classes for second-language work in a separate language group room. The number of staff seems particularly large for the number of children because of the provision of an additional teacher and two ancillary helpers from Section 11 funding. In all, the infant staff comprises a head, six full-time teachers, a part-time teacher in the spring term (who became temporary full-time, in the summer term), together with five ancillary helpers. Of these, one is full-time, and one also works part-time as the secretary. The nursery is staffed by a teacher and nursery nurse. A Hindi speaker (Mrs Kaur) visits the school for four hours each week to do mother-tongue work with small groups of children. The head, Miss Audrey Proctor (generally called 'Miss Proctor' by her staff), has been at the school for 20 years. She shares a long history with most of her staff, since all the full-time teachers have been in the school at least seven years, while Julia, the deputy head, has been at the school for thirteen years. There are four teachers with designated responsibilities: Rosemary, Margaret, Kath, who takes the second-language groups, and Patricia, the nursery teacher. In addition to Sarah and Jane, full-time teachers, and Rhoda, the part-time teacher, the ancillary helpers are Ruth, Sandra (also the secretary), Mary, Helen, and Mrs Kaur (who replaced Mrs Bains, a Punjabi speaker, halfway through the year). The nursery nurse is Rita. She is in her twenties; most of the rest of the staff are in their forties or fifties. Though many of the ancillary staff are relatively recent additions to the staff, all but one have previously been involved with the school as parents, dinner supervisors or volunteers. Finally, Frank, the caretaker for four years, is the only male member of staff. There are also regular volunteer helpers (parents and other community members) working in the classrooms. Apart from the change in mother-tongue ancillary, the staff remained unchanged throughout the year, though at the end of the summer term Mrs Kaur was appointed as a full-time ancillary for a child with special needs. The staff are mainly in their late-thirties to mid-forties, though Rita is in her twenties.

Table 2.4. *Lowmeadow Nursery and Infant School*

School	Number on roll (Sept. 1985)	Group size	Number of teachers (excluding head)	Number of ancillaries	Head's tenure	Staff changes during year	Number of classes
Lowmeadow Nursery and Infants School	210	4	7.3 (all f)	1 nursery nurse (f) 5 p.t. ancillaries (f) 1 secretary (f) 1 caretaker (m)	20 yrs (f)	additional 0.5 in summer term for reception intake. 1 ancillary change in summer term	5

Sedgemoor Primary School

Sedgemoor is a 5 to 11 primary school, built as a one-form entry school and opened in October 1975. It is housed in a low, single-storey brick building, on the edge of a council estate in a leafy modern town. Inside, the building is compact, with 210 children just about fitting into the open-plan design. Because of the school's sloping site, many of the teaching areas are linked by short flights of stairs, though one class space has stairs within it. Others have awkward corners which can make it impossible for the teacher to be visually in touch with all children at the same time. However, the small central court-yard, open-plan design, internal use of glass in preference to solid panels, and absence of corridors create an illusion of space. In practice, careful housekeeping is necessary to prevent chaotic untidiness.

Two-thirds of the children mostly come from the council estate, one-third from the private housing beyond, and a few from elsewhere in the town. The infants are organized into two vertically grouped reception/middle-infant classes in a single large open area with two small 'home bays'. The single top infant class is separated from the main infant area by a curtain and bookcases, and has become an enclosed classroom. The four junior classes are a few steps away, past the dining area and the court-yard, through a small junior library. Each class is a separate year group, working in two open but angular spaces, each containing two classes separated by a short flight of stairs. In the most challenging of these work areas, 37 ten-year-old children work in three linked sub-spaces.

Isobel, the head, is in her third headship, and opened the school ten years previously. She is in her forties, but most of her teaching staff are in their twenties and early thirties. Dennis, the deputy head, is the longest serving teacher, having been there five years. The rest of the teaching staff have been in the school less than three years. The infant staff consists of Veronica, who held the semi-official title of 'head of infants', Margaret, who is a newly appointed probationer, and Josie, who is temporarily in charge of the top infants until Sue returns from maternity leave in April (then Josie resumes as part-time teacher). In addition to Dennis, the other junior teachers are Peter (responsible for environmental studies), Sheila (temporarily responsible for games), and Sally (responsible for art and dance). Isobel always avoids defining responsibility areas too rigidly. The teaching staff is completed by part-timers Ann (music one morning per week), and Jane, who would leave when Sue returned. Molly is the part-time secretary and Polly is the ancillary. Molly joined the staff one year previously but Polly has been part of the school as parent, dinner supervisor, and now ancillary since the school's early days. Finally Mrs Aldridge, the cleaner-in-charge, was the only member of staff not to be referred to by Christian name.

Many of the staff are keen course-goers. Josie is on an advanced diploma course and Dennis is taking a higher degree.

Table 2.5. *Sedgemoor Primary School*

School	Number on roll (Sept. 1985)	Group size	Number of teachers (excluding head)	Number of ancillaries	Head's tenure	Staff changes during year	Number of classes
Sedgemoor Primary School	210	4	7.3 (7f) (2m)	1 ancillary (f) 1 secretary (f) 1 caretaker (f)	10 yrs (f)	1 teacher returned from maternity leave and the temporary teacher left.	7

LOOKING INTO THE SCHOOLS

Once we began to work inside the schools our knowledge grew. With growing familiarity we could observe the physical features of each school in greater detail:

> The building is an old one, adapted in the 1920s from community use and modernized in 1982. One enters it across a narrow asphalt playground up a steep flight of stone steps. The main door opens into a dining area, curtained off from the large, attractive, sunny hall, well-lit by large windows down one side, with a polished wooden floor and imposing, curtained stage at the far end. To the right of the dining area are the head's and secretary's offices, both very small. To one side of these are two classrooms, on top of one another and linked by a staircase, and a large, dark, but comfortable staffroom. To the other, along several right-angled corridors, are the remaining teaching areas, the nursery being the furthest from both the head's office and the staffroom. To reach it from the head's office one passes the language group room, and through three semi-open-plan teaching areas, two of them joined by a shared activity area. The whole school is warm, cheerful, well-lit and, in addition to children's work and other similar displays, is brightened by the plants and flowers which are regularly arranged by a volunteer helper. In addition, one is often aware of music; the hall is equipped with a good quality stereo and head and teachers make good use of their fine collection of tapes and records. Outside are two small asphalt playgrounds, one equipped with play apparatus, a small area of grass and a paddling pool. The nursery has its own play area. The school is generally well provided with good quality materials.
>
> (Fieldnote, October, Lowmeadow)

> Displays are in evidence in the corridors and classrooms. The school makes much use of computer/printer, TV/video, and the hall for PE. There is a swimming pool and a large field for sports. The hall is equipped with a stereo system and music is played at the start of each assembly.
>
> (Fieldnote, September, Greenfields)

Although we had lists of names, and we were introduced to all who came to the school, initially it was not easy to work out precisely who was who:

> Before I was introduced to the staff I went to assembly. . . . Judging by the number of adults there, ancillary staff must have been present, but there was nothing to distinguish them from teachers. . . . The staff list that I have been given, with staff addresses and telephone numbers, doesn't differentiate teaching from non-teaching staff.
>
> (Fieldnote, October, Lowmeadow)

Moreover, with voluntary helpers (usually parents) in attendance and part-time teachers and ancillary workers sometimes present, sometimes absent, it took time to understand who was who, who did what and when people might be in (or out) of school.

We had some factual notes on the staff and could make some generalizations. For example: the staff groups were predominantly female; their ages ranged from early twenties to over fifty; in some schools staff called each other by Christian names though there might be exceptions to this; some staff had specified responsibilities. Yet when we started to work in the schools and became teaching colleagues of the staff we quickly began to discover things about them as individuals — their training, experience, interests, personal backgrounds and social lives. Our interest in these details was sharpened by the fact that the behaviour of the staff was our fundamental concern, but in any case they talked freely of them. In short, during the early weeks of our fieldwork we were simply looking, noting and storing as many examples and instances of behaviour as we could:

> An early impression of meeting the Hutton staff was that they had a head with several names. He was usually addressed in school as Mr Handley. Away from school in social settings he was usually 'Rich' to his face and in his absence. But when mentioned in conversations in school he was invariably referred to as 'the boss.'
>
> (Fieldnote, September, Hutton)

> People have always thanked me for being in their classrooms, even when I felt my activities have been neither noteworthy nor notable. Parents get small considerations too. Use of first names with parents and between parents and staff is quite common.
>
> (Fieldnote, January, Greenfields)

> At breaktime whoever comes in first pours out the coffee for everyone else — today it was Molly — and hands out the cups.
>
> (Fieldnote, October, Sedgemoor)

> During the morning I work in Rita's and Sandy's areas, in the mornings they operate as two independent units, there is an invisible line which defines whose tables are which but this is flexible.
>
> (Fieldnote, September, Lavender Way)

> I spent part of the afternoon with Rita and Sandy in their area. In effect, it's one large room with one wall dividing it. This section, so they told me, had originally been intended as a junior end of the school and hence the area is divided into what is effectively two classroom areas. Thus, though they work as a pair, they find that in practice they have to divide the children (a) because the space separated the children into two groups naturally and (b) because of an influx of nursery-aged children. Currently Rita has the older children, that is, the top infants, and the older 'middles', while Sandy has the Reception and the younger 'middles'. At the end of the day they stop and chat. Rita says, 'We usually stop to chat for twenty minutes at the end of the day.'
>
> (Fieldnote, September, Lavender Way)

The staffroom is the one place where the staff meet as a group. Because all staff, including secretary and welfare helper, make a point of being in there three times a day, the passing interactions which might occur there and elsewhere at other times in the day are shared with the group. There are no alliances discernible from the seating patterns members adopt, and when staff drift singly to and from the staffroom in the middle of lunchtime or after school, conversations spring up between kaleidoscopic sub-groups whose most constant member is the head.

(Yeomans, 1986c)

All of the staff (but not the caretaker) use the staffroom and though the ancillaries talk less than the teachers they seem completely at ease there.

(Fieldnote, October, Lowmeadow)

Gradually then we built up more detailed pictures of the people and the schools. As these pictures were developing we also began to notice some habits and patterns:

There were many breaktimes when laughter filled the staffroom at morning break. Bill, the caretaker, always spent morning break in there, as did June, the secretary. It was unusual not to find Bill and Marion or Alison somewhere near the source of the humour. Frequently, they conducted a comic double act which Bill either initiated or in which he was used as a foil by Marion.

(Yeomans, 1987a)

Break duties, the tendency to spend time with music groups in breaks, moving and preparing for the next teaching session, were some of the reasons why all the staff seldom gathered together. Catherine usually spent some time in the staffroom, but was often delayed by school business. Staff often used this chance to talk school arrangements with her. The ancillary seldom spent break in the staffroom, the secretary and caretaker never.

(Yeomans, 1987c)

Pattern of the day.
Lunch time — Sally is in the staffroom at the beginning of lunchtime eating her sandwiches again and Peter has a quick cup of tea before going to his class. Otherwise the middle part of lunchtime sees the staffroom occupied by the head, Polly, Josie and myself until about five past one when the rest of the staff come in for the last ten minutes, having been in their classrooms.

Most lunchtimes, the teachers are out of the staffroom except for maybe the last ten minutes of the lunch hour. There are three or four of us who have lunch in there, so we're in there that bit longer than the others, but generally speaking you eat your lunch and then you're back to your classroom to sort things out.

After school.
Today all the teaching staff, except two (Peter being in the hall with the Badminton Club) are working in the dining area, this includes two, who are using the guillotine and mounting work there. At four o'clock Sheila goes, at four fifteen, Peter, and at quarter to five, Isobel, once she has run out of jobs to do (though she spent some time sitting in the staffroom and seemed reluctant to go). Dennis leaves about the same time. At quarter past five, Margaret goes and at half past five I leave, but two are still there. Veronica says she has still got her own room and the library to sort out but she says they often stay late and take a lot of care over display preparation because there is no point in doing it otherwise.

(Fieldnote, October, Sedgemoor)

We also studied the school's documents: brochures for parents, curriculum documents, and statements of aims. These documents contained each school's rhetoric about its guiding beliefs and aspirations. Since almost all documents were written by the headteachers, they gave us access to the heads' beliefs, and we could keep these in mind when we observed both them and the rest of the staff. Further, when we looked at what the heads did, we began to see whether their actions were consistent with their written words. Also, when we looked at the staff we could begin to see if they subscribed to the head's policies and whether they implemented them.

Communications and assembly soon emerged as major concerns and were observed in detail. As staff members we became part of the communication network and had to learn how to respond to it. As observers we recorded its nature:

> The subtle, familiar nature of staffroom communications creates difficulties for new-comers who do not, for example, realize that to keep up-dated they need to attend to letters on the staffroom table or to notices stuck to the mantelpiece. I give one example from my own experience:
> The deputy and the teachers I've been attached to have been extremely good about keeping me informed about important things like toilets, coat racks and tea money but there's a great deal about the *diwali* celebrations which I didn't know till Kath told me this morning. Even then, I didn't know how to behave appropriately in a sari and was terrified at appearing, through ignorance, to be undervaluing someone else's culture. I watched other people, copied them and hoped I wasn't getting it wrong.
>
> (Nias, 1986)

> The assembly is the time when I find out what the children are doing and tea and coffee is when I find out what the staff are doing.
>
> (Secretary, Lowmeadow)

> Lunchtimes are important, the way we all talk at lunchtime. That keeps Miss Proctor in touch with the children, because we are talking about them, as well as with us. And of course, she is moving, as you know, around the building all the time.
>
> (Teacher, Lowmeadow)

We realized that communications were fleeting, subtle, often non-verbal (conveyed through eye contact and gestures) and heavily coded. Sometimes we could recognize that communication was taking place, but we might not understand the message that was being signalled. Knowing that communication was taking place only led to other problems — what was being communicated and what did it mean?

Assemblies were fascinating events for a number of reasons. For one thing we could watch how people related to each other:

> Assembly was a very pleasant and warm affair, the governor was welcomed by name and so was the retired welfare helper who does all the flowers in the school. The music was cheery and the children swayed and sometimes half sang to it while we were waiting for the reception class. The adults were brought by name into assembly, with direct questions to them about their half-term activities . . . Adults were smiling across the room to each other and making a lot of eye contact. Miss Proctor made several remarks like: 'Isn't it nice to be back again. What a lot of things we do miss when we're not at school.' . . . There was a very positive feel to the whole occasion and I really had a sense of the school as a community coming back together and being glad to see one another.
>
> (Fieldnote, October, Lowmeadow)

> What happens is that teachers in turn take one assembly, it works out as one a week. The religious content is very low in terms of a sense of service and worship. Today, for

example, there was neither a hymn nor a prayer. Over the last five days of visiting I can't recall there being any prayers at all. However, the content of the assemblies is very much in the sense of applauding children's work in the school. What tends to happen is, to use Carol's assembly today as an example, she sat at the front, accompanied by all her class, and the children would in turn demonstrate some work they had been doing in the class that week.

Today, about eight children showed their interpretations from the Roald Dahl story *Charlie and the Chocolate Factory* of what an 'Oompa-Loompa' looked like, and there were also some written descriptions they read out. Then all the children showed the glove puppets they had made out of paper.

It was interesting to watch the reactions of the rest of the school, since all the children, sitting in random order and not in their class groups, always sit patiently, quietly and attentively.

It does serve functions, other than simply applauding the children's work. For example, what's also on display is at least one, if not two or three, of the teacher's lessons. Teacher colleagues sitting in the hall (since all teaching staff are always present) witness, at least in part, their colleagues talking about an aspect of their classes' work in the last five or six working days period. Teachers are effectively displaying at least one aspect of their activity before their colleagues. Whereas in larger schools where there is only a weekly class assembly it could take the best part of a term to get through the whole staff, at Greenfields it takes only a week for this to happen. At the end of term each teacher will have made fourteen or fifteen 'appearances'. This has significant implications for how teachers perceive their colleagues.

The atmosphere is very much a friendly one in assemblies, and also, between the teachers, it is largely non-competitive.

Also present in the assembly are parents. Parents have an open invitation to attend and today being a very fine Indian Summer morning there seemed to be more than the usual number of parents in the hall. The parents really seemed to enjoy the assembly.

(Fieldnote, October, Greenfields)

We also focused on the messages, implicit and explicit, which were conveyed during school assembly:

Morning Assembly — Tuesday is the one assembly taken by Catherine with all the staff present as well as the children. Although the children come in quietly there is general chat and murmuring from several children. The relationship with the children is exactly as in other parts of the school at other times, the only interventions by Catherine are 'shh', or 'listen' and these are said very quietly. The general tone is non-authoritarian and apart from the 'shh' to check the chatter, the only other intervention is when Ben moves to the back of the hall during the hymn singing. The assembly opens and ends with a hymn, Catherine's part is to ask the children questions about dates in the previous week which would have been half term and give clues to their significance. Getting back the answers that the important days were Shrove Tuesday, Ash Wednesday and St. Valentine's day, she then goes on to give their meaning and origins.

(Fieldnote, November, Lavender Way)

LOOKING INTO THE PICTURE

As we gathered evidence of this kind we began to try, in a provisional way, to make up pictures of the schools, but this was not easy because not all of the evidence was consistent or easily fitted together.

For example, in all of the schools there was talk of teamwork. Staff spoke of being a member of a team, or of working together. Yet during the school day most of the teachers worked apart from the other adults. They generally spent the greater part of each day working on their own with their class or group of children. If they did work with someone, that person was more likely to be an ancillary worker, a parent helper, or occasionally the headteacher. So what did teamwork mean? Similarly, we heard a lot of talk amongst the staff, but it was quickly apparent that talk was too general a category. There was 'professional talk' ranging across a number of categories: the behaviour of children (discipline, progress, special needs, successes, social development); curriculum (plans, evaluations, processes, development); in-service courses and careers; responsibilities and organizational arrangements. There was 'personal talk' about families, friends, social lives and interests. As these categories emerged we began to consider what they might mean for the staff and school. In short, the evidence was making us reflect upon it and analyse it. Also, the process of analysis began to show us that there were things to be discovered beneath the surface.

Our evidence was drawn initially from the audible and the visible but in trying to make sense of it we needed to think about the silent and the invisible:

> After several months in the school I still could not explain some of the nuances of interaction within the staff, nor account for staffroom phenomena. Silence, on some topics, spoke loudly — but I was not clear what the message was, except to realize that the relatively short time many of the staff had been together in the school meant that they must still be negotiating school-wide relationships.
>
> (Yeomans, 1986c)

It gradually became apparent that although we were working in primary schools with staff groups which in number resembled the size of the classic small group (6–12 members), use of the notion 'small' should not imply simple. Primary schools might be 'small' in comparison with larger institutions (e.g., a teaching hospital or comprehensive school) but our evidence was showing that they were not easy to perceive or understand (see also Southworth, 1987c).

The outline sketches we began with were broadly based upon each school's formal organization (e.g., staffing quotas, positions, responsibilities, class groupings). Yet the evidence we collected was often related to informal aspects of the school, in the sense that it frequently described the seemingly unplanned patterns of contact and association between adults. This distinction between formal and informal led us to consider the impact of structures *on* people and the creation of structures *by* people (Hoyle, 1986). Formal structures did affect people and sometimes explained why, say, heads and deputies and secretaries acted as they did. However, formal structures did not always explain behaviour. Our evidence of incidents, habits and routines (e.g., use of staffroom, patterns of the day, communications) seemed to offer glimpses of the structures created by people. In short, the former structures were easier to see and explain than the latter. Moreover, some informal structures might actually be invisible, as they were rooted in past experience, memories and history. Yet invisible did not necessarily mean inaccessible.

There were things that seemed to be particularly important to the staff. For example, the handing out of coffee cups at Sedgemoor, or the way children chose to sit for assemblies at Greenfields. We sensed that these might be symbols. A simple definition of a symbol is that it represents something other than itself, hence the handing out of coffee cups symbolized consideration for others, whilst the seating of children in assembly at Greenfields, with the older children being encouraged to mix with the younger ones, symbolized a 'family feeling', as the head later described it. As Hoyle (1986, p. 167) says, 'the school is a thicket of symbols' and

> . . . there is little doubt about the significance of the symbolic dimension of the school. Whilst management theory, and much organization theory, focuses on structures and management processes, these may well only be the surface features of the school. The 'reality' of the organization may inhere much more in the ways in which members utilize and respond to symbols.

We began to realize that coming to understand the schools was a slow and progressive process. To understand the symbols you needed to have close and sometimes long acquaintance with the underlying beliefs of the school. Our involvement as participant observers enabled us to have sufficient experience with the schools to identify some of each school's symbols (see Chapter 3) and to become acquainted with the beliefs which they represented (see Chapter 4). Moreover, our increasing awareness of symbols and beliefs caused us to realize that we were beginning to discern school cultures.

Just as we realized that we needed to appreciate both the formal and informal aspects of the schools' organization, so too did we come to appreciate that to understand the school as an organization one needed to understand its organizational culture. To do the latter one must understand the notion of culture at different levels, in different ways, over time and by being a member of the school. Hence, Chapter 3 looks at the factors which determine each school's culture whilst Chapter 4 considers the ways in which, in three of the schools, the cultures were alike.

Chapter 3

Individual School Cultures

In Chapter 2 we suggested that understanding the culture of each school was a haphazard and meandering process. But the longer we spent in each school the more we learnt about it. As we gradually 'became' members of staff, we made sense of events whose meaning had been obscure. In turn this fresh understanding enabled us to make sense of other previously unclear patterns of behaviour, to interpret the meaning of new events and gain access to further layers of meaning.

We began to realize too that the same range of factors seemed to be significant in all the schools, unique though each was. These were: the school's buildings and organizational arrangements; the people who worked there, their histories and that of the school. Each of these affected the school's culture, first, by determining the nature and extent of interaction between staff members, and second, by helping to decide who among them had authority and influence.

INTERACTION

Interaction is particularly important because, as Stenhouse suggests, 'Culture is a product of social interaction. . . . It is by taking part in the communication system of a group that one learns its culture' (1975, p. 8). Further, 'as well as being a product of social action, culture is also a determinant of it. It determines who can talk to whom about what. We talk to one another by virtue of what is common in the cultures we have learned; we are unable to talk to one another when we lack the common experience' (*ibid.*, p. 8). So having learnt the staff culture by participating in interaction with other staff members, individuals are able, in their turn, to shape the cultures to which they now belong. In this sense, to be a staff member is both to have learnt the culture and to be able to influence it.

We saw this dual relationship in the five schools which we studied: the culture of each adult group had been shaped by the nature of the interaction, especially talk, that had taken place between participants in the past, but it was also being changed continuously by interaction between present members. In turn that interaction was influenced by institutional and personal factors within each school, including patterns of authority and influence. Buildings and organizational arrangements affected inter-action by controlling individual opportunities for participation, whereas personal histories, particularly past experiences within the school and on other staffs, affected individuals' personal inclination to interact. In this chapter we discuss each of these factors in turn and consider the ways in which they can also contribute to the development of sub-cultures within sub-groups and cliques.

Buildings

Buildings could create natural meeting places and 'critical pathways'. The latter were routes through the building which staff had to use to get to places they needed to reach regularly, such as the hall and staffroom, and which brought some adults into unplanned but inevitable contact with other staff:

> Because it's so compact you're literally all over the school in minutes and I'm sure that's probably made a difference . . . if [the staff] are going into the hall they pass other classrooms and they call out to each other, they see what somebody is doing and make a little comment and say 'Oh, that's nice,' or a joke as they go past.
>
> (Head, Sedgemoor)

But buildings, especially temporary ones, could also reduce opportunities for interaction.

> The teacher who was in here before me used to tell me how isolated it was and said 'you will find out'. You are completely forgotten, and you end up feeling no one cares.
>
> (Teacher, Hutton)

> The only adult I see for most of the time is the teacher's assistant . . . I'm aware that I'm cut off from other members of staff . . . you don't feel that you're working as a team in the same way as you would if you were on a corridor with a row of classrooms.
>
> (Teacher, Greenfields)

Consequently they could encourage the development of sub-groups:

> The building divides the staff into two, unless they constantly choose to cross its bound-aries. Other than at breaktime, the first and second year staff would barely see the third and fourth year staff during the day, as the two parallel wings are separated by the hall or an outdoor space.
>
> (Fieldnote, October, Hutton)

> In working terms the school is a confederation of three elements, namely the two infant pairs, separated by a door, then the three junior teachers along a short corridor. The building is a major determinant of working relationships. It affects who will work with whom and also makes it difficult for some people to avoid working together.
>
> (Fieldnote, October, Lavender Way)

Similarly a change in building could affect the ease with which the staff as a whole interacted:

> It used to be everyone in their set classrooms with the door closed on them . . . it's become a much more open school, open to everybody's view and open to everyone's knowledge of what is going on in the areas.
>
> (Teacher, Lowmeadow)

Organizational Arrangements

Primary teachers, particularly inexperienced ones and newcomers to a particular school, learn most from those of their colleagues (teaching or non-teaching) who are easily visible or accessible, that is, people who have the same or adjacent teaching areas or who share with them responsibility for a school activity, such as an outing or a piece of curriculum development (Lortie, 1975; Nias, 1989b). Teachers generally lead working lives characterized by isolation from other adults, especially their colleagues. For most of the school day they are alone with a group of children, often enclosed in a classroom (or, more isolated still, in temporary accommodation in the playground). Even in their breaks they may find it difficult to meet colleagues — children, especially young ones, must be supervised in the cloakrooms, while preparation needs to be undertaken for subsequent teaching activities. Ancillaries are likely to work only with certain teachers and in some schools they, and their secretarial and caretaker colleagues, do not go into teaching areas except in breaks, and do not use the staffroom. In other words, teachers and ancillaries have, at best, limited opportunities to observe or talk to one another during the school day.

By contrast, arrangements which bring the staff together and cause teachers to co-operate create opportunities for meeting and talk. In each of the five schools some or all of the work was co-ordinated in ways which encouraged interaction. Sometimes these arrangements arose from informal agreements between sub-groups on the detail of how they would work together (for example, in the two pairs of infant teachers at Lavender Way). Heads exercised a particularly powerful control on staff interaction. By co-ordinating staff's work themselves, or by encouraging staff to plan and work together, heads increased or restricted staff interaction. But buildings, history, and the size of the school's pupil intake might increase or limit their room for manoeuvre. So Hutton's two-form entry encouraged the head to put parallel age groups in adjacent rooms and to require that year pairs plan together. The effect was to encourage limited interaction within pairs but not outside them. At Lavender Way the head had inherited a system of class and staff organization which reinforced the divisive effects of the buildings: four vertically-grouped infant classes and three similarly grouped junior classes, with a co-ordinating head of infants and a deputy head who co-ordinated junior classes. Consequently staff there interacted with some colleagues frequently and with others only fleetingly. In contrast history enabled the long-established Sedgemoor head, with a not dissimilar building, to choose informal co-ordination rather than a system of designated curriculum co-ordinators, which she thought divisive. Here, one of the first tasks of a new school year was to share some responsibilities amongst staff by open negotiation in staff meetings.

Some staff found that their particular jobs restricted opportunities for interaction. Caretakers were often not in school at times when other staff gathered together, whilst the hours of some part-time secretaries meant that they saw their colleagues regularly only at morning break. Neither needed to be part of educational meetings. At Lowmeadow the nursery staff worked to a different timetable from the rest of the staff so that 'Sometimes we do feel a bit left out down here and perhaps sometimes miss out on something that's been said in the staffroom at breaktime, simply because we don't have a breaktime.' (Nursery nurse, Lowmeadow)

In primary schools staff contact is often fleeting, so being able to predict when and where to find other staff also affected opportunities for interaction. Each staff had evolved its own patterns of social interaction, which over time had become a highly stable part of the daily routine. Unless staff worked in close proximity in shared or adjacent teaching areas, social encounters were concentrated in breaktimes, lunchtimes and at the end of the school day. Such encounters were particularly influential when they took place at the lunch table and staffrooms because, unlike classrooms and offices, these were territorially neutral places where staff could meet on an equal footing. For example:

> Arriving at the school any time after 8.30 a.m. you would usually find Graham, Victoria and Carol in the staffroom. By 8.50 a.m. almost all the staff would be in the staffroom. There exists something of a ritual of drinking coffee before school. Something similar happens at the end of the school day since many of the staff stay on after school.
>
> (Fieldnote, September, Greenfields)

Conversely, the absence of such traditions at Hutton and Lavender Way restricted opportunities for whole staff interaction in circumstances where buildings and organization encouraged sub-group contact. Such restrictions were particularly noticeable to people joining the staff and wanting to 'fit in'. New staff in both schools found themselves in situations where 'People seem to spend an awful lot of time in their classrooms. . . . Nobody seems to go in [the staffroom]' (Teacher, Hutton); and 'People didn't go into the staffroom as much as I had been used to' (Teacher, Lavender Way).

Personal Inclination

But interaction was as much a product of individual inclination as of opportunity, however much buildings and organizational arrangements encouraged contact. For example, in circumstances that encouraged close teaching co-operation at Lavender Way (buildings and organization) and Hutton (organization and planning arrangements), most staff nevertheless chose to work independently rather than to team-teach.

As a Hutton teacher said, interaction depended on staff 'actually making the effort to communicate with other adults'. Some people made the effort because they enjoyed the company of other staff. At Sedgemoor everyone found staffroom life rewarding:

> You'd miss a lot, you personally would miss out. I don't think the school would collapse or anything, but you as an individual would definitely miss out on a lot . . . in every way, I think, human contact, everything. It's part and parcel of the job, it's what makes teaching bearable because you're not cut off.
>
> (Teacher, Sedgemoor)

'Making the effort' was appreciated by colleagues too. At Greenfields a new member of staff was approved of because 'her attitude towards the rest of the staff is friendly . . . she's prepared to take her share of the conversation.' (Teacher, Greenfields)

In spite of the unhelpfulness of their working times and places, some non-teachers (whether ancillaries, secretaries or caretakers) also chose to play an active part in daily staff social life. At Lowmeadow the ancillaries always attended assembly and so did the secretary whenever she could; the Hutton caretaker was a prominent member of the staffroom and of staff social life who considered that 'If I'm to be treated as a member of staff, then I see it as an important thing to be able to come in and sit and talk'. But for others, such as the Lavender Way secretary, the demands of their job were a disincentive to 'sit and talk':

> During playtime there were always children lining up with bleeding knees at the office door with nobody to attend them. Invariably I'd sit down with a cup of coffee and the telephone would ring and I just gave up and found it more convenient to stay in the office.
>
> (Secretary, Lavender Way)

Most of the heads and deputies considered it part of their job as leaders to create time to talk to colleagues, both formally and informally (see Chapter 6). In addition they modelled this behaviour by talking to each other; their very partnership was a symbol of collaboration. The heads of Sedgemoor, Lowmeadow and Greenfields made a point of being in the staffroom frequently and of using it as an informal channel of communication. In contrast the Hutton head was often busy talking with one of his colleagues in his office at breaktimes, and at Lavender Way a relatively new head had to balance her breaktime priorities between staffroom interaction and administrative efficiency, because she spent much of her day as a teaching model alongside staff.

Although most staff enjoyed each other's company, in all the schools a few individuals preferred to be self-contained. One of two Greenfields staff who had worked in an isolated classroom enjoyed the experience, because 'It's nice to be able to do what you want without having to worry about what other people are doing.' A second Greenfields teacher spent little time in the staffroom because she was preoccupied with her teaching difficulties. The only ancillary helper at Lavender Way made little use of the staffroom because she felt isolated there: 'They're usually talking about some project . . . and if I've got a few minutes for idle chatter I usually go and see them in the kitchen.'

Past experiences within each school and in previous posts also affected each individual's readiness to interact with staff in general and influenced some individuals' interactions with particular colleagues. However, staff reactions to the same situations were not always identical. At Hutton, for example, not everyone responded similarly to the forceful lead given by the head.

> When I first started teaching it was 'Here is your class, there you are, get on with it.' You sink or swim, I was given no guidance at all. And when you start like that, it comes a bit hard when someone turns round and says, 'Right, this is the way it's going to be done.'
>
> (Teacher, Hutton)

can be compared with:

> I knew somebody very much like him [the head] before, so perhaps I warmed to him more because I had come across his sort of personality before, and what he said made sense to me.
>
> (Teacher, Hutton)

Individuals also had differing expectations of the nature and extent of the support they would receive from their colleagues and so sought the company of other staff to varying degrees:

> I came as a probationer, so in a lot of respects I was more open to new ideas and hadn't had the experience to tell me how I ought to teach . . . therefore I was willing to accept other suggestions.
>
> (Teacher, Hutton)

> [At a previous school] 'You would go in and say "I would like to shoot the lot of them". You don't mean it, but it's just a way of letting off steam and reassuring yourself that everybody else is struggling as well . . . people don't need to be reassured in that way here'.
>
> (Teacher, Hutton)

Experiences in previous jobs also affected the way staff viewed each other's professional roles and therefore how they interacted with one another. Assumptions were based on precedents not necessarily applicable to new situations. For example, at Lavender Way, Ben, the deputy head, thought his work in his previous school would fit him well for his new job:

> I never really thought I would find any difficulty doing it because I felt as if I had probably been at least as responsible, if not more so, than the deputy in my previous school . . . in fact it turned out to be infinitely more difficult than I could ever have imagined.
>
> (Deputy head, Lavender Way)

By the same token some of his colleagues took their previous deputy heads as a yardstick for Ben's performance:

> This is a first school and I do feel it is part of the job of deputy heads to put themselves about the school and to be seen by the infants and to work with them. The previous deputy heads used to spend time amongst the infants. Mind you, the previous one was a very extrovert type and was very hard to follow.
>
> (Teacher, Lavender Way)

Time and interaction were necessary before individuals could work out agreed ways of interpreting their jobs, because 'It's only through knowing people over a period of time that you know which role you're playing and which role they're playing and then you can respond accordingly' (Teacher, Lavender Way).

In contrast to Lavender Way, Lowmeadow staff had a long shared history, and few had been part of the culture of a different school. Interaction there was based on a shared set of experiences and expectations which influenced the behaviour of members:

> I think it's no accident that a large proportion of the teachers who are here came fresh from college or fresh on return, that, generally speaking, teachers who've taught a long time in other schools don't fit into the school.
>
> (Teacher, Lowmeadow)

The ability of the staff as a group to sustain its culture by influencing the behaviour of members is discussed more fully in Chapter 5. But some individuals had particular influence on a school's culture because they were seen to possess authority.

Authority

Chapter 8 argues that heads and deputies exercised formal authority, in that staff felt bound to accept certain of their decisions. But it is worth noting at this stage that because there was a considerable variation in the ways heads and deputies used their authority, they affected the cultures of their schools in different ways. It is instructive to contrast the comment of a teacher in a school where some staff perceived the head as tightly authoritarian, with one from a school where staff had considerable individual freedom over classroom decisions:

> For about the first term and a half I was doing one or two things which were technically wrong as far as what was expected here. I was politely told to change.
>
> (Teacher, Hutton)

> You are allowed, if that is the right word, to run your class as you wish, as you feel happiest working.
>
> (Teacher, Sedgemoor)

Moreover formal leaders had considerable informal influence over their colleagues simply because their views carried weight. But the exercise of informal influence was not confined to formal leaders. Just as individual histories affected personal inclination to interact, so the part individuals and sub-groups had played in the history of the staff and its culture affected their influence within the present staff.

The Power of History

Inherited traditions had a powerful influence on interaction. Staff who had been in a school for some time had helped create the existing culture, so they understood the origins of and justifications for customary patterns of behaviour. Because the logic of history was used to define 'reasonable' behaviour, staff who shared a common history within the school tended to define the present in similar ways, using their shared past as a yardstick for the success of the present. There was a temptation to create images of a past golden age:

> One thing that sticks in my mind is sitting on the floor with the children in assembly. It's only very recently that we've sat on chairs. We always used to sit on the floor with the children, which I thought was lovely.
>
> (Teacher, Lavender Way)

> He [the previous head] trusted us to get on and do things our way . . . we actually did the decision-making . . . it was more staff-centred.
>
> (Teacher, Hutton)

> Oh, we obviously had to get the OK from Mr Smith, but usually we had very sound ideas and that was very good.
>
> (Teacher, Hutton)

Heads who had been in their posts longer than their staffs controlled what the past meant:

> Those early days had shown what was wrong with the staff's approach and their attitudes and has helped me to crystallize what I'm looking for . . . I had to make Greenfields

into a school where all the parents would want their children to be educated . . . I said we would become a community school provided it didn't make any difference.

(Head, Greenfields)

New staff in particular had difficulty in questioning the legitimacy of traditions they had inherited, and since they had limited access to the meanings implicit in the latter, they could not easily alter them:

In my mind it's a thing to lose, that departmental identity . . . but it was well established when we came.

(Teacher, Lavender Way)

At Lavender Way one new teacher was confused that the staffroom was often empty for much of break and lunchtime because:

At other schools that I'd been in, as soon as the children were out to play everybody dashed and got their coffee and sat down . . . and I did notice once or twice that I went into the staffroom and there would be nobody there, and I thought 'Why is it that I'm the only one?'

(Teacher, Lavender Way)

Generally, newcomers had to accept the version of past events that was presented to them. Catherine recalled that one of the difficulties of coming as a new head to Lavender Way was,

Knowing what the real situation is, not what you're told the situation is. . . . There were certain things I was told about particular staff, in the way to approach them, which was not my way of approaching staff. So I didn't approach them in that way, but it inhibited the way I would normally want to do it.

(Head, Lavender Way)

But the heads' authority was also reinforced by the general assumption that the school belonged to those who had created it (Chapter 6). They could reasonably expect their policies to be accepted as the yardstick by which newcomers' suitability for membership would be judged. When at the start of her third full school year Catherine began to feel in control of the past, she used that feeling of control as an index of having made Lavender Way 'her school':

Nobody now makes a reference to 'We used to do it like this', and it's nice to be able to say 'Last year do you remember, we did something like this.'

(Head, Lavender Way)

NORMS AND SHARED MEANINGS

So far in this chapter we have suggested that each school's culture was shaped through interaction, that the nature of interaction in each staff was a product of its buildings, organization, people and history, and that these factors affected interaction both by controlling individual opportunity and inclination to interact and by determining whose influence predominated. Now we shall consider the specific ways of behaving which emerged from interaction.

As staff talked, worked and relaxed together, they began to negotiate shared meanings which enabled them to predict each others' behaviour. Consequently each staff developed its own taken-for-granted norms. Because shared meanings and ways of behaving became so taken for granted, existing staff were largely unaware of them. But they were visible to newcomers, whether probationers or staff who moved from another school and encountered unfamiliar ways of behaving and meanings which initially they found difficult to understand. Researchers moving between schools were constantly reminded of the uniqueness of each school's norms.

Because new staff are normally anxious to fit in with acceptable ways of behaving in their new schools, they are receptive to the clues offered by behaviour and readily learn, by modelling themselves on their colleagues, what it is to be a staff member. For these reasons norms and shared meanings can best be perceived through the eyes of newcomers. For example, a Sedgemoor teacher recalled how she learnt that staff there shared each other's problems.

> I think that when I came here I tended to think about it in terms of how it had been at the other schools. It took me a good four months to realize that everybody was quite willing to help with problems and that when you had problems you didn't hide away, you voiced them.
>
> (Teacher, Sedgemoor)

By contrast a Hutton teacher had learnt the opposite at her school: 'I've just learnt that because nobody else does it, I don't, and so I take all my problems home.' (Teacher, Hutton)

Influenced by norms of this sort, new staff sometimes adopted practices they found bizarre, because they needed to show they belonged. For example at Lavender Way, everyone brought their own brand of breaktime drink:

> I think I would have found it disconcerting if it wasn't for the fact that someone said, 'Oh crikey, there are so many different lots of coffee here. You'd be much better to bring your own.' I find it a bit of an odd arrangement but I think it's 'if you can't beat them join them' . . . as soon as I'd got my jar there with my name on, I was one of the gang and I didn't have to worry any more after that.
>
> (Teacher, Lavender Way)

Through the process of learning what to do, staff began to share the sophisticated meanings implicit in routine behaviour, simple statements and actions. As one teacher said:

> Relationships are putting yourself in other people's shoes, not so much what they say, but picking up the signals about what they mean.
>
> (Teacher, Lowmeadow)

The researcher's comments bear out this observation:

> Throughout the preparation for the day's work, putting on shoes, settling the children down, going in and out of assembly, etc., I was once again impressed by the extent of eye contact and hand signalling between the teachers and ancillaries and between them and Miss Proctor.
>
> (Fieldnote, October, Lowmeadow)

In particular, the existence of shared meanings was often revealed by humour and laughter, especially at actions which seemed, to an observer, to carry intentions contrary to those of the initiator:

> Polly, the ancillary, has been tidying the store cupboard in the hall. Isobel comes to inspect it, is impressed and says, 'I'm going to put a notice on for a joke.' The notice is duly written: 'Entry to this stock cupboard is verboten.' Shortly afterwards Isobel says

to a passing child, 'Tell the teachers that I'm going to have a stock cupboard inspection tomorrow and that there will be points for the best ones.'

(Fieldnote, July, Sedgemoor)

The humorous implication of these exchanges is revealed when:

> At camp, Dennis deals with the organization of the children who are members of his class. We watch him at the end of the afternoon, herding the children into the shelter to write their camp diaries. He adopts Hitlerian poses, marching up and down in parody of the values implied by his actions, for the amusement of the watchers – and to dissociate himself from those values.

(Fieldnote, May, Sedgemoor)

In the same way foreknowledge of how her colleagues would react to a plea for help gave the Lowmeadow head the chance to provoke laughter:

> Miss Proctor came in and stood in the middle of the staffroom and said 'I've got a problem.' Everybody stopped to listen and make sympathetic noises. Then with mock seriousness she described how she'd brought a pavlova left over from a dinner party last night into school, meaning to share it with the staff at lunchtime, but had forgotten to do this, and now what could she do, because they were all full up with someone's birthday cake? Amid laughter, they all offered to eat it up.

(Fieldnote, May, Lowmeadow)

Over time, shared definitions or shared meanings became so refined that they were expressed in culturally specific language. Sometimes this took the form of regularly used words, phrases, or references whose meanings were obscure to outsiders. At Sedgemoor, 'flapping' referred to the school's emphasis on not making a fuss. 'Shall we have a school meeting?' was understood as the deputy's way of offering to give colleagues an end-of-week recuperative time, whilst he took the school in the hall. At Greenfields 'a hepic' was a term of disapproval referring to an over-elaborate assembly, 'marching children about' also conveyed disapproval. At Lavender Way regular references to 'infants', 'juniors' and 'our area' indicated to all participants the distinctions between staff which were masked by the open-plan nature of the building.

SYMBOLS, RITUALS AND CEREMONIES

We have suggested that the shared meanings which grew from interaction were largely taken for granted. But some meanings were so important to the culture, yet so deeply internalized and therefore difficult to articulate, that staff had evolved symbolic acts, rituals and ceremonies through which to express them. The more extensive the shared meanings, the more staff relied on rituals and symbols.

For example, as Chapter 4 makes clear, in several of the schools individuals were felt to be important, but so too was the fact of belonging to a group. These values were frequently symbolized in rituals of sharing food or drink. At Lowmeadow all manner of personal events from moving house to birthdays were celebrated by bringing a cake. At Greenfields there was a glass of wine during staff meetings. At Sedgemoor such rituals included the 'family' morning coffee together, then after school anyone making a pot of tea took a tray of cups round to colleagues working in classrooms.

Meeting socially also had symbolic implications. At Greenfields when staff were anxious to spend time talking through school problems together, but union action precluded formal staff meetings, Carol suggested a get-together at her house:

> It was a meeting which Carol, Victoria, Graham, Jim and Mary attended to discuss next term . . . very much the five members of the 'family' in the school getting together for a kind of staff meeting, but more a family meeting at which they wanted to discuss things.
>
> (Fieldnote, March, Greenfields)

At Hutton the suggestion of a staff cricket team expressed a similar need:

> Early in the Autumn term the staffroom conversation turned to the idea of getting together one evening and having a social game of mixed indoor cricket. From casual beginnings came an institution which became a source of shared enjoyment for several of the staff.
>
> (Yeomans, 1987a)

Other rituals such as the celebration of birthdays in assemblies reaffirmed that individuals were important to the group.

Assemblies were particularly significant as cultural ceremonies because only then did the whole school, staff included, meet (see Nias, 1989c). Events there emphasized the unity of the school and the interdependence of its members, so that even routine patterns of behaviour which carried shared meanings had ritual importance (King, 1983). Assemblies were also occasions when staff's attentive presence implied their support for public statements to children about attitudes, values and beliefs.

Though by its very nature, the fact of assembly symbolized the existence of a school and therefore of a school culture, every stage of a particular assembly was replete with symbolic implications. Specific aspects of the way assemblies were conducted emphasized their ritual importance, indicated assumptions about relationships or taught attitudes and values, both implicitly and explicitly.

Sometimes entry revealed attitudes to relationships and discipline. At Greenfields adults and children walked into assembly and sat randomly rather than lining up and sitting in classes. Staff and children at Hutton, Lowmeadow and Sedgemoor were bound by a convention of strict silence whilst they waited for assembly to begin:

> Assembly was used to remind the children of the standards expected of them throughout the school, thus when one child slid on his seat, the head sent him out with a 'Come in sensibly'.
>
> (Fieldnote, October, Hutton)

Similarly, membership of audiences revealed staff attitudes to the school's community (for example, parents and governors were regularly invited to join assembly at Lowmeadow, Greenfields and Hutton).

Assembly was also a time when leadership could be reaffirmed, though in different ways. The head or deputy took all assemblies at Hutton but the Greenfields head seldom did so, usually closing them instead with reflections on the shared experience. Children with their teachers regularly took assemblies at Greenfields, Lowmeadow, Lavender Way and Sedgemoor. Most assembly leaders sat in a chair, though the Hutton head usually stood.

The manner in which headteachers took assembly revealed to staff as well as pupils their attitudes to children:

The head begins his assembly by saying in a friendly tone to the children 'Sit up', and there was an immediate response. He illustrates his story by involving children as demonstrators, and by questioning the children who are seated . . . directing them into the right paths, but in a benevolent way.

(Fieldnote, October, Hutton)

We sang 'Maytime', and since half the children didn't know it we needed to learn it. After the first or second attempt Miss Proctor called out R. (a Sikh) and asked him to go on the stage and sing the chorus by himself because he was doing it so beautifully . . . he stood about nine feet tall, with joy and confidence radiating out of him.

(Fieldnote, May, Lowmeadow)

Content was often important too. For example, cultural values were often made explicit in stories, and through the morals that were drawn from them. Silence and listening to appropriate music before an assembly also emphasized the importance of the occasion, of what all were gathered to hear, and respect for the people they were about to listen to:

Beethoven's Moonlight Sonata and the children, once all assembled, sat for quite a long time to the end of the recording.

(Fieldnote, July, Lowmeadow)

Similarly endings, usually with ordered and silent departures, again often with music, maintained, for staff and children, the sense of having participated in an occasion of importance.

Finally, assembly was also a time for those ceremonies in which the head spoke as the voice of the school, leading the applause for those who exemplified the school's values in some notable way:

The assembly was devoted entirely to giving out the swimming certificates . . . and every single child was applauded for their certificates.

(Fieldnote, July, Greenfields)

or conveying to staff who were leaving the affection and goodwill of the whole school, thereby affirming its unity:

It was a 'going day' because it was a chance to say goodbye to Violet (the caretaker). Graham gave her the wrapped present . . . inside was the engraved fruitbowl which had a picture of the school engraved and some words saying 'To remind you of your time at Greenfields School from the children and community of Greenfields'.

(Fieldnote, March, Greenfields)

SUB-GROUPS AND CLIQUES

We have seen that symbols and rituals were an important means by which the norms and shared understandings of a culture were expressed. But because the influences on patterns of interaction operated in different ways from school to school, not all schools had a single culture. Under some circumstances sub-groups could develop, each with their own sub-culture. When a sub-group developed particularly distinctive and exclusive patterns of interaction, it might become perceived by other sub-groups as a clique. By definition, members of a clique placed greater value on their sub-group relationships than on their relationships within the wider staff group. Such unequal valuing of colleagues inhibited the development of a single staff culture because, just as talk could encourage staff-wide shared meanings, so restricted inter-action created in-group understandings:

> When we first got to know each other we always talked about school, but since we've settled into a relationship at dinnertimes, school is almost banned unless one of us has a problem. We talk about poetry, books, all sorts, so you get away from what you are doing and leave your little molehill.
>
> (Teacher, Hutton)

As a clique developed a particular shared perspective on school situations, other individuals and sub-groups could perceive it as having all the hostile characteristics of an 'enemy'. The staff at Hutton were afflicted late in the year by internal divisions which originated in two such sub-groups who were mutually perceived as cliques. It was the apparent exclusivity of such sub-groups that made them harmful to the staff as a whole. One Sedgemoor teacher recognized that out-of-school contact which was not accessible to all staff had the potential to generate division in school. His words are an apt commentary on events at Hutton:

> It is not a terribly social staff in the sense of going out. If that started it might go against the working of the school because you can get 'us' and 'them' cliques forming in the staffroom and that can cause problems . . . they can get on well outside school, so they tend to mix in school as well. Whereas when we go out . . . that's not brought into the staffroom, everyone comes feeling on an equal footing with everyone else.
>
> (Teacher, Sedgemoor)

The origins of the Hutton sub-groups were innocent. Membership of the evening staff indoor cricket team created a sub-group which included the head:

> Once the cricket has finished all stay for a drink. There is a strong cohesive feeling. Everyone wants to stay and chat. They begin to stray back to school issues.
>
> (Fieldnote, September, Hutton)

The natural tendency to discuss their games in the staffroom meant that:

> We are really boring to people who are not in the cricket team because it can be 90 per cent of our conversation on the morning after we've played.
>
> (Teacher, Hutton)

Moreover, non-members were confirmed in their belief that they were being excluded:

> I did offer to play one night when they were short, and they said, 'Yes'. So I got all psyched up, and then this person decided they would play after all. They are a bit closed shop about it, which is a shame. It has set the staff apart from each other rather than bringing them together.
>
> (Teacher, Hutton)

During the year a second clique emerged, one of whose members was the above speaker. It consisted of three staff who spent their lunchtimes together at a member's home during the periods of union action, and its existence points up three ways in which social differences could mirror and deepen professional divisions within school. First, each sub-group had a fixed membership and there was no overlap between groups. Secondly, both sub-groups met away from school in circumstances which excluded other colleagues. Thirdly, when school issues were debated at staff meetings, it was by reference to the cliques rather than the whole staff that members validated their beliefs and attitudes. Moreover, because attitudes became fixed, views on contentious issues were less likely to be stated openly within the staffroom, and more likely to be aired in places where they would receive a sympathetic hearing.

> I didn't want to say anything because I thought 'They are going to see me as being provocative because I'm leaving'. . . . Someone else said 'I thought they would say I was the old-fashioned one who wasn't willing to change.' We talked about it afterwards and we'd all got reasons why we didn't say anything. Yet everyone felt they should have said something.
>
> (Teacher, Hutton)

At Lavender Way too, there was a phase when latent differences between established members, exacerbated by the building's divisive effects on interaction, threatened to polarize the staff into sub-groups, and created an 'open secret' which hampered the growth of a single culture:

> There was a stage when I came here that you got whisperings in corners. Somebody would come and tell you something that you weren't supposed to let anyone else know and vice versa, and you ended up piggy in the middle, knowing all the bits, but not knowing what to say to whom.
>
> (Teacher, Lavender Way)

> The atmosphere got icy at times and I just kept a low profile.
>
> (Teacher, Lavender Way)

SUMMARY

Each school had developed a culture whose unique quality was determined by the influence of its buildings, organizational arrangements, the people who worked there, their histories and that of the school. These factors affected opportunities and inclination to interact. Each culture was further shaped by the formal and personal authority carried by individuals, the latter often legitimized by history. Norms and shared meanings grew from interaction, the latter in particular being expressed through the symbols, rituals and ceremonies which reflected the underlying values, attitudes and beliefs of the culture. The factors determining patterns of interaction could also however encourage the emergence of sub-groups (at Lavender Way) and cliques (at Hutton), each with separate sub-cultures. In contrast, at Lowmeadow, Greenfields and Sedgemoor there had developed strong and unifying cultures which had important common elements. It is to this particular form of culture that we now turn.

Chapter 4

The Culture of Collaboration

In the previous chapter we argued that all the project schools evolved their own dominant staff cultures, as over time individuals with different amounts of authority and influence chose or happened to interact with one another. But soon we also became aware that three of them — Greenfields, Lowmeadow and Sedgemoor — were so similar in many respects that they could be described as having a particular type of culture. To be sure, this was manifested in different ways; 'the way we do it here' in relation to, say, assembly, staff meetings or the distribution of curricular responsibilities was unique to each school. But we began to discover that, as we penetrated below these surface differences, we encountered similarities, particularly in regard to staff beliefs about the relationships which existed or should exist between individuals and groups. In consequence, the values enshrined in much of the practice of these schools were also similar.

The fact that Greenfields, Sedgemoor and Lowmeadow shared a common type of dominant culture was emphasized by their differences from Hutton and Lavender Way. In both the latter schools, relatively new headteachers, supported by recently appointed deputies, were attempting to change the ways in which their staff worked together. It is clear, as this chapter demonstrates, that, in terms of beliefs about the nature of social relationships, the directions in which they were trying to move their schools were similar to those already existing in the other three schools. At Hutton the situation was complicated in two ways. The head's main purpose was to change his teacher's curricular and pedagogical practices, and his attempts to do this included putting pressure on them to work together more closely in their implementation of school-wide educational policies. Yet his aims were often expressed to them as directives, the effect of which ran counter to his intentions. Therefore, although in this chapter we often emphasize the similarities between Greenfields, Lowmeadow and Sedgemoor by contrasting them with Lavender Way and Hutton, this should not be taken as meaning that staff relationships in the latter two schools were steadily moving throughout the year in identical directions or at the same rate. Generalizations always distort the fine detail of individual cases, and we have been unable to do justice here to the complexity of relationships at Hutton, particularly given the number of staff changes that the school experienced during our time there. Nevertheless, it is fair to make two claims: that at the start of the year the staff cultures at Lavender Way and Hutton were qualitatively different from those at the other three schools; and that the leaders of each of these schools were attempting to change their staff culture so that it became more like that which we identified in the other schools. This gave us the opportunity (see Chapters 5 and 7) to examine staff groups where the culture was altering and to identify the means by which heads and deputies, in particular, sought to initiate and sustain appropriate changes.

We need to stress that in none of the schools were staff groups homogeneous or totally cohesive. Individuals were rooted in their own sub-cultures (e.g., religious, class, regional, gender) and brought these into the schools with them. They were also members of varied occupational sub-cultures (e.g., caretaker, teacher) whose interests were not always identical. Third, teachers themselves sometimes belonged to separate professional sub-cultures (as, for example, 'infant' or 'junior' teachers). Finally, neither teachers nor ancillaries subscribed all the time or to the same extent to key cultural beliefs. The extent to which individuals participated in the dominant culture of their schools was subject to a constant process of negotiation. Individual interests had always to be reconciled with membership not just of the institution but also of the staff group (see Chapter 8). Indeed, one characteristic of the culture of collaboration was that it facilitated the reconciliation of individual and group aims, since differences were tolerated or resolved rather than being submerged.

In addition, in Hutton and Lavender Way, sub-groups existed at the start of the year, each with its own sub-culture (see Chapters 3 and 5). Faced with their leaders' determined efforts to install a new culture, dissentients had three choices: to leave their schools (at both schools some staff left during the year, though not all were unsympathetic to their heads' policies), to isolate themselves within their sub-groups (as some at Hutton did) or to move in the directions in which the heads and their deputies were pointing (as happened with some staff in both schools). Differences were therefore more noticeable in these two schools than in the other three, and negotiation was more overt and often more intense (see Chapter 8).

In this chapter we identify the beliefs and values which underlay what we have called the 'culture of collaboration', as it existed in Greenfields, Lowmeadow and Sedgemoor and was developing in Hutton and Lavender Way. We examine in particular the ways in which similar values were expressed through speech and action, in customs, habits and accepted ways of behaving, by individuals acting in their own right and as members of groups and teams. In the process we touch upon assembly. Symbolic ways of representing the culture are dealt with in greater detail in Chapter 5, 'culture-founders' and 'culture-bearers' in Chapter 6 and the importance of shared perspectives in Chapter 8.

We argue that the culture was built on four interacting beliefs. The first two specify ends: individuals should be valued but, because they are inseparable from the groups of which they are part, groups too should be fostered and valued. The second two relate to means: the most effective ways of promoting these values are through openness and a sense of mutual security.

THE CULTURE OF COLLABORATION AND EDUCATIONAL PRACTICE

Now these four beliefs relate more obviously to personal relationships than they do to children's learning or to teachers' classroom practice. Yet these were schools rather than other types of institutions in which adults work together and the behaviour towards one another of staff, particularly but not exclusively of headteachers and teachers, was inescapably educative in outcome and sometimes in intention. It therefore seems important to comment on the relationships which existed between the 'culture of collaboration' and the educational tenets and behaviour of the staff.

Teachers, as people and as practitioners, hold many beliefs. Some of these impinge on their practice more obviously than others. In general, there appears to be a broad consensus among primary teachers about what children should learn. Most stress literacy and numeracy and beyond that pay at least lip service to the need for a broad and balanced curriculum (Alexander, 1984). Certainly, in all the schools we found agreement, enshrined in curriculum documents and guidelines, about curriculum content. Differences in staff culture between Greenfields, Lowmeadow and Sedgemoor on the one hand and Hutton and Lavender Way on the other cannot be explained by reference to conflicting beliefs about the nature or organization of knowledge.

Teachers do, however, vary widely in their views on how children learn. As teachers we have encountered schools where all or the majority of the staff espoused the same set of beliefs about, for instance, the way reading should be taught or the importance to children's learning of direct experience and discussion. Much of the polemic literature of the 1960s and 1970s suggests that some staff groups do build a shared culture upon such pedagogical beliefs and that it can have a powerful effect upon its members.

But the 'culture of collaboration' had a different emphasis, being primarily concerned with personal relationships rather than pedagogy. As a result it seems to have had an indirect rather than a direct effect on educational practice in the schools in which it existed. This effect was most obvious in four main areas of school life and practice.

First, it worked in several ways to produce a very broad consensus among the staff about teaching methods. A simultaneous concern to encourage the expression of individual differences and to foster the unity of the group encouraged open but constructively critical discussion of varying opinions and practices. A majority viewpoint began to emerge, which legitimated individualism but not extremism. Those who held extreme educational views, or who defended particular beliefs extremely, tended to become marginalized and eventually sought posts elsewhere. As this happened, heads were able to increase the likelihood of educational consensus by gathering round them staff who held similar pedagogical beliefs to their own, and who were prepared to act in accordance with these beliefs (see Chapter 7).

In time, a combination of open, friendly discussion and judicious recruitment policies tended to bring everyone's views into line with those of the head and of the staff majority:

> We probably have got the same basic ideas about education, and from the things that we say to each other, we are all working on more or less the same lines now.
>
> (Teacher, Lavender Way, at the end of the year)

That's what I really noticed once I'd stayed here for a while, the way everybody . . . worked to the same goal.

(Teacher, Lowmeadow)

Of course, such pressures could have acted to produce schools with highly cohesive and constraining policies on classroom organization and teaching methods. But the nature of the 'culture of collaboration' ensured that this was not the case. Provided that the speech or behaviour of individual teachers did not threaten the collective sense of interdependence, everyone was encouraged to hold independent views and to translate them into action in ways that suited him/her individually. Teachers and ancillaries were expected to be aware of the likely effects of their behaviour upon the school as a whole, but not to be clones of their headteachers or of one another:

> On important issues, we do work things out together and I suppose we're lucky that by and large we are of like minds over general things, even though in our classrooms we do it our way.
>
> (Teacher, Sedgemoor).

> One of the first essentials in a school with aims of this kind is harmony and respect among the staff. We felt it important for each to consider the school as a whole as well as to be absorbed in the working of a single class. We felt that we must be prepared to share our ideas, and not to reach the stage of over-competition at any level. Teachers must work as a team and be prepared to cooperate, to ask advice, to use a colleague's experienced knowledge with courtesy and without affectation as one friend to another . . . It is recognised that teaching methods and approaches are highly individual assets and that it is virtually impossible to copy these, although there are some details which can be employed over a wider range. We feel, therefore, that to try and impose a single blanket teaching method would be injudicious.
>
> (Greenfields, Introduction to *School Schemes of Work*)

There was a second and rather different way in which the existence of a 'culture of collaboration' affected the content and practice of education in these schools. The central beliefs of this culture reflected a particular view of what the relationships between individuals and groups not only were but should be. On the one hand, every individual should be perceived and treated as unique and valuable. All five schools saw themselves in broad, ill-defined terms as 'child-centred' and the staff believed that they were all 'absolutely interested in what each individual [pupil] is doing' (Teacher, Lowmeadow). In a sense familiar to all students or practitioners of liberal, humanitarian values and richly described in Hargreaves' (1982) account of the contemporary comprehensive school, these teachers all participated in what he describes as the 'culture of individualism'. Yet they also believed that 'moral ends are to be seen as collective not individual ends' (Hargreaves, 1982, p. 108). In all the schools, the staff felt that education should create in pupils a disposition to act in the light of other people's well-being and interests, that children should learn to treat one another with 'caring, concern, interest' (Teacher, Lowmeadow). As the Greenfields *School Curriculum Document* states: '[We aim] to set our children on the way to becoming competent adults, socially aware, considerate of others, feeling confident, secure and able to meet a variety of situations'.

Further, all the school documents stress the importance of perceiving the school as part of the community, and in all of them links were actively built with the surrounding neighbourhood, whether through the church, the governors, parents or, for example, 'the old people across the road' (Head, Sedgemoor). Members of the community were regularly welcomed into every school, especially for assembly, and the two male heads, both of whom lived locally, were personally involved in village affairs (e.g., through cricket or music). Lowmeadow was described by its head as a 'community school', and the head of Sedgemoor spoke of 'the conscious effort I made in the early days, and to a certain extent still do, to keep a village school in mind, because that was my sort of ultimate aim when we first opened, I wanted this to be as near to a village school as it was possible for a school on a new council estate to be . . . where everyone is involved'. As the head of Greenfields said, 'My belief that community education is good for the children is actually founded on experience, it isn't something I got from a book, I don't ever remember reading it . . . it's something I actually saw happening. . . .'

Moreover, as his comment suggests, the group (whether family, class, school, team or larger community) was not seen as a moral burden but as the means by which and the context within which individuals could achieve their maximum development. In Hargreaves' words (1982, p. 111): 'Genuine individuality must be rooted in group life.' Accordingly, talents and abilities of all sorts could best be fostered within an atmosphere of mutual concern. Interdependence was not only morally inescapable but educative in its effects:

> It's the kind of caring community of children and adults which leads to the maximum progress, socially and educationally, for everybody and that includes adults. So that nobody ever stops progressing . . . I want to see everyone achieving high academic results and going on to make their lives the best that their character and ability is capable of making . . . [with] feelings of concern for other people. I don't want them to turn out the kind of people who would trample on everybody else's susceptibilities.

> (Head, Greenfields)

In this context, we do not know whether or not it is significant that Hutton was a voluntary aided school, Lowmeadow, though a maintained school, was strongly Christian in ethos and at Greenfields the head, though an agnostic, spoke of wanting to foster 'the kind of community Jesus would have established'. Be that as it may, the staff in all of the schools were concerned to foster not simply independence and the exercise of initiative but also a sense of mutual obligation and responsibility. Their conception of moral education was Janus-like, simultaneously looking inwards to the person and outwards to the group.

Yet in the social and moral areas of the curriculum English primary schools have very little tradition of direct teaching, other than through assembly (Alexander, 1984). Instead, such teaching usually takes place through the hidden curriculum (that is, through school organization, rules, rewards and punishments and the like) and through example. Appropriate attitudes and behaviour are often felt to be 'caught' rather that 'taught'. Certainly, in the project schools, the staff recognized the educative potential for children of the relationships they displayed towards one another. They were aware that they needed to behave towards one another in ways consistent with those whose value they wished to impress upon children:

> I do believe that the atmosphere in the school moves outwards from the staffroom or wherever the staff meet, like ripples on a pond. If you've got a happy school you've almost certainly got a staff who work together well, who can relate well to each other, and a reasonably happy staffroom. That leads straight out to the rest of the school and affects the children and the parents and everything else.

> (Head, Greenfields)

Participation in the 'culture of collaboration' had a third effect upon its members' professional practice. Within each school it resulted in a strong sense of commitment to a common task: the twin facts that headteachers, teachers and ancillaries valued the contribution each could make, while being aware of their interdependence, encouraged them to develop a sense of collective responsibility for the education of their pupils. In turn this enjoined upon all the staff the need for a high degree of occupational competence. When a weak teacher who was being given a last chance at Greenfields failed to prove, despite a great deal of help, that she could cope, the rest of the staff sadly but unanimously agreed that she should leave the school, and so the profession. As the head said:

> I would have said a year ago, someone who is simply prepared to work hard would have been accepted, but that has proved to be not true, because Julie works ever so hard, yet she hasn't really been accepted. This is partly because she doesn't enhance the reputation of the school and that's resented by the rest of the staff. They get their strokes not just out of their own personal success, but out of the success of the whole school. That's something that has struck me very forcibly this year.
>
> (Head, Greenfields)

Similarly, at Lavender Way the caretaker discovered to his cost from the new head that to count himself, as by implication he did, as 'one of the family' was no substitute for maintaining a clean school. As a result:

> Generally [in the past] it's other teachers that have given up, not the school. They're the ones that have said, 'Oh I can't do it.' They've in effect said, 'Well I'm not going to be able to keep up the standard you want here' and they have decided to go, one way or another.
>
> (Teacher, Lowmeadow)

> It's hard to tell why, but people take their job seriously and do think things through.
>
> (Teacher, Sedgemoor)

The standards within the staff group were achieved only through long hours of hard work. As a new appointee to Greenfields said,

> When the permanent job came up Graham did say to me would I be interested and I think he maybe wondered why I didn't bite his hand off and say 'yes'. I was a bit hesitant about it, not because I didn't want to stay, but because they seemed such a committed and hardworking staff. I think I'm quite conscientious – I work in my lunch hours and I take stuff home, and I pop in at weekends if I need to — but I really felt that with a young child I couldn't be here for half past eight in the morning or an hour or so after school at night. So I had to give it a lot of thought and I did put all this to Graham. I said 'I can give you 100% while I'm here and I'll do the preparation, but I can't always be about.' I didn't know how the staff would see it. They might have thought 'she's not pulling her weight', or that sort of thing, so I talked to Graham about that. I wanted to be fair to everyone.
>
> (Teacher, Greenfields)

Isobel, the head of Sedgemoor, was reported (October, 1985) as saying to the researcher 'I keep telling them to go home but they don't take any notice', while at Lowmeadow, 'To work here you have to be very conscientious and hardworking and dedicated . . . you have to set high standards' (Secretary, Lowmeadow). A fieldnote from Hutton reads:

> A colleague comes into Teresa's room and talks with her about the experience of being

at a previous school, she describes how everybody had gone by 4 o'clock, the head by 3.45 p.m. and how depressing it was. They look at and discuss some of Teresa's work. Teresa is already becoming important to the staff as an encouragement to standards by example.

(Fieldnote, February, Hutton)

For headteachers, teachers and ancillaries in the 'collaborative' schools, shared responsibility and hard work resulted in the feeling that theirs were unique institutions — 'different' (Lowmeadow), 'special' (Sedgemoor), possessed of an *esprit de corps*' (Greenfields). This belief that the product of their joint endeavour was different from and by implication better than that of other schools, helped to confirm the staffs' team pride and shared pleasure, both in the process of working together and in its outcomes. In turn, this tended to confirm them in further, largely untested beliefs that they all shared a common approach to teaching or, where differences obviously existed, that individuality was collectively enriching.

In Greenfields, Lowmeadow and Sedgemoor, and increasingly during the year in Lavender Way, this awareness of being engaged on a common task, coupled with a broad consensus on teaching methods and a respect for individual differences, made it relatively easy for staff to share the job of teaching. They often put two or more classes together for one activity, exchanged children for a particular purpose, and knew and talked about what was happening in one another's classrooms. Pupils, for their part, moved between one class and another without any apparent anxiety and without encountering major discontinuities. Teaching, though still construed as a personal activity, was not necessarily a private one. By contrast one pair of teachers team-taught at Hutton and, in the earlier part of the year, at Lavender Way, yet in neither did there exist a school sense of collective responsibility. Now team-teaching, it may be argued, requires close agreement on more areas of professional practice than do looser, more pragmatic forms of co-operation. One can share the process of teaching and learning only with those who have similar beliefs about curriculum content, pedagogy and discipline. As a member of a team-teaching pair at Lavender Way said: 'You need to be very much on the same wavelength . . . so that you can interrelate with children.' At Hutton, one teacher said of her partner:

> You don't take long to find out that you're sharing the same sort of philosophies, that the standard of work and the level of discipline that you expect is the same and that you both share things like, the children come first, you've got to give them opportunities right across the board.

(Teacher, Hutton)

Similarly, another teacher gave this explanation for why she could not team-teach with a colleague:

> [She] does some super work and gets some lovely things from the children, it is just totally different from the way I do things and there is just no way that I would do them, I just couldn't do it.

(Teacher, Hutton)

A paradox seems to exist: where there is a school-wide culture which encourages teachers to think of themselves as individually different but mutually dependent they may, but often do not, teach in tandem. By contrast, in the absence of such a culture, like-minded colleagues have an incentive to create their own sub-culture. When this is based on shared pedagogical or epistemological beliefs, and the physical setting is propitious, teachers may choose to team-teach. But sub-groups, especially those which are built upon or incorporate team-teaching, impede school-wide acceptance of particular practices and inhibit the open discussion that might eventually lead to the creation of a whole-school perspective (Nias, 1989b). In other words, there is no reason why team-teaching cannot be undertaken in a school characterized by a collaborative culture, but equally, its existence may indicate the presence among the staff of divisive sub-groups rather than of a school-wide sense of common purpose. Put another way, team-teaching is less rather than more likely to exist among staffs who participate in a 'culture of collaboration', though pairs or groups will feel free to teach together if they choose and they will certainly co-operate with one another whenever the need or opportunity arises.

To sum up, the 'culture of collaboration' arises from and embodies a set of what may broadly be described as moral beliefs about the value of the relationship between individuals and groups. It does not grow from shared beliefs about the nature or organization of curriculum content or teaching methods, but it has an impact in several ways upon educational practice in a school. It leads over time to the formation of a broad curricular and pedagogical consensus, tolerant of difference and divergence. It is an instrument of social and moral education, through the hidden curriculum and especially through the attitude and behaviour of staff towards one another. It encourages a sense of team pride and so of hard work, and it facilitates relaxed, spontaneous co-operation over teaching and other professional responsibilities.

We turn now to look in detail at the central beliefs about ends which underlie the 'culture of collaboration'. These may be expressed in the following way: individuals are valuable both in their own right and because they have the potential to enrich the communities of which they are part. Moreover, since neither individuals nor communities can exist independently of one another, each is equally important and interdependence is as much to be valued as independence.

VALUING INDIVIDUALS AS PEOPLE

In the schools where this culture existed, even the most mundane and apparently insignificant details of staff behaviour were consistent with its values. Respect for the individual cropped up in many guises. There were few signs of status consciousness within the staff groups. Headteachers freely used the staffrooms and joined in the informal conversation, joking and teasing that were commonplace there. Probationers and newcomers to these schools were quickly made to feel valued by their colleagues (e.g., 'They [the staff] treat me as an individual here to do a job, not to be looked down upon or anything like that. I'm like anybody really' (Probationer, Sedgemoor). At Sedgemoor, Lowmeadow, Greenfields and Hutton, the secretary and ancillary workers used the staffroom, while at Hutton the caretaker and the ancillary were members of the informal staff cricket team:

> During the evening cricket match Bill the caretaker was very prominent, not just as a player but as a member of the group. He enjoyed it hugely, saying 'I'm not competitive; but I do get involved.' He is deferred to as the expert on how to play and on the laws of this particular form of the game. Diane the ancillary is brought into the proceedings.

Although she is officially reserve, she comes along and so that she can have a full part she and Maureen share the eighth place on the team, each playing for half the time.

(Fieldnote, October, Hutton)

At Lavender Way, however, the caretaker was not invited to use the staffroom, and the ancillary, who had previously been a dinner supervisor, did not feel comfortable there, choosing instead to take her breaks in the kitchen because 'I was missing the company of the girls in the kitchen.'

Everyone coming to these schools was made to feel welcome:

I don't think it matters who it is and again we say this to the children, it doesn't matter if it's the dustman, or somebody who looks terribly important, or somebody's mum, we treat them all alike and they are all made to feel welcome.

(Head, Sedgemoor)

The staff were so nice, it's a very open school, you know, 'Come into the staffroom', there was no waiting around in the corridor, straight into the staffroom. Somebody was making a cup of coffee and they involved me in the conversation. They don't just do that with someone like me who came to look around the school, they do that with all the parents and with everybody. They make everybody very welcome, it's marvellous and I like the way they've got time for parents and involve the parents a lot in the school. I like the attitude towards the children. They care, and that's what came across to me.

(Recently appointed teacher, Greenfields)

The health visitor was in this afternoon, the governor this morning and the special needs teacher from the Special Needs Unit was also around. All these visitors were warmly welcomed, all of them are on first name terms with all staff, including the head, and first names are used with them too, so there is this easy-going informality.

(Fieldnote, November, Greenfields)

The fact that staff saw one another as people rather than purely as role occupants or colleagues was also evident in the 'person-centred' nature of much of their talk. This topic is explored in detail in Chapter 5, so just two brief examples are given here:

Staffroom talk at breaks is almost always domestic and personal, e.g., broken ornaments, shopping, holidays, weddings, pets. Today, after lunch, two teachers discussed some workcards for about three minutes. It was the first curriculum conversation I've heard in the staffroom and it was rapidly overtaken by talk of a television programme shown last night.

(Fieldnote, January, Lowmeadow)

In the discussions at lunchtime there was a sense of the staff group re-convening [after a half-day strike]. It was also the first time Mary was back in school since her hospital appointment. She was warmly welcomed by both Carol and Victoria. Victoria and Mary then talked at some length with Carol about teenage children. Jim happily said hello and in a warm way noted how long it had been since they had seen each other.

(Fieldnote, November, Greenfields)

Newcomers too were politely offered the opportunity to reveal something about themselves — interests, family, hobbies and the like — and were given plenty of opportunity to talk. Listening was seen as important:

I would try very hard to say, 'Look I do understand', and to really listen so that I'll understand her situation as far as I possibly can.

(Teacher, Lowmeadow)

Yeomans (1987c) commented, at the start of his year at Lavender Way, on the absence of casual conversation in the staffroom and noted that when it did take place, 'Talk was cordial rather than convivial, and mostly work-focused rather than people-focused'. Yet as the staff there came to work more closely together, the amount of interpersonal chat increased. Similarly, when the new deputy at Hutton looked back on her first term's efforts to bring the staff closer together, she reflected:

> Different relationships have become forged between most of the staff . . . much more one to one, friendly, not just concerned with the school, but in general terms.
>
> (Deputy, Hutton)

Regard for individuals was signalled by respect for their right to privacy as well as by a readiness to be interested in their personal lives:

> They are very determined people here, with principles, not necessarily all the same. There's also a respect for privacy; people, as personalities and as individuals, although they're very close, they respect each other's lives.
>
> (Teacher, Greenfields)

Accordingly, only if people wanted to talk in school about their home lives or see one another outside school did they do so. Staff accepted, and often liked, one another as people with whom they worked but not, of necessity, as companions for their leisure activities. At Lowmeadow one teacher suggested that their friendly co-operation in school 'might well be due to the fact that we live in different places, we don't all live on top of one another'. At Sedgemoor too the staff freely accepted one another's right to draw boundaries between personal and occupational lives. To talk freely about one's out-of-school experiences and the emotions engendered by them was to share oneself at work as a person; it was not to abolish all distinction between one's personal and professional lives.

Furthermore, differences between people were recognized:

> [The day after the staff party at the head's house] Kath asked me if I'd enjoyed it. I told her I had and we chatted about it for a bit. I asked her if these kinds of events often happened and she said no. 'I used to think it would be nice if they happened more often; I even suggested we might all go to the theatre together or something like that but we never have and it's probably just as well. It'd be hard to find something we'd all enjoy, because our tastes are so different.'
>
> (Fieldnote, July, Lowmeadow)

Because the lives of staff, however private, were seen to extend beyond school, allowances were made at work for domestic circumstances such as a husband's or son's redundancy, invalid relatives, children's half-terms, moving house and for the immediate health and happiness of the individual. Staff were tolerant of each other's taciturnity, irritability or unaccustomed inefficiency, they were quick to anticipate the help which might be needed because of, for example, a fit of depression, a painful back, a broken car or a sleepless night. When someone was having a bad day, the appropriate response was to be sympathetic rather than offended. In the collaborative schools there was a pervasive atmosphere of consideration for others. Although it had begun to develop in the other two, it is instructive to compare:

> [In the last week of term] the staff are all looking very tired and I am frankly exhausted, but everyone still deals with one another with total courtesy and painstaking consideration. I haven't heard an irritable exchange, grudging comment or expression

of impatience and they continue to take a loving interest in one another's domestic doings.

> (Fieldnote, December, Lowmeadow)

with the remark made by a teacher at Lavender Way as she looked back at the start of the year: 'It felt like a conscious effort to be courteous and kind to each other' (Teacher, Lavender Way).

Personal kindness sometimes also extended beyond school:

> It's nice to sort of socialize really outside school . . . I've been out to people's for meals and that kind of thing. Personally I like getting to know people of all age groups — things like Josie's husband's been wonderful for mending my hoover and putting plugs in, and I've taken Sheila's little girl swimming and that kind of thing. So we do tend to do things together.
>
> (Probationer, Sedgemoor)

Knowledge and acceptance of people as individuals was further strengthened by getting to know and like one another's families, a reciprocal process which enabled staff members to gain insights into the broader social context in which their colleagues were set:

> We all know each other's families and we've shared our problems. . . . We've all managed to share and advise each other and commiserate with each other and I think that's got a lot to do with making us into a closer community. Because of the things we know about each other . . . we've all tried to be supportive to each other and just listen. All of us feel that if we've got any problems at home we can always talk about them here and somebody will say, 'Oh that happened to me', or commiserate or help or advise or whatever.
>
> (Teacher, Lowmeadow)

Networks of out-of-school relationships similar to the one revealed in the following extract occurred in all the schools:

> *Int:* You have quite strong, informal social links with Jim, you're going to stay at his parents' and he's met your parents, I think, so there's a kind of outside school 'getting to know you'.
> *G:* His daughter is my god-daughter.
> *Int:* Right, so that's another link. I know you see Carol, because you sometimes call round of an evening to have a chat, you've said that in the past. I wonder if there are any such links with other staff?
> *G:* The four of us, Victoria and her husband and Sally, my wife, are quite close friends and Victoria and I have been involved in activities together like school journeys which have involved chats in the evening, so there have been evening meetings with Victoria as well, probably as much as with Carol. But certainly there are times outside school when we meet — Carol, Victoria, Jim and me — not so much anybody else. We go on courses together in twos and threes and that usually means some form of socializing after the course, so there are those kinds of links.
>
> (Head, Greenfields)

However, as Chapter 3 makes plain, when a collaborative culture did not exist within a school, close or frequent out-of-school contact between individuals who were also friendly at work could be read as exclusivity rather than cohesion. Similarly (see Chapter 8) although friendship groups of the sort described above existed in Greenfields, Sedgemoor and Lowmeadow, they overlapped in membership with different working groups within school. In other words, the existence of complex networks of professional and personal relationships prevented cliques from forming.

VALUING THE INDIVIDUAL'S CONTRIBUTION TO OTHERS

In addition to respecting and nurturing others as individuals in their own right, headteachers, teachers and ancillaries in the collaborative schools perceived the differences between them as a mutually enriching source of collective strength:

> Working in a team doesn't mean that everybody's the same and everybody's so busy saying yes, yes, yes to one another that nothing happens. That deadens it. You've got to have different personalities and different ideas to spark other people off, but it can be done without aggression.
>
> (Teacher, Lowmeadow)

> You're certainly given free rein to introduce, innovate, to do new things, to carry out what you want to do without interference and you carry it out with the encouragement of the rest of the staff and with the head.
>
> (Teacher, Greenfields)

> I've come to terms now with the fact that I am free to put my ideas forward. I offer my ideas and that's it, and that's the way everybody works here anyway.
>
> (Teacher, Lowmeadow)

> I think people here have very individual ways of doing things and I think if you tried to fit somebody into a framework of doing things then you're not going to let out their talents, as it were.
>
> (Teacher, Sedgemoor)

Again, it is interesting to note that as the staff at Hutton moved towards greater collaboration, one of them said:

> The topic areas are laid down but we're breaking away from that and the staff have got more responsibility for choosing their own topic . . . I think that, within this laid-down philosophy, the teachers are becoming freer now to interpret it in their way.
>
> (Teacher, Hutton)

Nor was this freedom confined to teaching staff. In all of the schools ancillary workers used their dexterity, aesthetic sense, practical skills and knowledge of children to make suggestions about classroom work and displays, to make apparatus and, when they had particular skills (e.g., in flower-arranging), they were invited to share these with the children. In some of the schools caretakers too were encouraged to enrich the life of the whole organization. At Lowmeadow, for example, children without a stable male figure in their families were often sent to show particularly good work to the caretaker, and at Hutton Bill was a leading figure in the social life of the staffroom.

There were other ways too of indicating that everyone's contribution to the school was valued, of whatever kind it was and however it was made. Gratitude and appreciation were regularly and openly expressed:

> It's never taken for granted and it's never left to just one teacher – all staff make the point of expressing their appreciation to whoever they are thanking. Consequently it's

never just Graham who says thank you to a parent, but whichever members of staff are around at the time will also say thank you and similarly it wasn't just for Graham or Victoria to say thank you to me today, but it was both of them who said it.

(Fieldnote, January, Greenfields)

Rosemary hurried back into the classroom, caught Helen [an ancillary] just as she was going off at lunchtime, thanked her and said what a marvellous job she'd made of the display.

(Fieldnote, November, Lowmeadow)

So too was praise. As Nias (1986) describes in her case study of Lowmeadow,

The school is characterized by positive reinforcement, reassurance and praise . . . I frequently noticed teachers praising work undertaken by welfare helpers, admiring children's work done for other teachers, sending children to their colleagues with good work, especially when they knew the latter had had a hand in it, sharing each other's delight in a child's achievement, prompting another teacher or a welfare helper to share tiny but hugely significant improvements in a particular child's work, praising one another's assemblies and offering reassurance about them, commenting enthusiastically on the accomplishments of other adults around the school.

Greenfields and Sedgemoor provided many similar examples. By contrast, lavish use of praise by the staff in general was not so characteristic of Lavender Way or Hutton though, as the staff at the latter school moved closer together, one teacher reported of the head:

He is beginning to give positive feedback to people, which is something that they have said they haven't had. He went to one teacher the other day and said how much the people at the PCC meeting they had on Saturday had admired her room.

(Teacher, Hutton)

VALUING INTERDEPENDENCE: BELONGING TO A GROUP

So, individual staff members at Greenfields, Lowmeadow and Sedgemoor valued one another as people, each with his/her own identity, personality, interests, skills, experiences and potential, but they also appreciated the diversity which this brought to the school. Similarly, the sense of collective dependence on which the 'culture of collaboration' was also built had two sides to it. Together the members of each staff made a group which they valued because it gave them a feeling of belonging. At the same time, they accepted a collective responsibility for the work of the school, so creating a strong team in which people helped, encouraged and substituted for one another.

The staffs' awareness of belonging to a group characterized by social or emotional interdependence was expressed in two main ways. First, they saw one another as 'friends' and even, sometimes, as 'family', phrases that they repeatedly used:

I regard them all as being friends. . . . I could go to them if anything was wrong.

(Teacher, Sedgemoor)

[The head] is like a friend, not that she's boss, she's more a friend.

(Ancillary, Sedgemoor)

I don't just look upon it so much as job as an extension of family . . . everybody is so close . . . I know I would miss it terribly if I didn't come.

(Teacher, Lowmeadow)

There's a great deal of warmth between us and it's almost like a family that closes ranks against outsiders when it's being attacked by a piece of gossip or an occasion of vandalism. We come together very closely.

(Teacher, Greenfields)

I think the friendliness more than anything else. I've worked for a long time in industry and only a short time in school, comparatively, and I don't think in industry you get the friendliness that you get in school, from the staff and pupils.

(Caretaker, Lowmeadow)

I think we are friends, not just colleagues, I think it's more than just working together.

(Teacher, Greenfields)

I like to think that when a teacher walks into my classroom, the children see that we are friendly towards each other. For instance I will call all the teachers who come into my room — I think perhaps with the exception of Graham [the head] — by their Christian names in the children's hearing . . . I think the children then see that we are mutually supportive and I think that does rub off on them. I think it helps promote the family atmosphere in the school.

(Teacher, Greenfields)

Significantly, individuals at Lavender Way increasingly came to regard one another in this kind of way, as the head and deputy worked during the year to break down the barriers that had historically kept staff apart. For example, late in the year, a teacher said:

It is certainly a lot more fun in the staffroom these days. I think people do go in more because it is a lot nicer in there. You've not constantly got ears out for those little barbed comments and arguments over television, pencils and scissors and tissue paper and things like that. People have got a lot more friendly towards each other now. Much less reserved. They open up a lot more.

(Teacher, Lavender Way)

Secondly, the fact that the staff saw one another as friends spilled over into the way in which they tackled their work, making it hard to maintain a distinction between personal and professional interdependence:

I went in with her and helped her put up her display that she's got to do for assembly tomorrow . . . I would have gone and helped her anyway because that's part of my job. Aside from that, I know she's not feeling very well. I know that she's got to go to the dentist at quarter to five and that she's been struggling on during the afternoon to do things, but that reinforced what I was going to do anyway. So the professional side of me going to help her is reinforced by the social side of me liking her and wanting to help her.

(Deputy, Sedgemoor)

If I just came and did the cleaning and teachers just saw you as that, just the person who comes and does the cleaning, perhaps they would treat me different, but if you give them a bit extra, then it must make your own job more enjoyable, it certainly does mine. I would hate just to be the person who comes and does the cleaning.

(Caretaker, Hutton)

VALUING INTERDEPENDENCE: WORKING AS A TEAM

Although group membership was affectively satisfying, this is not the whole story. At Greenfields, Lowmeadow and Sedgemoor the staff also felt a sense of collective responsibility for their work and saw themselves as a team. As Isobel wrote in the Sedgemoor Curriculum Award folder: 'We feel that the consideration and closeness which characterizes relationships between adult members pervades the school as a whole. . . . Thus issues like infant–junior liaison are less important than the sense of the school as a whole team.' To be a 'team' meant to recognize and value the unique contribution of each member, teachers and non-teachers alike, to a joint enterprise. Being a team did not necessarily mean doing the same job nor working in the same teaching space, but it did mean working to the same ends. At Sedgemoor:

> Everyone has a function and the value of that is acknowledged — for example Josie for her language expertise, even though she is 'only' part-time, Molly the secretary for her ability to deal with administrative concerns that teachers find difficult, Polly the ancillary for her ideas and personal support.
>
> (Yeomans, 1986c)

Similarly, at Lowmeadow:

> Another thing I agreed with was to try and bring the caretaker and cleaning staff into the team. I firmly believe that to get the school working properly you have to have everybody working as a team and here it really works. . . . When it was Janice the cook's 21st birthday, we had a present for her and she came into the assembly. Sandra, the secretary, comes into assemblies, and when it's her birthday, she has her candle.
>
> (Teacher, Lowmeadow)

The sense of collective responsibility on which the teams were built showed itself in many ways. Most obviously everyone advised, supported and helped one another so habitually and regularly that it has been difficult to select a few illustrations from among the multitude of daily examples:

> Rhoda said to me, 'I haven't done reception teaching before, could you help?' And I said, 'Absolutely, I'd love to'. So we had lots of chats at lunchtime, but it became apparent very soon that she didn't need any further help. . . . To give it and then take it away because it's not needed is much preferable to running after someone with a crutch after they've fallen over. It's too late then, it's the wrong way round.
>
> (Teacher, Lowmeadow)

> If you say 'I'm doing such and such, I haven't got any good ideas', there will be six or seven different ideas thrown at you instantly. Or if you get halfway through doing something and you happen to say 'Oh, it's not working or it's going wrong', there's always someone who is willing to help in any sort of situation. And in dealing with the children you never feel, if you have a problem, that you're cut off, there's always somebody else who is willing to help you. It's often the case [in other schools that] there is someone around who is capable of helping, but not always that they will help, but in this school that doesn't seem to be so. Everyone seems very ready to help.
>
> (Teacher, Sedgemoor)

> It is the sort of school where you can say 'I don't know what to do' in such and such a subject or how best to tackle this, or what do you suggest with this child to get him reading? And everybody will jump in with advice and help and try to be helpful, which is nice.
>
> (Teacher, Greenfields)

I work with a small group of children finishing off the deputy head's section of the large hall picture. As I work in the dining area the deputy head comes up from time to time to see how things are going and offer suggestions. The welfare helper passes and suggests to the deputy a better method of painting leaves. He suggests how he would like the poppies to be painted, but the head and welfare helper come by and say they don't like the idea at all. I add a little paint to the place where I think the children perhaps haven't quite finished. As Peter walks by he catches my eye and I guiltily hide the brush. He laughs.

(Fieldnote, November, Sedgemoor)

There was a general awareness that any member of staff might need the others at some point and that this need would be met, as a matter of course, by anyone who was available. As one teacher said:

[You've got to be] adaptable and friendly to work here. Everyone is prepared to help everyone else out, as and when they can. If they ask you for something, you are prepared to do it, or you're prepared to volunteer something when it's required.

(Teacher, Lowmeadow)

This sense of mutual dependence can be contrasted on two counts with the situation at the start of year at Lavender Way and Hutton. First, where interdependence existed (that is, within the team-teaching pairs) it was limited to them:

The rewards are that we can interrelate with children and we help with workloads. You do get days when you don't feel too good, perhaps when you've not slept well or you've had a near accident with the car or you've had a late course, so you've not prepared yourself as well as you should. . . . One will pick the other up.

(Teacher, Lavender Way)

Secondly, outside those pairs, people did not feel secure enough to enter one another's teaching space, let alone ask for help:

[When I arrived] I spent my time watching other members of staff but it's difficult; you can't just barge into somebody else's room and say 'can I just have a look?' I couldn't do that and I wouldn't expect anybody else to come in and see my room.

(Teacher, Hutton)

It took time before I could ask, as a new teacher. I don't think it helps in some ways having a list of 'this person being responsible for this', 'this person responsible for that', I think time is the answer.

(Teacher, Hutton)

It was significant that one of the first things the staff at Lavender Way noticed as they began to work more closely together was that they were sharing ideas and asking each other for help:

What I think has happened, is the business of openly adopting each other's approaches to things. I think it's right that you should imitate other people when you see things that are good and enjoyable and it's a mutual process. There are things now that we do collectively — I think that's much better. And we certainly share our enjoyment or disappointment at the progress that the children make in different things much more openly than was ever the case before.

(Teacher, Lavender Way)

Phyl [the new teacher] is using [her colleagues], she says to me 'You said to me, Catherine, I have got to ask and hopefully they will all help me, so I am asking everybody and they are.' I know Sandy, especially, says 'Phyl comes and asks me about this and that' and I say 'Well, that is how it should be, Sandy. You don't mind her coming and asking you?' And she says 'No, and I am asking her things' and I say 'Great, because she has got a lot to offer'.

(Head, Lavender Way)

Teamwork meant sharing successes as well as concerns. The staff were as ready to show and tell one another what they were proud of as they were to seek help, as prepared to accept praise as they were to give it:

At the end of the day Julia listened attentively to what Rhoda had done with her group and was full of praise for what she accomplished. Later in the day she drew Rhoda out in the staffroom so that we were all able to share her pleasure in the progress being made by the children.

(Fieldnote, June, Lowmeadow)

As I go out, Josie is showing Margaret some work she is particularly pleased with, through the space that separates their two working areas.

(Fieldnote, March, Sedgemoor)

Further, the common task often took precedence over individuals' concern for status or for the limelight:

You have to overcome the competitiveness . . . schools are run on competitive lines, in a way. People work individually, they resolve problems in the classroom individually and the tensions that arise by controlling children . . . I think that people here do work not to be like that . . . there is an awareness that you don't need to be like that in a school. I can think of a lot of instances where people haven't been concerned about their status and their position in that sort of a way. . . . People here consciously try not to be like that.

(Teacher, Sedgemoor)

Leader of visiting German party to Isobel: 'In Germany we have competitions in school to see who has the most beautiful classroom. Could you do that in your school?' Isobel: 'No, it wouldn't work here. We work as a team and try to support each other.'

(Fieldnote, June, Sedgemoor)

The teachers work together, they are concerned for each other. There's no one really pushing for their own ends the whole time. There's a lot of give and take, a willingness to co-operate with each other.

(Ancillary, Lowmeadow)

A sense of shared endeavour could even override the traditional, and treasured, relationship between teachers and their classes. It is interesting to compare the situation at Lowmeadow illustrated in this fieldnote:

Mention was made at one point of a child and I said to Jane, 'Is that your Sarah' — I nearly said 'our', meaning to identify myself with her because I'd just spent a week in her classroom. She said, 'No, do say 'our', I never think of a child as mine.'

(March)

with the comment made by a teacher at Hutton who was reluctantly about to embark on a change in classroom organization suggested by her head:

I will try it, though probably through gritted teeth and digging my heels in, as I did with team-teaching last term. I was very reluctant at the beginning to let my classroom go and let my children go. I felt very maternal about them all, and to let go of them was very, very difficult for the first week.

(Teacher, Hutton)

Individuals were also willing to modify their plans and activities in response to the perceived needs of others:

> With the top two classes leaving the school, just three classes were left in the school. Instead of having an assembly, Carol suggested, why don't the rest of us wave them off? . . . So the whole school was gathered at the front, two classes waiting to embark on the buses, and the rest of us there to wave them off, and a good few parents around as well.
>
> (Fieldnote, July, Greenfields)

Teachers and ancillaries fitted flexibly round one another's activities and took whatever role seemed appropriate at the time:

> [In the last week of term] Helen obviously wanted to clean a cupboard near where Rhoda was working. The latter noticed this, without saying anything moved her group to another table and continued her word game. Helen moved swiftly in and signalled to Rhoda as soon as she'd finished.
>
> (Fieldnote, July, Lowmeadow)

> If anybody sees that something needs doing, they will do it. It's not generally one person that does it. We all do it, if we see that something needs doing, whoever sees it will do it.
>
> (Ancillary, Lowmeadow)

> After school the new infant entrance hall display is prepared. Isobel [the head] is there and although she isn't responsible for the display, she is very important as a support. First of all she sweeps the rubbish clear with a mop. Then she goes and makes tea for everybody. Dennis [the deputy] brings it round. Next she gets out and arranges plants for the display and starts wiping their leaves. Fourthly, as the display begins to develop she comments on various things that look particularly attractive. Fifthly, she also comments on the odd item which she feels isn't very well mounted and so Veronica changes it.
>
> (Fieldnote, November, Sedgemoor)

An awareness of shared responsibility for a common task led people to expend their own resources. Despite union action which during much of 1985–6 restricted many teachers' participation in work-related out-of-school activities, teachers frequently discussed their work with one another in their own time. Often they telephoned one another at home to talk shop; sometimes they met there. Typically,

> At lunchtime, Josie to Sue 'Do you want to sort out the spelling programme during the holiday?' Josie, 'Yes, that's a good idea, Wednesday or Thursday, better at my house, then I don't have to bring my child with me.'
>
> (Fieldnote, May, Sedgemoor)

Nor was it only teachers who behaved in this way. Ancillary workers took children's painting overalls home to wash and provided cookery ingredients from their own grocery cupboards. In their spare time caretakers mended equipment, made apparatus or did odd jobs in preparation for Christmas activities or summer fairs. Secretaries too blurred the distinction between work and home:

> I work every morning, I work Monday and Wednesday afternoons and usually I mentally reserve Friday to stay on until I've sorted out anything that needs doing. There are times when I've got a whole pile of stuff when I think, 'oh, I could do this at home' and I've got my electric machine at home. So I do that, I don't mind doing that, that's fine. I'm not going to rush off at twelve because it's twelve and I'm supposed to leave.

Usually I'm talking too hard anyway but I will do what is required and also I feel part
of the school.

(Secretary, Sedgemoor)

In a world as shifting and elusive as the primary school (see Chapter 7), successful
teamwork depends crucially upon the acceptance of collective responsibility for communication. Paradoxically, the very nature of the collaborative culture made this
more difficult because, although staff spent most of each day working apart from
one another, they expected information to pass by word of mouth. As a result,
mistakes were sometimes made. Nevertheless:

People are very good at communicating with each other. I mean, if one person knows
about something, they tell other people. It doesn't just come from Isobel or me or one
person. Someone will make sure that they tell somebody else what's going on. And
they'll come and ask, they'll send children or come into your classroom or nip down the
steps, you know, to say things like that.

(Deputy, Sedgemoor)

I know that news will catch up with me in the end, if I haven't been told instantly or
first hand, I know that between one or other of the teachers they will let me know so
that there is no fear that you will be floundering completely on your own somewhere.

(Ancillary, Lowmeadow)

Formal communication, though relatively sparse, also displayed a sense of common
concern for a shared task:

At this point I noted some of the patterns of the meeting. One teacher talked at a time,
there was very little cross-talk and only one or two occasions where the discussion wasn't
focused on the agenda; very few asides, no difficulty of two or three simultaneous
conversations, just once there was some cross-talk.

(Fieldnote, June, Greenfields)

Overall, then, in Sedgemoor, Greenfields and Lowmeadow mutuality was the norm:

We've got to be looking for someone who will 'fit in' with the rest of the staff. They
don't actually take kindly to anyone who is too shy. They don't mind somebody taking
a little while to settle down, but once they've settled down the rest of the staff here are
the kind of people who are delighted to help and give help, they like to be asked for
it.

(Head, Greenfields)

You can go round supporting everybody and expect everybody just to listen to what
you suggest and you not to take ideas, but that's unrealistic. . . . As far as supporting
and influencing people [goes], it's important that it's mutual because otherwise it doesn't
work.

(Deputy, Sedgemoor)

What was less clear from our evidence was whether a sense of personal interdependence preceded or followed the decision to work together, that is, whether groups
became teams, or teams developed into groups. As someone rhetorically reflected
at Hutton,

Alison and Marion stand out, obviously, you don't really see it [team-teaching] anywhere
else. Did the friendship come first or did the partnership come first?

(Teacher, Hutton)

The answer seems to be that sometimes liking led to sharing work and thence to a sense of belonging to a team, while at others working with colleagues resulted in a feeling of social cohesion, and a group was formed. Either way, '[to work closely together] you've got to respond to someone *and* develop a good working relationship with them.' (Teacher, Hutton) Moreover once a 'team-group' had become established, membership of it was so rewarding that it tended to be self-perpetuating (see Chapter 5).

VALUING SECURITY

In this section and the next we examine the two beliefs embedded in the 'culture of collaboration' which specify means rather than ends: that security is a necessary condition for the growth of openness, and that openness is the best way of simultaneously fostering the individual and the group.

The link between beliefs relating to ends and to means lies in the notion of interdependence which we have so far discussed as if it always and necessarily enriched those who experienced it. There is of course another side to this: mutual dependence also means mutual constraint. To accept that one is dependent on anyone else is to admit that there are limits to one's autonomy. These limits might be unspoken, as they were in the team-teaching pair at Hutton and for all the staff at Sedgemoor, they might be spelt out by curriculum documents (such as those at Hutton and Greenfields) or be implicit in curriculum materials (e.g., the mathematics scheme at Lowmeadow). They might be relatively open to negotiation, as at Greenfields, or rather precise, as was the case in the Jayne–Stella partnership at Lavender Way. Whatever their exact nature or extent, acceptance of them was mandatory:

> If you've made a conscious decision to be in the school, then you've got to make it work, you can't say 'Oh, I can't work like this and I'm not going to', because nobody has forced you to actually come to the school. You make the decision to come here, so then you've got to say 'I'm going to do my best and work with this situation as it is and not try to make it into something completely different'. . . . You can't just come storming in and do your own thing. . . . So that was it, really. I did learn a lot from Jayne and got to know her very well.
>
> (Stella, Lavender Way)

> These schemes were drawn up as a result of several staff discussions. They are not intended to be comprehensive directives, but rather to form a framework within which members of staff are free to exploit their strengths and to experiment with methods. In some cases, however, it was felt that teachers would welcome a more explicit approach as an aid to continuity. We felt that freedom of method would only be desirable within a well structured scheme, and that we should try to ensure that such freedom did not lead to omissions in the course of the school year.
>
> (Introduction to *School Schemes of Work*, Greenfields)

> To work here you'd *have* to be prepared to work as part of this team. If you persisted in not being part of a team you could exist here, but you wouldn't be happy. You could make it, but not in any satisfying sense. . . . If you're not prepared to submit, in the Biblical sense, you're not going to be an effective team member. But once you can see it's in the best interests of the children, it's easy.
>
> (Teacher, Lowmeadow)

There is no inconsistency in this position. Though to submit is to accept another's power over oneself, when all the members of a team make this submission to one another, their power over each other is evenly balanced and becomes influence instead (see Chapter 8). So within a situation of agreed interdependence, 'We're all influencing each other, I'm quite convinced of that' (Teacher, Greenfields).

But even this statement, by a member of a staff group in which dependence seemed to be evenly spread, does not reflect the whole truth. For, as we have repeatedly claimed and Chapter 6 makes plain, the 'culture of collaboration' rested upon beliefs which emanated from and were exemplified in the headteacher:

> They [the staff] feel free in staff meetings or discussions with me, to make their opinions known quite clearly and they know that I'm going to accept their opinions, but that I'm not going to be swayed by them in the 'wrong way', if you like. There is no one on the staff who is going to express an opinion which will push me in a way that I don't want to go.
>
> (Head, Greenfields)

> I think you must accept that things that are done in certain classrooms . . . will be done in your classroom too. I think you have to be fairly accepting of the situation as it is. Individualistic teachers tend to leave quite quickly.
>
> (Teacher, Lowmeadow)

The answer to this apparent contradiction between mutual constraint and deference to the head appears to lie in three interrelated facts. First, headteachers are the main 'culture-founders' in their schools (see Chapter 6), and provided that they exemplify in their personal and professional behaviour the beliefs that underpin this culture they have a degree of personal authority which transcends that of other staff members, even though they can exercise effective leadership over the latter only by becoming one of them. Secondly, the mutual influence which characterizes the 'culture of collaboration' is exercised within boundaries which are themselves set by and respected out of deference to the head's authority (see Chapter 8). Thirdly, primary headteachers and teachers are members not just of their schools but also of an occupation which traditionally sets much store by its members' ability to control pupils and which is, perhaps in consequence, hierarchically structured. Teachers exercise authority over others but are often themselves authority-dependent (Abercrombie, 1981; Nias, 1987a). In other words, the 'culture of collaboration' co-existed in the project schools with a wider occupational culture that served to limit the extent to which teachers expected to be able to influence their heads. Similarly, the latter remained and expected to remain *primus inter pares*.

The fact that the heads' responsibility for the main policies in their schools was virtually unchallenged and that the staff exercised a good deal of mutual influence over one another made the collaborative schools very secure places in which to work. In addition, interpersonal familiarity helped people feel professionally at ease with one another. The personally self-confident were more disposed to speak their minds and to invite reciprocal comment than were those who felt insecure:

> It's a lot to do with self-confidence, whether people can open themselves to you. If they are not very self-confident, they can't open themselves because it makes them vulnerable. But if they can, then you can have an insight into their personality and you can respond to them much better.
>
> (Teacher, Hutton)

As the researcher at Hutton commented, after participating in a cricket match:

Those you are socially at ease with may be those to whom you are able to tell the truth more easily, even when you disagree with them.

(Fieldnote, September, Hutton)

Lack of professional self-assurance could also be inhibiting. At Hutton some teachers hesitated to admit to failure in the classroom because other people seemed more successful than they were, even though, in the absence of general candour about classroom matters, they could not tell if their perceptions were accurate. One put it this way:

I've felt for a long time that I couldn't tell anybody about it because I thought they would think I was failing, although I am sure I'm not the only one. I'm sure everybody feels that way. I am sure everybody feels frightened to admit that something has gone wrong in the classroom in case anybody else confirms their belief that they are failing. Teachers are generally very insecure. . . . I couldn't rush into the staff room and say 'oh, so and so's just done this, I feel like stringing them up from the beams in the classroom'. I couldn't do that because I'd feel as if it was my fault . . . The other members of staff didn't really seem to be complaining about their children . . . and that reinforced the feeling that I was failing which contributed to that point at the end of the second term where I felt 'well, I can't teach'.

(Teacher, Hutton)

Nor did anyone in Hutton and Lavender Way have sufficient confidence in the resilience of the personal or professional relationships which existed among the staff as a whole to risk a direct challenge to the headteacher or to one another:

In my previous school we had 14 teachers at one stage and conflict meant just that: an argument about something. And you could have those arguments. . . . But here I've never had the confidence that relationships are strong enough to stand it.

(Deputy, Lavender Way)

I was just thinking though, nobody ever comes into the staff as a whole and makes complaints about the way the school's run, or anything like that, and yet we will do that to each other in smaller groups. I don't know what that says really?

(Teacher, Lavender Way)

Everybody is capable of feeling threatened at some time and some people feel threatened more than others. That is a very important consideration when you consider free discussion at the staff meetings, I think that is the biggest hurdle to get over . . . If people leave the staff meeting here and talk about the same point in smaller groups, they feel quite able to discuss it very honestly and very openly, because they don't feel the person they are talking to is a threat. By choosing sympathetic listeners it becomes a reinforcement of their own ideas rather than a threatening situation.

(Teacher, Hutton)

Chapters 5 and 7 suggest the ways in which heads and others helped to build and maintain among their staffs the senses of personal and professional security without which openness was difficult to achieve.

VALUING OPENNESS

Many of the day-to-day attitudes and actions of the staff demonstrated the value which they attached to openness. Headteachers, teachers and ancillaries were ready to admit publicly to a sense of failure:

This is a very unusual school because normally you don't do that. In the other schools I've taught in you *didn't* fail. It you did you kept it very quiet. It took me a good four months to realize that . . . when you had problems you didn't hide them away, you voiced them and you got them sorted out instantly instead of taking them home and worrying about them.

(Teacher, Sedgemoor)

Rosemary said, 'I don't know what all the problem is, I don't have any trouble with playground duty', but in a way that wasn't putting down and Jane felt able to respond by saying 'I feel terrible when it can take a minute or more to get the children to attend to the Stop board when I'm out there, whereas when Rosemary is on playground duty, I see her holding it up and everybody is quiet at once'. Margaret chipped in to support Jane. 'It takes me a long time too.'

(Fieldnote of staff meeting, May, Lowmeadow)

We all have to accept that mistakes are made. If that happens, we learn by our mistakes. You usually only notice that you've forgotten something if something bad happens from it. If you forget and later on it turns out that it was important, because of the atmosphere of trust in the school, you're not afraid to say, 'Well, I'm sorry', and then it becomes a point of discussion and helps everybody to see the importance of communicating carefully.

(Teacher, Lowmeadow)

Staff were also ready to display other negative emotions, such as guilt, anxiety and anger:

We can all go in the staffroom and let off steam if we want to with each other, and really know that it's not going to go any further. You can get rid of your pent-up anxiety or whatever it happens to be, you can really let fly and they'll sympathize or agree with you. You don't have to bottle it all up and take it home with you, and take it out on somebody at home, you can talk about it here.

(Teacher, Lowmeadow)

You feel you can tell them, you're not letting yourself down. . . . You feel they will understand . . . if you didn't have the staffroom and your colleagues to go and let steam off, that's when things would get a bit much. We've got that, it's our safety valve, isn't it? Being able to sit in there at dinner time over a cup of coffee and chat about everything and anything, whether it's related to school or not, to get things off your chest. It does help. If you've got to bottle everything up, that is when you get uptight.

(Teacher, Greenfields)

I remember once somebody saying that in one school the staff didn't think it professional to talk about the children in front of other members of staff, if they were having problems. I just said 'that's a load of nonsense', because I think that's one of the ways of getting rid of your tension, screaming about a child or joking about some child and their impossibilities.

(Teacher, Sedgemoor)

It was also regarded as normal for individual staff members to voice irritation or dissent directly to one another. Disagreements were accepted as part of human intercourse:

Differences of opinion do emerge but we're all very open, straightforward. If we don't agree with someone we do say so. You know, you just state that you didn't agree and that you thought such and such . . . it doesn't need to be argument.

(Teacher, Sedgemoor)

Some reference was made in the staffroom to politics and a teacher said, 'We have a range of opinions here. You should hear us at a general election'. [Later] I took the opportunity of asking her how 'the group of sisters' coped with differences. Her answer can be summarized as follows: 'We talk a lot, all the time, so when differences occur they can be dealt with naturally. Also, because we respect one another and respect one another's differences it's usually quite easy to talk quite openly about things. People are not afraid of speaking their mind.'

(Fieldnote, March, Lowmeadow)

By contrast, at the start of the year at Lavender Way and Hutton few people felt they could be direct with one another:

I didn't know the school he came from, but he said the staff there really did communicate with each other and you could say something to a member of staff and they didn't feel offended or you could really shout at somebody and they would bounce back the next day. It's not like that here.

(Teacher, Lavender Way)

However, would-be 'collaborators' at these schools worked during the year to establish an atmosphere in which it was seen as normal for people to disagree:

The key factor in the personal relationship side is trying to help people to understand somebody else's perception of that particular thing that has caused whatever it is. I mean, you can't possibly go through the school day term in, term out without there being problems between people. But I would hope that you could actually improve people's relationships with one another by helping that person to face it.

(New deputy, Hutton)

At Greenfields and Lowmeadow the expression of dissent was sometimes quite impassioned. From time to time pairs of teachers, or a head and a teacher, would have what they described as 'disputes', 'rows' or 'violent disagreements'. These were not, however, allowed to disrupt relationships permanently:

There was quite a severe argument between Jim and Victoria, which seemed to indicate that tempers were becoming quite frayed. We had had a very difficult couple of weeks with changing the caretaker, staff being appointed elsewhere and so on. . . . What happened was that I mentioned to Victoria that there had been an advertisement in the school list for a temporary deputy head teacher in a school at Castleton. So she was looking for the list and Jim said he had tidied it away. Victoria's rather waspish comment was 'That's the sort of thing you used to do when you were a deputy head', to which, of course, Jim took exception. . . . There was an outburst from both sides. . . . By lunchtime Jim had invited Victoria to go and have lunch with him and I went along and they both apologized and I was impressed with . . . the fact that they could be extremely angry with one another over a small thing and yet by half way through the day things had been smoothed over and they seemed to be perfectly all right.

(Head, Greenfields)

[After describing a heated difference of opinion with her head] As with all relationships, it's not having the row that counts but how you deal with it afterwards, whether you're able to build on it and go forward with the relationship.

(Deputy, Lowmeadow)

The emotions that people felt free to express were however positive as well as negative. Reflecting on the amount of open emotion he saw at Greenfields, Southworth (1986) wrote:

There is . . . affection. First there is affection for the children. . . . Second, there is affection amongst the adults. . . . Staff actually like each other, as professionals and as people. To talk of the school as a family is not merely to use the family as a metaphor for how the school works as an organisation, it is to imbue the school-as-an-organisation with affection. It is to recognise that working together involves an acceptance that everyone in the school has feelings, and is making an emotional as well as a professional investment. . . . On the last day of the year the emotional side of the school became particularly visible. Affection was breaking out everywhere.

Learning from Difference

The direct expression of views or feelings was not valued only for its therapeutic effect or because it eased interpersonal communication. Experienced staff members saw that it also enabled people to learn from one another in enjoyable ways. The free exchange of work-related information and ideas contributed both to the professional development of the whole staff and to its social cohesion, that is, it simultaneously built up the team and developed the group:

> In other schools I've worked in there would be talk, but it would be more general in nature, of what you were all doing in your spare time, whereas there's an awful lot of professional talk here. I did find it very strange at first, not having been used to it. To be expected to contribute an opinion or articulate what you've had an intuition about is very different because not every head expects his staff to have a view. Obviously this is a school where they like you to have ideas, which is rather nice.
>
> (Teacher, Greenfields)

> The way that we discuss things too, I think that's important and the way that people are prepared to say what they believe in and how they understand children, that's the bit I enjoy.
>
> (Teacher, Sedgemoor)

Significantly, as the staff at Lavender Way drew closer together professionally the absence of open dialogue began to worry them:

> I'm feeling my way along a bit now, because I'm having a new maths scheme, and I've got to find out what people feel about it. One of the most difficult things is getting people to say what they really feel about things, that they're not just saying it on the surface and thinking something else, getting them not to be afraid of saying what they feel about things, because then we can discuss things. There's nothing wrong in saying, 'I don't agree with that.' So I've had to work my way into that a little bit and I know I've got a lot more working away to do.
>
> (Teacher, Lavender Way)

Evidently the 'culture of collaboration' contains a potential for professional development, through the free exchange of opinions, which makes it particularly well suited to schools.

A GENDER-SPECIFIC CULTURE?

The claim is often made that primary schools are 'female' institutions, characterized by compassion and care and dominated by the interests of children. By extension, it could be argued that the 'culture of collaboration', with its emphasis on concern for the individual and on cohesion, its legitimation of emotionality, its validation of control both by peers and by the head, its denial of competition, is a 'woman's culture'. To be sure, in one of the schools the only male was the caretaker, and he did not play a dominant part in the adult life of the school, while in all the others women were in a large majority. Moreover, two out of the three schools where the culture was well established had female heads. In addition, there was evidence in all the schools that some at least of the female staff did from time to time see themselves as a 'women's group' (Teacher, Greenfields) or as a friendship group of women (e.g., 'the group of sisters' referred to in Lowmeadow). Gender was clearly not an unimportant factor in the social fabric of these schools.

Nevertheless, to argue that a collaborative culture is gender-specific is simplistic. In the first place any job focused upon children and their well-being is likely to attract humane individuals, of either gender. Kindness, warmth and a relative lack of competitiveness are not peculiar to women, though cultural conditioning may encourage us to think in these terms. More fundamentally, to defend this claim one would have to argue that females rather than males place an equal value on individuality and interdependence, security and openness, and that the men in the schools, being in a minority, had adopted a 'female' set of attitudes and behaviours — assertions for which it would be hard to find any evidence in our case studies. It would also be necessary to dismiss as false consciousness the claim made by women in these schools that shared beliefs about the aims and means of education were more important in determining whether or not they could work with someone than gender was. In this respect the Lowmeadow case study is unequivocal:

> Finally, at various times during the year, I asked all the teachers if they felt that the fact that all the staff except the caretaker were women made any difference to the way they worked together. Several suggested that the presence of a man would sometimes alter the topics and possibly the nature of the conversations in the staffroom. Otherwise, however, they were all of the opinion that they worked together despite rather than because of their shared gender. Some had previous experience of working in all-female institutions and did not have happy memories of this experience. Most lived in mixed-gender family groups and claimed that they would not normally have chosen to work in a single-sex establishment. All felt a school staff's ability to collaborate and to form warm, open interpersonal relationships had nothing to do with the gender of its members.
>
> (Nias, 1986)

Further, in all the schools there were effective and mutually rewarding head–deputy partnerships between two men, two women, a woman and a man and a man and a woman. Gender did not appear to be a relevant factor in this crucial but sensitive pairing.

Yet it is certainly reasonable to suggest that many of the means by which staff — being predominantly women — expressed their values and beliefs were influenced by their gender, especially in those schools with female heads. In some staffrooms there was a tendency for interpersonal conversations to centre round topics such as family photos, grandchildren, clothes or shopping, and the nature of the gifts chosen to express gratitude or appreciation sometimes reflected their female donors and recipients. Emotion was more often expressed through touch or with tears than would probably have been the case in male-dominated institutions, and the hospitality of the schools (e.g., at the end of term) had a 'home-making' feel to it.

By contrast, in conversations about educational or professional matters or in action relating to them, gender did not seem to be a relevant factor; men and women expressed their views with equal vigour and force. Women exercised authority when it was needed, initiated and handled confrontations, coped with conflict. But they did all these things in a way consistent with the underlying beliefs of the 'culture of collaboration'; it was the latter, not the gender of the staff, which made interactions between them positive, open, non-competitive, person-centred and predictable and which created an atmosphere within the staffroom and the school that members themselves described as 'trusting', 'happy', 'warm', 'secure' and 'supportive'.

TRUST AND RESILIENCE

Now it was these characteristics which also led many staff members at Greenfields, Lowmeadow and Sedgemoor to describe themselves as a 'family', a choice of term which reflected their subjective experience of school relationships. From these relationships, as from a family, they drew strength to withstand the frustrations, disappointments, irritations, ambiguities and endemic tensions (Nias, 1989b) of their shared endeavour.

This state of affairs headteachers, teachers and ancillaries often described as 'trust', a word which Elliott *et al.* (1981) also found, in a study of accountability in secondary schools, to be in frequent use by parents, teachers and governors. To talk of trust as if it explained everything is, however, to make it into a 'black box', an abstract word packed with individual meanings. Nias (1981) therefore attempted an analysis of the term, arguing that it has two dimensions — predictability (of the other's personal and work-related behaviour and occupational competence) and common goals. For trust to exist, people must find one another highly predictable and share substantially the same aims. In such a situation much can be left implicit in interactions between participants; the occasional misunderstanding can usually be resolved by a personal exchange. But when people do not find others predictable, or do not have the same ends in view, they cannot be said to trust each other. Instead they attempt to resolve differences of aim or policy through formal procedures, such as rules or meetings.

When the culture of a school is collaborative the conditions necessary for the existence of trust are obviously satisfied. Members share the same beliefs and values and therefore have similar aims. Norms are built upon these beliefs and shape the behaviour of participants, so members' actions become highly predictable to one another. Moreover, one of these sets of norms — acting in ways which show people that they are valued as individuals — ensures that staff members become very familiar with one another as persons, not just as fellow workers; and another — acting so as to foster interdependence and cohesion — further increases both predictability and an awareness of common goals. In other words, trust is the almost inevitable outcome of participation in the 'culture of collaboration'.

So too is resilience. Because mutual support and encouragement were taken for granted, the staff in the collaborative schools were able to cope with exceptional events with very few signs of strain ('Don't make a fuss' was the unofficial Sedgemoor motto). Interdependence created networks of overlapping roles and responsibilities, which dispersed strain and encouraged adaptability. Staff themselves attributed their individual flexibility and collective strength to the habits which had become part of their normal way of life:

> It's quite remarkable [this week] that we've all gone on with teaching, nothing has fallen apart, everything has just gone on, assembly, playtimes, lunches . . . there were points in this week that could have been a crisis, because the balances have been shifting so much, but people have been pushing in added support, quite unconsciously this must have been happening all the time, in order for there not to be things sinking.
>
> (Teacher, Greenfields)

> I commented to a teacher on the smoothness with which the classroom move had been accomplished. She said, 'It would be impossible for it to happen like this unless we were all used to helping each other out.'
>
> (Fieldnote, July, Lowmeadow)

Finally, organizations in which this culture is dominant are well adapted to coping with uncertainty because they can build up a certain amount of what organizational theorists describe as 'slack', that is, spare resources (in this case, personal ones) which can be used to deal with unpredicted events. Because the ways of behaving enjoined by the culture result in a subtle blend of instrumentality and affectivity, cognition and feeling, simultaneous attention to task and personal concerns, almost every word, gesture or action exchanged between individuals serves more than one purpose. At the same time, the interdependence characteristic of staff relationships enables them, if the need arises, to act on one another's behalf, a safeguard that results in a situation which Landau (1969), in a description of commercial airliners, describes as 'redundancy' — that is, every vital function can be, or is, performed by more than one person. The overlapping, duplication or substitution which result make staffs such as these relatively impervious to shock and disruption of routine.

SUMMARY

Three of the project schools — Greenfields, Lowmeadow and Sedgemoor — shared a common type of dominant culture, though it was expressed in each school in slightly different ways. The heads and deputies of Hutton and Lavender Way were trying to move their schools towards this 'culture of collaboration'. Its existence made it possible for headteachers, teachers and ancillaries routinely and unself-consciously to work as a team, that is, to behave, despite all their differences, as if they all shared a common goal, to feel collectively responsible for its attainment and always to be ready to help one another towards it. It was also this culture which helped staff members, including the head, to identify as a group, that is see one another as friends and to feel a satisfying sense of social cohesion.

This culture arises from and embodies a set of social and moral beliefs about desirable relationships between individuals and the communities of which they are part, and not from beliefs about epistemology or pedagogy. It does however have a multiple effect, over time, on the educational practice of the schools in which it exists.

Its two main beliefs are that individuals should be accepted and valued, but that so too should interdependence, because individuals exist only in a social context. Within both beliefs one can distinguish two threads. Individuals are to be welcomed, appreciated and fostered for their own sakes, but also for the mutual enrichment which comes from diversity. Similarly, interdependence is valued because it celebrates both the group and the team. The culture also embodies beliefs about means. Interdependence leads to mutual constraint, and it is the resulting security which encourages members of the culture to be open with one another in the expression of disagreement and of emotion.

Shared understandings and agreed behaviours enable staff in schools where this culture is dominant to trust and to learn from one another. The relationships which they create in the process are tough and flexible enough to withstand shocks and uncertainties from within and without. 'Collaborative' staffs tended to be both happy and resilient.

We may so far have given the impression that the existence of this culture was fortuitous. Since this was not so, in the next chapter we explore the means by which it was developed and maintained.

Chapter 5

Developing and Maintaining the Culture of Collaboration

So far we have attempted to explain the main factors shaping the nature of individual school cultures and have suggested that we were able to identify a distinctive type of dominant culture in three schools. We have also suggested that Hutton and Lavender Way appeared to be moving towards this culture, largely under the influence of their heads. In this chapter we consider how that culture was developed and maintained in all the schools.

We must emphasize that at first sight the 'culture of collaboration' seems to emerge from similar influences to those involved in the evolution of all school cultures (see Chapter 3). But there are important differences. Because the heads consciously wanted to encourage collaboration they fostered certain forms of behaviour and the patterns of influence associated with them. They also took steps to inhibit activities which might have prevented the culture from developing. Moreover, the intentionality of the heads' actions makes it difficult to distinguish between behaviour which developed, and that which sustained, collaboration. 'Developing' and 'maintaining' should be seen as different in degree rather than in kind. The 'culture of collaboration' began when the first leadership acts of openness, sensitivity, tolerance and flexibility were reciprocated by other members of the staff group. From then on, it was sustained whenever members behaved consistently with the collaborative norms which the group was developing. In other words, once the culture of collaboration was established, it tended to become self-perpetuating. Consequently, similar types of action by head or staff members had different implications for a staff culture in different phases of development, and the implications of particular actions could only be understood in context and by members who had access to shared meanings. For these reasons we have tended not to differentiate factors contributing to 'development' from those helping with 'maintenance'.

Although the heads consciously initiated and fostered the 'culture of collaboration', cultures cannot be built by one person. They therefore relied extensively on their staff to follow their lead and upon the schools' other leaders for support. Whilst staffs' personal characteristics influenced their attitudes and their actions, and hence the development of the culture, their behaviour was also modified by a process of socialization, largely through talk. Through chatting, staff negotiated shared meanings and developed norms. These were in turn sustained by subsequent interaction and by humour, which was important because it made membership of the culture pleasurable. Regular meeting at predictable times and places also encouraged extensive talk. Teams and groups grew from all these kinds of interaction and proved both professionally and affectively rewarding. Celebrations were regular reminders of each staff's interdependence. Finally, the presence of an internal or external 'enemy' could give a false impression of unity which was not based on the values characteristic of this culture.

MEMBERSHIP

Our evidence suggests that in all of the schools the task of developing a collaborative culture was a subtle and complex one and that in three of them its maintenance required constant attention and activity. When Isobel described how 'the Sedgemoor way' was developed and sustained, she emphasized that regular interaction was a conscious achievement constructed from apparently trivial everyday behaviour. However happy the outcome, it was no mere accident:

> We all tend to sit round after school and chat. I think that is a very important element of the school, that we create sessions when we are all together. For example, before school in the morning people drop in and have a coffee and chat, and at lunchtimes and after school.

> (Head, Sedgemoor)

The important part leaders play in initiating and encouraging collaboration is discussed in detail in Chapter 6. Their attempts to develop the culture of collaboration depended for their success on the heads' clarity of purpose and their ability to communicate implicit values and attitudes through the personal model they offered to their staffs:

> Rather than run the school by verbal or written edict, the head's style is to co-ordinate the efforts of individuals and groups, identifying needs which are not being met, and helping to meet them. In this way she seeks to influence teachers but not dictate to them.

> (Fieldnote, November, Lavender Way)

But no whole-school culture can develop without the active co-operation of staff members: they are continuously involved in negotiating their relationships in response to the forces of change acting upon them (see Chapter 7). Even in schools where a culture of collaboration has been established, it is not stable, depending for its continued existence upon the ability of the staff group to respond to each change in ways consistent with the culture's characteristic beliefs and values. As one Hutton teacher said, 'You still have to have your Indians, don't you, and you have to have good Indians, otherwise the chiefs don't do very well.'

So headteachers depended in the first instance on the perceptiveness and sensitivity of their staff, on their ability to discern their leader's purposes and follow them:

> Those members of staff who are most successful . . . have taken the trouble to get to grips with what he really wants . . . it's people who really want to learn who learn,

people who don't want to learn won't . . . I think I'm always willing to try things if people suggest them . . . if it doesn't work, then you can say so.

(Teacher, Hutton)

But once staff understood how to be active followers, each appropriate action that they took reinforced and developed the values underlying the culture. In time they became members of it, interacting with other members and adopting and exemplifying the values and norms that they all shared. This enabled them to become models for other staff, especially new ones:

Isobel depends on people who have been here knowing what's wanted and how to go about things, and the information is disseminated through them rather than from her . . . which again helps because it's not seen as coming from the top.

(Teacher, Sedgemoor)

In addition, because individuality was valued, members could and did sustain the culture by the initiatives they took and by demonstrating their readiness to accept responsibility for joint activities:

I think there is a rubbing-off process. Once one person says 'Look, this is what I've been looking at, somebody else says 'Oh yes, maybe we ought to think about it.'

(Teacher, Sedgemoor)

Isobel tells me that collaborative work is frequently organized in a very informal way. 'An example is the large hall picture. It had become very tatty . . . so we were talking about what to do about it at a staff meeting. Sally said "What about . . ." and she could obviously see the whole thing quite clearly, so we said "right, you're in charge".'. . . Later in the day Sally said to Isobel 'can we have a quick meeting one lunchtime so that we can make sure everybody knows what they're doing for the hall picture'.

(Fieldnote, May, Sedgemoor)

Heads reinforced such efforts by showing that they too valued individual initiatives:

We've all got our own ways of caring and Miss Proctor allows us to show that in the way we want to. We don't all have to be alike, though we all want the same things for the children. I think that's where Miss Proctor is so clever, because it must be very easy when you go into a headship to make people try to fit into a mould and say 'I want things done this way'. But she doesn't do that.

(Teacher, Lowmeadow)

Everybody is allowed to be an individual, you are allowed, if that is the right word, to run your class as you wish . . . But at the same time there is this overriding idea of interaction between the staff over the sorts of things that are going to affect everybody.

(Teacher, Sedgemoor)

Yet heads themselves could lead a collaborative culture only from within it, so once it had been established, their behaviour was often difficult to distinguish from the active membership of their colleagues; actions which had once been characteristic of leadership became the ways in which every member typically behaved. However, heads' position and authority meant that their behaviour remained conspicuous, and they continued to act as models:

This term Catherine is on duty once a week. It creates a chance for her to be seen to be a teacher like everyone else.

(Fieldnote, November, Lavender Way)

Deputies too were important models, especially because they could use their position as class teachers to complement the example of the head (see Chapter 6).

PERSONAL QUALITIES

Although the existence of a collaborative culture depended on members bringing with them, or learning, behaviour which conformed to shared values, the contributions of staff as individuals were very influential. Because individuals were valued and individuality was encouraged, 'who' staff were was important. Further, without the contributions of particular members, each staff might have become a sterile and limiting copy of its head. So the personal attributes of individuals helped to give each staff its unique quality. Moreover, since maintaining the culture depended on individuals' willingness to consider, help and work with others, personal qualities mattered in this context too.

Because the central beliefs of this culture related to relationships between people rather than on the jobs they did, particular individuals could transform the quality and nature of staff relationships. Differences between schools were partly therefore a reflection of differences between people. Colleagues behaved and reacted to each other as persons rather than as practitioners, so liking was important:

> [Of a new member] She is good fun, placid, and you can pull her leg. Yes, it's a happy atmosphere. It is different. There is no doubt about it.
>
> (Teacher, Lavender Way)

But liking itself was affected by other attributes. Provided that they had the opportunity and inclination to participate in the staff culture, probationers, ancillaries, secretaries or caretakers could be as valuable as heads or deputies as humorists, carers, sympathetic colleagues, sources of praise, sharers of outside lives, empathizers with personal difficulties and educators of new staff into the staff norms. For example, the Hutton caretaker was a prominent source of staffroom humour. In contrast, at Lavender Way, the caretaker was criticized as much for being a disruptive personal influence as for his lack of cleaning:

> I don't always want to enter into his jolly banter every night after school, because I do find it very trying to have him in there at the end of every afternoon.
>
> (Teacher, Lavender Way)

The contribution of non-teachers to each staff group was particularly affected by their personal characteristics, because unlike teachers they were often the only person doing their particular job — 'A banana between the apples and the oranges'. (Caretaker, Lavender Way) But their relative isolation also had advantages for the rest of the staff. Secretaries, for example, would listen, could be trusted and confided in and brought a different, non-teacher perspective:

> I do find that I get somebody coming into the office ready to tear their hair out and scream . . . they just want to get something off their chest . . . Once they have had a good shout about it, it's all back to normal again.
>
> (Secretary, Lavender Way)

Heads consciously chose staff for their personal qualities as well as their professional expertise. When they were seeking to develop a collaborative culture, they sought staff who could be leaders in and models of the values they wanted to establish:

> One teacher starts to impose on Teresa [the new deputy head] the role of channel of information from the head, by asking 'Do we have to hand in a forecast next week?' Teresa says 'i'll say no, and if I'm wrong you can blame me . . .' and she laughs. She has managed to convey that she is friendly and cheerful and that she is prepared to carry the can. Her general approach is to invite them to come to her if they want to.
>
> (Fieldnote, January, Hutton)

Similarly, when heads were selecting staff to work together they considered personal compatibility. In the collaborative schools the culture was strengthened by the selection of staff who shared its existing values, and who showed the perceptiveness and sensitivity to understand how to become a member:

> I was looking for somebody who would fit in with the existing team, have enough experience to be able to lead, and have the right sort of personality.
>
> (Head, Sedgemoor)

But to write of 'personal qualities' is not to suggest that these were seen as fixed. In recruiting new staff heads looked for the capacity to adapt and to adopt culturally appropriate ways of behaving rather than for particular kinds of personality. Heads' emphasis on the need for sensitivity and flexibility in new staff reflected their view that 'fitting in' was a matter of behaviour, and that new behaviour could be learnt or developed. Consequently they tried in the first instance to educate existing staff into collaboration, rather than attempting to get rid of them. They undertook this education themselves and they also relied on the socializing power of the staff group. But since tolerance of individuality was part of the culture of collaboration, normative control did not mean that all staff became alike. A group which was developing this culture needed and valued the idiosyncratic contribution that individuals could make to particular roles (e.g., deputy). Once the culture was more fully established, different members were likely to perform varying functions at different times so that, for example, tolerance, supportiveness or a willingness to confront the disagreeable were norms which anyone could confirm through individual behaviour.

'CHAT IS A HIGH-LEVEL ACTIVITY'

One of the main ways in which a fresh culture was created and an existing one developed was through talk. Two related features of the collaborative schools were that the staff spent a great deal of time talking to one another and that their conversations were usually a mixture of chat about themselves and discussion of their teaching. These activities were among the chief means by which the culture was developed and they were crucial to its maintenance.

Our evidence suggests that in all the project schools everyday talk was the medium through which shared meanings first evolved and then were continuously and implicitly reinforced. These day-to-day exchanges often appeared trivial in content and in their short-term significance probably were. Yet they had important long-term implications. First, talk is a process which reveals individuals' attitudes, values and beliefs, that is, their perspectives. Second, because it can facilitate the development of trust it can lead to mutual openness. Third, the development of a shared language which is rich in inferred meaning enables apparently mundane exchanges to convey complex ideas. Moreover, the significance of such interactions is obscured to outsiders who are not a party to the shared meanings. Understanding of cultural language comes only with membership, and is a sign of it.

Lavender Way illustrates the first two of these processes. There, a staff which had been together a relatively short time were tentatively negotiating relationships. The initial encounters of new colleagues were characterized by a kind of guarded cordiality, avoidance of contentious issues, transaction of routine business, and silences:

> Breaktime.
> There are references to class assembly, with Amanda, the newcomer, asking how often they take place. She comments on the children's quietness in the hall. We move on to Sir Keith Joseph. Catherine tells what she has heard him say on television about the teachers' industrial dispute.
> We talk about how warm the school is. This stimulates talk of the merits of different home heating systems. Catherine takes the conversation as a hint that the school is too hot and goes to ask the caretaker to switch the heating off. Jayne asks for contributions to the ancillary's leaving present and tells the head of her concern about the work of some children.
>
> (Fieldnote, November, Lavender Way)

But, in time, talk led to the sharing of outside lives and so became self-revelation; this in turn was the first step towards openness and reciprocal confidences, so that within a year staffroom talk at Lavender Way was beginning to change:

> The talk at morning break shows a continuing opening up. Several staff have had the first meeting of courses they are attending. Stella talks about the teachers she has met who have two and a half hours free per week. When I suggest that this reflects the idea of having a supernumerary teacher, so that everybody can pursue their specialism, Amanda's response is 'And those of us who don't have a specialism can just go and chat.' Ben replies 'Chat is a high-level activity.' It's a comment on what they are doing: they are talking far more openly and are beginning to understand each other far more clearly. Chat has *become* a high-level activity.
>
> (Fieldnote, September, Lavender Way)

Talking about outside interests also offered colleagues a window on the sort of person a teacher was, so that common interests and experiences could be discovered and shared attitudes perceived:

> When you're on duty you don't just talk about education. You talk socially . . . you just pick up snippets of conversation, you just think 'Yes, I would say that' . . . I've never actually seen any of her drama lessons, yet I know through what she says about them that we would approach drama in the same way . . . we were so in tune it was just unbelievable.
>
> (Teacher, Hutton)

In Chapter 3 we showed how shared meanings which are developed through interaction are expressed through culturally specific language. As Bernstein (1971) has suggested, talk becomes characterized by speech forms and codes which reflect, sustain, and can modify the form of social relationships from which they evolve. Moreover, within a closed culture speech forms are likely to become 'restricted' because talk happens in a context laden with shared history, interests and assumptions. By contrast when meanings are not shared, speech has to be 'elaborated' and meanings made explicit. Bernstein's discussion of speech codes emphasizes the complexity of meaning carried by 'restricted codes' and, by implication, suggests that a group such as a primary school staff may develop a restricted communication code as they develop greater mutual understanding. This was certainly the case in the project schools, a fact which suggests that we must be careful in accepting Pollard's (1987, p.106) contention that sometimes primary school staffroom talk 'revolves around topics which are "common denominators" ' and that 'the discourse of common denominators is inherently insular, relatively static and sometimes reveals a tendency to decline to the lowest common denominator.' Sometimes, it appears, the kinds of topics to which he refers should not be taken at face value but should rather be seen as coded indicators of deeply shared cultural understandings.

However, sometimes Pollard is right. Certainly at Hutton and Lavender Way there were occasions when 'educational issues of fundamental importance are often excluded from discussion because of the controversy which they might cause' (*ibid*). As a result individual perspectives were not revealed nor meanings shared among the whole staff group, and a coded language was therefore slow to develop. Staffs who found openness threatening often confined themselves to safe and superficial banter:

> Marion described herself as 'feeling seraphic'. Bill asked her what on earth that meant, to which she answered, 'It means feeling like a heavenly body.' General laughter follows.
> (Fieldnote, October, Hutton)

Such exchanges avoided the public airing of privately acknowledged differences in educational perspectives: in spite of the cheerful tone of conversation at times such as morning break, several staff felt that informal occasions did not bring them together. In particular the major concerns that might have been prominent staffroom topics – children and teaching – were seldom raised:

> I think it comes down to the question of we're all very polite and we've got to work together, so a good friendly relationship on a social level is important, but when it comes to a professional level, I think people expect different things and people need different things, and that's why it falls down.
> (Teacher, Hutton)

Under these circumstances, avoidance of difficult areas became a staffroom norm to which new members were expected to conform:

> You just don't discuss problems, nor things that haven't worked . . . I don't know [why] . . . I've just learnt that, because nobody else does it, I don't.
> (Teacher, Hutton)

The development of a climate in which, by contrast, openness was the norm was contingent on individuals being prepared to take risks. Risk-takers were often heads, especially when they first joined a staff:

> After several weeks I decided we needed to sit down and discuss their concerns. I was opening myself up, I was prepared to do so because I felt that they might open up a bit.
> (Head, Lavender Way)

Sometimes deputies too performed this function:

> Everybody needs to feel wanted and that people are interested in them, even the abrasive people who at first push you off; very often that's even more of a reason that you should find out some way of getting to talk to them, to get to know them as people.
>
> (Deputy, Lowmeadow)

> Julia [the deputy] is so natural, she's so disarming, she's prepared to make fun of herself. Sometimes she makes herself look silly deliberately, to put us at ease I suppose. I find that's very infectious, very catching. You suddenly think, 'Oh yes, it's open, I'm accepted and there's no need to hide behind barriers from one another.' We can be who we are, then in turn we are more relaxed and in turn we pass on that relaxation to the children.
>
> (Teacher, Lowmeadow)

Some staff also realized that their willingness to take the first step towards self-exposure might encourage others in this direction:

> [In my last school] we all worked together as a team, you could always walk into that staffroom and see somebody to smile at you. Somebody would say 'come on, sit down, I'll make you a cup of coffee'. It makes a big difference and it wasn't just every once in a while like it is here, it was every day. It makes a much happier working relationship. But it's what you make it. A lot of the effort has got to come from within yourself. You can't just walk in and expect everybody to start talking to you and making cups of coffee and asking you questions if you are sitting there or reading a book or something. You have got to make a move.
>
> (Teacher, Hutton)

Indeed at Hutton, as talk between all the staff increased during the year, so too did openness:

> [Staff meetings] have made me relax more because somebody is actually saying 'I've got this problem' . . . they have taken away the stress which I wasn't even aware was there . . . we gas before meetings, contribute during the meeting and chat after.
>
> (Teacher, Hutton)

At Greenfields, Lowmeadow and Sedgemoor extensive, densely coded talk had long since developed and now continued to sustain the culture of collaboration. Personal and professional topics often mingled, conversation was characterized by openness and a willingness to talk about outside lives:

> Sally recalls how 'Sunday was really enjoyable, as it seemed to go so slowly because Monday was a holiday.' Isobel says, 'Yes, by Sunday lunchtime normally time seems to go faster and faster with school coming.' As Isobel and I sit in the staffroom after school, staff come in and talk about themselves. Sheila talks about the new puppy she has taken on. Veronica tells us about her husband's wisdom tooth operation and the terrible pain he's in. Then she talks about the successful farm visit that morning.
>
> (Fieldnote, February, Sedgemoor)

> Over lunchtime the conversation ran through a variety of topics: children's handwriting, presentation skills; whether education was about finished products of a high standard, or whether the process and thinking behind them is more important. There was talk about television, the role of books in society; what people thought about the current Booker Prize winner . . . whether parents should help with computers, given the problem of using computers whilst running the rest of the class; a governor offering to bring a pony to school to show one of the classes.
>
> (Fieldnote, November, Greenfields)

The staff themselves recognized that such day-to-day chat had been the way in which they had discovered common attitudes and learnt to understand each other as people:

We get on very well and I think it's because we talk so much. If you have got to work with somebody all day, you've got to find out how they work and think.

(Teacher, Lowmeadow)

As they had learnt more about each other's lives, classrooms and professional attitudes, they had also begun to 'realize that other people are human like you and can get things wrong' (Teacher, Sedgemoor). They had discovered that 'If you talk to someone it helps you to see the way they think and the reasoning behind what they are doing' (Teacher, Lowmeadow). Consequently colleagues learnt to anticipate actions and predict responses because they defined situations similarly:

> You do say what you think because you're familiar with your surroundings and you are familiar with the people. You know what their reactions are going to be. You know that you can say something to somebody and not upset them, or if you do say something that upsets them, you can say 'Look, I didn't mean to upset you. Why have you taken it the wrong way?'

(Teacher, Lowmeadow)

Once openness was established, conversation could range widely. In addition, as meanings became increasingly elaborated, brief exchanges enabled complex understandings to be established with great efficiency. For example, the relaxed staffroom conversation of a single lunchtime at Sedgemoor served many purposes. It: (a) communicated task-related information; (b) acknowledged professional fallibility and thereby legitimized failure; (c) asked for help and support; (d) offered it; (e) accepted it and thereby attached value to interdependence; (f) carried out specified responsibilities informally; (g) revealed personal beliefs and values; (h) used humour both to cement relationships and to make a serious point; (i) manifested caring concern for children and adults.

> At the lunchtable Josie tells Pete about a child's reading levels last year when she took him. 'He was only on the whites then.' Pete says, 'he's still on the whites but he can cope with them well now' (a), (i).

> Peter tells Josie and myself about another problem. 'I couldn't get John to see how many centimetres there were in one and a quarter metres', and then he continues to explain exactly what he said and what the child's responses were (b), (i).

> Margaret gets feedback from Josie on her farm visit, which confirms to her that it is well worth going (c), (e).

> Veronica overhears the discussion of which day to go to the farm and says, 'I shouldn't change the day, your mums will have already arranged to go Tuesday' (d).

> This confirms Veronica's watching brief over the Infants (f).

> When we get back to the staffroom, Sally and Peter chat. Pete makes flippant suggestions to Sally about a trip she might try for her Holland project. 'Why not try Walton Fen', he says with a laugh, 'or even Spalding?' But Sally says firmly, 'I want a canal trip and a windmill visit' (h).

> Dennis is in charge because Isobel is away on a course and he goes out of his way to check with me that I am prepared to take the Infants on Friday afternoon (i).

> He uses his lunchtime to make arrangements to work on maths with some of Sheila's class (f).

> Josie and I have a long conversation about racial discrimination experienced by her
> daughter and her coloured friends at secondary school (g).
>
> (Fieldnote, March, Sedgemoor)

The arrival of new members was particularly important to a well-established culture, since they were a possible threat to its norms until they had learnt, accepted
and adopted them. However, since the culture was largely implicit, the assimilation
of new members depended on their sensitivity to cues coming from the interactions
of their colleagues. 'Correct' relationships and the values these reflected were not
usually specified in curriculum documents. They had to be perceived in staff behaviour and understood from it. Talk was particularly important in this context because
it was the main medium through which the culture was conveyed. So, becoming a
member meant learning the language of the culture and then using it to show
one understood shared meanings and was prepared to adopt culturally appropriate
behaviour:

> You suddenly realize what you can and can't do (except you can do more or less
> anything), but the way it's done and not done. It's never that it's a stated thing, it's
> more a discussion in the staffroom usually. It's not even necessarily addressed to you,
> but it's there and it's said, and if you're in there and switched on you'll hear it, and
> then it comes back later. It isn't set out as the rules of the school, it's just an ongoing
> thing. You pick up bits and pieces here and there.
>
> (Teacher, Sedgemoor)

If potential members proved insensitive to obliquely expressed normative control,
various degrees of explicitness were used to convey to them the fact that their actions
were unacceptable:

> The head talked about the previous secretary who 'used to leave notes around when
> people owed coffee money and I used to surreptitiously chuck them in the bin because
> I'm against that'.
>
> (Fieldnote, July, Sedgemoor)

> After the staff meeting Graham turned to Alexis, and said 'Don't worry about the
> children in assembly, I think they were sitting very well'. During assembly Alexis had
> gone up on two or three occasions and talked to a trio who were restless, and on the
> third occasion had gone and brought the troublesome child to sit by her. Graham was
> soothing her concerns that the children's behaviour might not be congruent with the
> rules of the school, and he was saying he thought it was fine. I interpreted Graham's
> actions as giving both advice and gentle guidance, by showing her his values.
>
> (Fieldnote, April, Greenfields)

Further, once individuals had learnt the language of their culture, their participation
in the communication network helped to maintain it by emphasizing the exclusivity
of membership. Access to information about everyday gossip and arrangements kept
colleagues in touch with events of importance in each other's lives. Moreover, 'being
in the know' reinforced commitment to the culture, since it was a sign of being
valued as an individual and as a member of the group. Consequently, as Chapter 6
shows, deputy heads who ensured colleagues were kept informed of changes in
routine arrangements when they were not present at relevant times performed two
functions simultaneously. They helped the school run efficiently and maintained its
culture:

> At the end of the afternoon break there was the suggestion of an *ad hoc* meeting

tomorrow lunchtime. This was arranged by Julia going round each member of staff saying 'Is tomorrow all right?' and then as she reached me she said 'Now it's only Sarah who's on playground duty.'

(Fieldnote, May, Lowmeadow)

By contrast, a Hutton teacher who felt undervalued used as her criterion lack of consultation and uneven access to information:

Decisions are made that most people don't know about. If a book went round . . . they could know that everybody had or hadn't seen the note . . . we're often the last to know if things have been decided, and that's not nice when parents know things before you do.

(Teacher, Hutton)

HUMOUR

Schools with collaborative cultures were places where staff laughed a lot. Of course, in many cultures laughter is important as an indication that shared meanings exist and as a reminder that the culture is exclusive, but at Greenfields, Sedgemoor and Lowmeadow humour was particularly prevalent because there were so many shared meanings. By the same token, these meanings were often obscure to an outsider:

Deputy head: We were joking that after I had done two assemblies Isobel was going to spend the whole week preparing an assembly where she was going to dance herself and I would do a puppet show.
Int: What did that mean?
Deputy head: What were we joking about? That we didn't want assemblies to become high-profile, status-oriented.

(Deputy, Sedgemoor)

Humour was also actively used to create and maintain a sense of belonging, by making work and interaction with colleagues pleasurable fun. There were times when laughter represented genuine enjoyment of the company of friends with a similar sense of humour:

Carol came in with some very old books which Jim had found in a classroom when tidying out. We sat around giggling and laughing at these 1940s children's stories and the illustrations. Carol was 'camping it up' quite happily. Jim brought in another entitled 'On the train with Uncle Mac'. Carol was delighted at this and proceeded to read in a haughty 'home counties' voice. A great deal of fun was generated by the books.

(Fieldnote, March, Greenfields)

At Hutton and Lavender Way laughter served a slightly different purpose; it helped the staff take tentative steps toward openness because,

Humour simply oils the wheels. If you've got something humorous to say and people are relaxed, the message that comes across afterwards is more effective. Besides which, it's a lot more fun.

(Teacher, Lavender Way)

Interviews have dominated much of the conversation. At morning break there are extensive comments on Keith's shirt, pink with a white collar. Everyone thought this was very suitable for interviews, but told him there was a horrible clash with his fawn jumper.

(Fieldnote, October, Hutton)

It was also important as a sign that colleagues were learning not to be threatened by open relationships, so that late in the year a teacher commenting on developing closeness at Lavender Way used laughter as a yardstick:

> If you can't have a few laughs and a few jokes to lighten the day, it's a poor do isn't it? You can't go around being serious all the time and thinking 'Dare I say this? Dare I say that?'
>
> (Teacher, Lavender Way)

Self-mockery was an important way of legitimizing openness, because it gave one's colleagues an opportunity to see that fallibility did not result in exclusion from the group:

> Everyone was in the staffroom and it was already two or three minutes after the end of playtime. Carol suddenly said 'Oh dear! I'm supposed to be on yard duty.' She had spent the whole time in the staffroom. She then bobbed back for the bell and said 'Do you know, I've been standing there thinking "I wish somebody would ring the bell soon, because I've got a lot to do" — which brought the house down in gales of laughter.
>
> (Fieldnote, May, Greenfields)

It also encouraged people to admit openly to their own failings and so avoided the tensions and frictions which could arise from defensiveness:

> Vera wasn't in school, so Jim would be teaching her class. He is very much a junior teacher, less comfortable with infants, and particularly the reception class. There were a few jokes flying around the staffroom before 9 o'clock about him coping . . . There was continued teasing of Jim when, having survived half the morning, he came in for his coffee. There was some talk that Vera wouldn't be back this afternoon and some leg-pulling. In Jim's absence during lunchtime nobody broke the tease that the staff had now concocted for him. Carol even said that there had been a phone call from Vera saying she wouldn't be back. There was quite a lot of fun at his expense. When he did return, the tease was sustained, and Jim looked rather worried until 1.15 when Vera returned, and he confessed that he had been nervous about the afternoon. There had been humour at Jim's expense, but it was now laughter with him, and he took it in good part.
>
> (Fieldnote, March, Greenfields)

Similarly, humour was often the means by which sensitive concerns, problems, and difficulties were brought into the open. For example at Hutton:

> At break time all the talk is about a deputy headship candidate who has been touring the school. There is growing hilarity which masks, yet indicates, the genuine concern about the sort of person the deputy head is going to be.
>
> (Fieldnote, September, Hutton)

> The head mentions that a staff cricket game has been arranged. This provides an opportunity to reduce the possible tension over industrial action, and the NUT representative says 'Would a practice be against NUT regulations?' Laughter follows.
>
> (Fieldnote, September, Hutton)

Indeed it may be significant that staff relationships at Hutton tended to become more acrimonious after the departure of the teacher who led the staffroom laughter.

Humour also enabled minor irritations to be mentioned in a manner which did not threaten individuals' dignity:

> Confrontations don't happen, because we talk about things, usually on a casual, half-joking basis in the staffroom and the message is conveyed that way.
>
> (Teacher, Lowmeadow)

Pete's always teasing me because I hate going outside [on playground duty] when it's cold . . .

(Teacher, Sedgemoor)

Further, the heads' willingness to be the butt of colleagues' humour was confirmation that openness left self-esteem undamaged.

It emerged that Carol would be helped throughout the day by myself and Jim the deputy. The headteacher, in humorous plaintive tones, said 'Well, you've got two helpers today. No one ever helps me.' To which one of the staff replied 'Well, Graham, you've got to be doing something before you can be helped.'

(Fieldnote, November, Greenfields)

Breaktime talk in the staffroom — Isobel [the head] on giving up drink for Lent: 'I found it really hard.' Peter: '*You* found it hard, how do you think the rest of us found it !'

(Fieldnote, March, Sedgemoor)

MEETING EACH OTHER

Building and maintaining the culture of collaboration was a continuous process which happened when and where need and opportunity arose. Casual, unplanned encounters in classrooms and corridors helped to sustain contact between individuals, but the extensive talk and humour which had enabled understanding to grow and norms to be developed and by which these were collectively reaffirmed depended on the existence of predictable times when, and places at which, all the staff could gather together. Such predictability also made it more likely that everyone would participate.

Staff gatherings were important to the development and maintenance of the culture in several ways. First, they were occasions for interaction. Second, they were the forum in which shared values could be translated into action. At informal meetings in particular, individuals were able to make their contributions to the group irrespective of their formal status and could confidently expect to receive help and support when they needed it. Third, when culturally appropriate interaction took place in the presence of an audience, it provided an example on which newcomers could model themselves. Fourth, they sometimes testified explicitly to the importance of the culture or, more powerfully, fifth, they sometimes celebrated it. Gatherings where people could talk together, usually in the staffroom, could achieve all these outcomes. But so too could more formal occasions, such as assemblies and leaving ceremonies, where most of the staff were indirectly involved as an audience.

The Staffroom

The staffroom played a crucial part in the culture of the collaborative schools. It was the place where staff could go and know they would be together. Gatherings there were a centre for talk, with all its implications for revealing perspectives, conducting negotiations, sharing meanings, forging understandings, developing and sustaining relationships, giving and receiving support and maintaining the flow of routine task communication:

> That's how most of the staff conversation takes place, especially at lunchtime. That's when the group is all together and they are able to bring things up.
>
> (Teacher, Lowmeadow)

> The staffroom is the place to be, to find things out, to be yourself, to share and learn things. The staffroom is unquestionably the hub of the communications.
>
> (Southworth, 1986)

> The fact that there isn't competition amongst us as professional people means that when we go into the staffroom, we can just treat it as a place to relax and be ourselves, not just as teachers, but as people, and I suppose that's something to do with the feel of the school in general. I think we mix professional discourse with ordinary conversation quite well.
>
> (Teacher, Greenfields)

Each school had developed customary times when staff gathered, and members knew that 'belonging' to the staff meant appearing in the staffroom at those times. Newcomers who wanted to achieve membership needed to be aware of and adopt the practice. Lowmeadow was typical of the collaborative schools in that

> My field notes continually emphasize the importance of lunchtimes, both for those who eat at the staff dining table and because there is an unwritten understanding that teachers will gather in the staffroom about 15 minutes before the start of the afternoon session.
>
> (Nias, 1986)

Heads' regular presence in the staffroom served several related purposes. Decisions about various aspects of work could be made informally:

> Graham came into the staffroom and looked as if he was going straight out, so Victoria said 'If you're coming back, Mary's got something to ask you' . . . Mary put the problem forward by saying there were insufficient pencils, what are we going to do with the students? Graham responded by saying 'We'll get the pencils.'
>
> (Fieldnote, May, Greenfields)

Similarly, staff could 'have a private word' without the formality of an interview in the head's office. At Lowmeadow the sink was a popular venue:

> A teacher said to me 'It's a good place to have a private word. It's very difficult to talk privately in this school without it being apparent that you want to be private.'
>
> (Fieldnote, June, Lowmeadow)

To be present in the staffroom also gave heads the opportunity to exemplify the kind of behaviour they wanted to establish as taken for granted (see Chapter 6). Moreover they showed that simply being there was a valuable and legitimate use of time:

> Graham doesn't do yard duty, so he is always in the staffroom, doing introductions, bonding people together, keeping the discussion calm, soothing if necessary; picking up the 'vibes' is, I suspect, what he's also doing.
>
> (Fieldnote, January, Greenfields)

Because they believed the staffroom was important, the heads of the collaborative schools took an active role in encouraging teachers to use it regularly. They ensured that staff needed to be there by using staffroom gatherings as informal but essential channels of communication. They also consciously tried to make the staffroom a pleasant environment so that it was a place which encouraged the staff to linger and talk:

> It may sound ever so silly, but I think things like having the right sort of crockery available in the staffroom, glasses if you are going to have a bottle of wine or have a glass of sherry together [are important]. It sounds a very small thing, and in some ways it is, but it's all part of developing this feeling that we do these things together. It's not something exceptional, it's just the way we behave, an extension of home in a way.
>
> (Head, Sedgemoor)

They paid attention to the furnishings and layout. For example, at Sedgemoor a single circle of chairs enabled anyone to join in any conversations and excluded no one:

> There were just enough chairs for everyone, so that intermittently, a flurry of minor conversations broke out concurrently between neighbours, no matter who came to sit next to whom. There was a single low square table in the centre, a small shelf with books and plants, and on the end wall a glass-fronted cupboard with an array of glasses, cups and saucers, which suggested that hospitality sometimes flowed freely. Altogether it was a comfortable environment which encouraged relaxation.
>
> (Yeomans, 1986c)

By contrast, at Lavender Way, the staffroom discouraged talk because eye contact with all colleagues was difficult:

> The chairs were usually set along one wall. This meant that anyone sitting at the end had to move their chair so that they could see their colleagues. The television was regularly on in preparation for recording programmes. Staff seemed loath to reorganize the seating, since this was the room used for classes watching television. Thus there were times when we sat in silence before a flickering screen.
>
> (Yeomans, 1987c)

Moreover, within a divided staff no one was prepared to take an initiative towards transforming the environment:

> The only thing I don't like about [the staffroom] is when we're all sitting in a row . . . unless you make a specific move to pick up your chair and walk about with it, and I'm far too lazy to do that. I just tend to sit down wherever I happen to be.
>
> (Teacher, Lavender Way)

Assemblies

Assemblies were highly significant cultural occasions, involving adults and children. In all the schools, all teaching staff and some ancillaries attended regularly. Though heads took most of them, regular class assemblies also allowed teachers the opportunity to confirm their participation in the culture. Assemblies offered head and staff jointly a chance to express in various ways their shared acceptance of the beliefs underlying the culture of collaboration and of the values it incorporated (see also Nias, 1989c).

Sometimes the content of assembly was the important part:

> Monday assembly was on the theme of community and unity. The main part of the head's assembly was a story about a father and his three sons who were given a stick each. The story showed how easy it was to break the stick singly, but how much harder

that was when they were bound together and gained strength from each other. As all the staff come into assembly, both they and the children are potential audiences for the head's view of relationships in the school.

(Fieldnote, September, Hutton)

Julia did an excellent assembly with the aid of her class on 'friends'. She had us all holding hands and feeling each other's hands with our eyes shut, both adults and children. Then, with her children, she described the things they had done yesterday to get to know each other and to show what friends do.

(Fieldnote, March, Lowmeadow)

At other times it was the manner in which they were conducted:

The atmosphere is very much a friendly one in assemblies, and between teachers it is non-competitive.

(Fieldnote, October, Greenfields)

Assembly started with Miss Proctor saying to the children 'I did miss you yesterday.' Later she told them, but really the staff, what she had been doing yesterday.

(Fieldnote, March, Lowmeadow)

There is a birthday ritual which involves children coming and blowing out a candle, taking a sweet from the jar, receiving a badge, and having 'Happy Birthday' sung to them. Assembly ends with the closest thing there is in the school to a telling-off for the children. Catherine tells them quietly about the slide which has been made in the playground, points out that she had previously asked them not to slide, and gives reasons why they shouldn't use it — because a child had cut her chin previously.

(Fieldnote, November, Lavender Way)

Assemblies also gave teachers an opportunity to reveal the values they shared:

I commented that Sheila didn't seem to be panicking about her assembly. Veronica said 'It's not like that'; in other words, doing assembly isn't meant to be a detailed scrutiny of you and therefore isn't perceived as a threat.

(Fieldnote, June, Sedgemoor)

They were important for another reason too. Since the 'culture of collaboration' set parameters within which individual freedom operated, class assemblies could show whether each teacher understood and accepted those parameters and worked within them in the classroom:

The audience of staff and children is arranged in a horseshoe with Sheila's class at the front. There is a small display of work there. The theme is Space. It is reflection of the work done within the classroom over a period of weeks. What follows is a twenty-minute performance which integrates every aspect of the curriculum. There's movement, singing, tuned percussion, writing, information about the planets. Children demonstrate science experiments. One boy shows how a flame needs air in order to burn, and there's an audible sigh of relief when the candle finally dims under the jar. A girl demonstrates rocket propulsion by sending a rapidly deflating balloon along a taut string. At the end several children play space music they have composed. The teacher sits calmly at the side marking off the items as they are completed. The inference is that the assembly is not about the teacher but about the children and what they have achieved, but it does show that Sheila operates an integrated curriculum and that she's an effective teacher. It also confirms to anyone who wants to know that this is the kind of teaching and learning that is appropriate at Sedgemoor.

(Fieldnote, February, Sedgemoor)

Valuing and Celebrating Membership

As we explained in Chapter 4, when the staff of the collaborative schools spoke of their working relationships they often referred to the staff as a 'team'. But they also frequently emphasized the warmth of belonging to a group whose members they regarded as friends or even a 'family':

> We work together as a team within the school, but it's a sort of friendship really.
> (Teacher, Lowmeadow)

The distinctive nature of team relationships within this culture meant that people and their contributions were valued both personally and professionally. The occupational rewards of team membership stimulated the affective rewards of group membership, and in turn commitment to the team was strengthened. A cycle of constant reinforcement evolved, as the personal benefits of collaborating professionally encouraged staff to want to continue collaboration. Staff felt that belonging was a privilege and that they were 'special' as a group:

> I think the staff feel very special themselves, as a staff. They feel they have a special relationship with each other which other people don't understand and they don't want other people to understand it, because they want it to be special.
> (Head, Greenfields)

> I don't know another school like it really, and that plays an important part in its success. Everyone gets on, everyone is relaxed because they get on.
> (Teacher, Sedgemoor)

Because they found membership professionally and personally rewarding, collaborative staffs often created special occasions which celebrated and reinforced both the value of individuals and of the interdependence they felt. So, for example, all staff, including part-time teachers, ancillaries, caretaker and secretaries were included in occasions such as Christmas dinners and farewells. It was not oversight that the caretaker at Lavender Way, a frequent target for complaint, never participated in end-of-term buffets. At such occasions, leaders often retold the history of their institutions as 'stories' which assumed the stature of 'organizational sagas' (Clark, 1983). These served a threefold purpose: to affirm the solidarity of existing members and to remind them of their capacity to triumph over adversity; to celebrate the beliefs on which the individual culture of the school was built, and to alert newcomers to them (see Chapter 6).

Relatively minor occasions were also used as a reason for a staff celebration. At Greenfields, Lowmeadow and Sedgemoor members were expected to bring in a cake or bottle of wine on their birthdays, a custom which enabled the whole group to show its affection and goodwill towards individuals and to emphasize the ties of friendship binding them all. Consequently when the Sedgemoor deputy head forgot to mark his birthday, the head considered this an oversight worthy of comment:

> As today is Dennis' birthday Isobel wants to know why he hasn't brought the staff a cake. He says he hasn't had time but will bring a bottle tomorrow.
> (Fieldnote, July, Sedgemoor)

In the same way, the start of birthday rituals at Lavender Way had a symbolic importance which Catherine, the head, recognized, but other colleagues were still learning:

> Catherine comments that she had had to rescue from the bin the surprise birthday flower arrangement and candle that Rita had made for her.
>
> (Fieldnote, July, Lavender Way)

In the collaborative schools, staffroom celebrations were preferred to the relative formality of dinners at which spouses and partners were present. By contrast when, as at Hutton, the 'culture of collaboration' had yet to develop fully, staff dinners were defined by some people as a duty rather than as a celebration of cohesion. And at Lavender Way, as staff began to develop more open relationships, they chose to have a meal out together, but without husbands and wives.

End-of-term and end-of-year celebrations which offered an opportunity to look back and forward could also be used to mark joint achievements and to emphasize the continuity of the staff group over the coming holiday:

> Ten or fifteen minutes after school had closed the staff gathered in the staffroom. Bottles of wine were opened and we sat and drank. Jim immediately began talking about the fact that he wasn't sorry to see the end of many of his class and he related one or two stories about the children that were leaving. Then he started to talk about the ones he was receiving and complained about them and was making many jokes. Victoria said she liked September and starting again with a new class because it showed how far you'd got with the last lot and so by comparison you could tell if you'd done a good job in the previous year. Some of the chocolates were opened and were passed round. There was a toast to Julie . . . I left with the staff group sitting together, sipping drinks, talking, laughing, with mixed emotions; some sadness, some tiredness, but still very much a happy staff group.
>
> (Fieldnote, July, Greenfields)

When staff were leaving, presents and farewell parties marked the group's care and affection for the departing member and, by inference, for all other members. These were the only occasions when speeches were used; the relative formality of the ceremony perhaps showed the significance of the occasion for the departing member and the group. At Lavender Way saying goodbye heightened staff awareness that a sense of interdependence was developing:

> Jayne said at the end of the week 'I've had an absolutely lovely week. I've never known it where we've all sat and talked like that.'
>
> (Teacher, Lavender Way)

and that the group would survive:

> This group seems to have found the cohesion not really there previously, and has not wanted to waste any time before Jayne goes.
>
> (Fieldnote, July, Lavender Way)

Moreover, as Sedgemoor's tenth anniversary celebrations show, membership of the group did not necessarily lapse when an individual left the school:

> The staff are very quiet today. They have all been at the school's tenth anniversary party last night. There were about thirty staff there, which is all the staff who have been there in the school's life.
>
> (Fieldnote, October, Sedgemoor)

Everybody who has been part of the forming of the school is always part of it, and I think they feel that, because they've actually said so when they come back . . . they are aware that they've played a crucial part in the early stages.

(Head, Sedgemoor)

FINDING AN 'ENEMY'

It would be misleading however to assume that every display of staff unity signified the existence of, or a move towards, the 'culture of collaboration'. In some circumstances in Hutton and Lavender Way groups and sub-groups developed a unity which was not based on its characteristic beliefs and which diverted attention from the efforts being made by some of the staff to develop it in those schools. In particular, a tacitly or openly acknowledged 'enemy' could give a staff a transient feeling of cohesion which could be used as a diversion, allowing them to avoid resolving their own internal differences and offering them a spurious unity derived from agreeing on what they disliked. It temporarily absolved them from the task of working to negotiate open, and where possible, trusting relationships among themselves. Such 'negative' cohesion offered colleagues a shifting foundation on which to build. Essentially ephemeral, it remained only as long as the 'enemy' did. So, for example, when Hutton's new deputy head was appointed from the 'enemy' school, it was difficult for the staff to sustain the illusion of external threat, and cliques began to emerge internally.

Both Hutton and Lavender Way had 'enemies'. At Lavender Way the scapegoat was the caretaker who could be criticized openly because he never used the staffroom:

> There was uncertainty about who had asked a workman to come to repair a lock. Ben thought it had been Charlie the caretaker, though it simply needed oiling — as he had suggested to Charlie. Ben had oiled the lock himself, and it was working perfectly.
>
> (Fieldnote, October, Lavender Way)

> Have you ever known a caretaker like it? He said I couldn't go into the hall because the floor has been polished. So I said I was going to go in. So he said 'Oh well, I expect the floor will only be a bit sticky by now.' It was hardly worth going in by the time we had waited for the floor to be dry enough.
>
> (Teacher, Lavender Way)

At Hutton a neighbourhood 'show' school provided an external enemy and was used as a semi-humorous yardstick of Hutton's standing:

> Comments about imitating Derngate go on even when we're mounting a display for the entrance hall. . . . 'You're not even double mounting, you're triple mounting' . . . or 'That was very Derngatey'. In fact some staff even went to a meeting just to see what Derngate School was like, and came back saying we do just as well if not better.
>
> (Teacher, Hutton)

> I suppose it's because it's a show school, the people that count think it's the bees' knees, and it gets visited a lot, and I suppose if you put something on a pedestal you have got to expect it to be knocked down.
>
> (Teacher, Hutton)

Yet collaborative schools sometimes had 'enemies' too. At Greenfields and Lowmeadow there were instances when a sense of being under attack from some of the parents strengthened the existing unity within the staff. But their reaction was not characteristic of 'negative' cohesion, because it did not distract members for long from the need to nurture their in-school relationships and did not prevent them from facing internal disagreements when these arose.

SUMMARY

This chapter has suggested that the culture of collaboration was deliberately fostered by heads who depended on the active support and participation of members, particularly to socialize newcomers. They were greatly assisted by members' personal qualities, inherent or learned, especially their sensitivity to others. Much also depended on regular everyday conversations which enabled staff to establish and reaffirm shared meanings in relation to their personal and professional attitudes, values and beliefs. Humour was a prominent feature of such interactions. Predictable meeting times and places enabled all staff to share in and be influenced by the staff culture; staffrooms at breaks, lunchtimes and after school were particularly important. So too were assemblies.

The fact that members perceived themselves to be an effective team which was also a supportive friendship group made membership of the culture a rewarding experience and helped to render it self-sustaining. The existence of the culture was recognized symbolically in regular celebrations, particularly at the ends of terms. Finally, the development of authentic collaboration could be impeded by transient unity generated by a perceived 'enemy'.

So far we have acknowledged, but not explored fully, the part leaders played in all aspects of the 'culture of collaboration'. To this topic we turn in the next chapter.

Chapter 6

Leadership

It will be apparent from all that has been said so far, in particular in the previous chapter, that the establishment and maintenance of the culture of collaboration owes a great deal to its leaders. Most obviously these were the headteachers in all the schools but, as this chapter sets out to show, they shared many aspects of their leadership with other staff members, notably their deputies. Before we explore in detail the part played by headteachers and others in founding and fostering collaborative cultures in their schools, we need to examine the concept of leadership. This, we suggest, has six dimensions important to an understanding of staff relationships in primary schools: initiating structure and consideration (Halpin, 1966); decision-centralization (Yukl, 1975); contingency (Fielder, 1968; Handy, 1981); example (Coulson, 1976; 1986; Southworth, 1987a); and 'mission' (Peters and Waterman, 1982; Hoyle, 1986). Each of these itself requires clarification because similar concepts have been identified by other writers (often from fields other than education), using slightly different terminology. Accordingly, this chapter falls into three main parts. The first examines significant dimensions of leadership, the second uses the distinctions suggested by this examination to illuminate the work of headteachers in the project schools, the third looks at the part played by other, often informal, leaders.

THEORIES OF LEADERSHIP

Leadership has been studied by many analysts and from a variety of perspectives. Early studies considered leadership as a function of personal characteristics (the trait approach) whilst other work looked at leadership style (e.g., democratic, autocratic, laissez-faire). Later work has shown the limitations of both approaches (see Hughes, 1985; Hoyle, 1986) and since 1950 research has focused on the dimensions of leadership, particularly task achievement and personal relationships. The effective leader, it is assumed, ensures that tasks are accomplished and, at the same time, helps colleagues to feel that their social needs are being met (Hoyle, 1986). A bewildering number of terms have been coined to describe these two dimensions, but two terms have proved popular: initiating structure and consideration. They have been defined as follows:

> *Initiating structure*: refers to the leader's behaviour in delineating the relationship between him/herself and members of the work group, and in endeavouring to establish well-defined patterns of organization, channels of communication and methods of procedure.
> *Consideration*: refers to behaviour indicative of friendship, mutual trust, respect and warmth in the relationship between the leader and the members of his/her staff.
>
> (Halpin, 1966, p. 86)

A third dimension was added by Yukl (1975), who noted that the twofold typology did not take account of the extent of the followers' or subordinates' participation associated with the leader's behaviour. Yukl proposed a third dimension, decision-centralization:

> *Decision-centralization*: refers to the degree of leader influence over group decisions.

These three dimensions have been shown to have relevance to primary school leadership (see Nias, 1980; Lloyd, 1985). Clearly primary school heads initiate structure (e.g., timetables, pupil groupings, meetings, curriculum organization), and the extent of their consideration can be observed, as can whether their decisions are more or less centralized. Moreover, because individual primary heads behave differently on each of these dimensions, as Lloyd (1985) has shown, heads need to be rated in terms of their combined behaviour on all three dimensions. Behaviour on these three dimensions is, however, an insufficient description of leadership because (at least) three other factors need to be taken into account. First, Fielder (1968) and Handy (1981) suggest that different types of situation require different kinds of leadership and that effective leadership is, in part, contingent upon the context within which the leader and the group are working. The effects of a school's situation does affect leadership in a primary school (see Open University, 1988). To be a teaching head in a small, one-form entry primary school like Greenfields is different from being the head of a two-form entry junior school such as Hutton where the head did not, for example, have the same teaching requirement as the head of Greenfields. The pen portraits of the project schools in Chapter 2 demonstrate some other situational factors (e.g., school size, type, catchment, buildings, staff) which Chapter 3 shows as affecting the school's culture.

Second, because of his/her position the leader is inevitably a model for the group, whether in terms of attitudes and behaviours to be imitated or those to be avoided (see Hughes, 1985; Handy, 1981). Coulson (1976; 1986) and Southworth (1987a) have shown that primary school headteachers are exemplars not only because of their position but also because they put faith in example as a way of influencing others.

Third, recent work on leadership suggests that leaders identify and articulate a sense of 'mission' for their organization (see Peters and Waterman, 1982; Peters and Austin, 1985; Hoyle, 1986). Although this is a rather nebulous idea it seems to be concerned with identifying, transmitting and gaining acceptance of an image or vision of where the school is heading. It is to do with providing a sense of direction, a feeling of going somewhere. Seen in this way the idea has neither a military connotation (e.g., the achievement of a clear objective within a finite time scale), nor a religious one (i.e. it is not evangelicalism or zealotry) (Hoyle, 1986). Rather, mission is to do with the beliefs, usually of the headteacher, and normally in relation to the nature of personal relationships and therefore about the social and moral purposes of education, and the nature of effective educational practice. The leader's mission helps to guide the school.

Leadership is evidently a construct in which dimensions, functions and context all play a part (see Hughes, 1985). In this chapter, leadership in the project schools will be discussed in ways which enable the reader to identify the ideas discussed above. Despite the fact that leadership remains too complex and elusive a topic to define in a single, simple statement, the five project schools revealed valuable insights into the nature of leadership in primary schools. This is particularly true in that previous studies have tended to equate leadership with headship (e.g., Coulson, 1976; Nias, 1980; Whitaker, 1983; Lloyd, 1985; Southworth, 1987a). Although these, and other writers, have contributed to our understanding of the role of the primary head their narrow focus has restricted our understanding of the leadership roles that other staff occupy and perform. This chapter will therefore look at leadership in primary schools, first by considering headteachers and then by looking at other leaders. Furthermore, previous work has underestimated or overlooked the connection between leadership and culture. This chapter will consider the links between the two.

HEADTEACHERS

Studies of the primary head's role focus on the headteacher's formal, managerial functions (Coulson, 1986; Open University, 1981; 1988). These studies and others (Alexander, 1984; Campbell, 1985) recognize the head's substantial, if not formidable, concentration of power and authority. However, it is acknowledged that these formal functions and power are discharged and transacted in an informal manner (Coulson, 1976). In addition, the head's managerial job involves deeply felt self-expectations (Southworth, 1987a; Myer, 1987). The picture which emerges from the five project schools supports much of this existing work.

But there are some new findings. In three of the schools (Greenfields, Lowmeadow and Sedgemoor) the heads had been in post, in the same school, for at least ten years (and in the case of the heads of Greenfields and Lowmeadow for almost double that length of time). The head of Hutton had been in post for five years whilst the head of Lavender Way had only been in post for one and a half years. At Greenfields, Lowmeadow and Sedgemoor the heads felt 'their' schools were now congruent with their individual aspirations, whereas the two other heads felt there was still some way to go before their aims were translated into action. Part of the significance of this relates to the idea of mission. To a large degree the heads of Greenfields, Lowmeadow and Sedgemoor were satisfied that their principal beliefs both about personal relationships and about effective educational practice were now installed, whereas the heads of Hutton and Lavender Way were still moving practice in their schools towards their beliefs on either or both fronts (social and moral purposes and/or effective educational practice). The fact that longer-serving heads, with feelings of 'mission accomplishment', were in the three schools where the culture of collaboration was firmly and widely established supports a connection between leadership, mission and culture. It also suggests that there is a need to explore these connections.

Moreover, because the heads of Greenfields, Lowmeadow and Sedgemoor felt that their schools were broadly in line with their mission, part of their leadership function was to sustain the culture of collaboration. By contrast the heads of Hutton and Lavender Way saw their job as developing their schools towards their missions and therefore towards the development of a school-wide culture of collaboration. Hence the leadership of these five heads was different. They were either sustaining or developing 'their' schools according to their perceptions of the school's situation in relation to their mission and its phase of development. Yet, regardless of whether the head felt his/her job was that of sustaining or developing the school, all five heads subscribed to two views: that the head's job was to provide a direction for the school and that it is the head who sets the underlying philosophy (see Coulson, 1976).

A Sense of Mission

During the early phase of our research we read a number of documents that each school made available. We studied the brochures for parents, statements of aims, schemes of work and, in one school's case, the school's 'Curriculum Award Folder'. Each of these documents, being written by the heads, revealed in its individual way, the latter's guiding beliefs (about the social and moral purposes of education, and/or the nature of effective educational practice):

General Aims (in the school's brochure to parents)
I have found it impossible to condense into a few sentences the aims and objectives of our school. To write them down under numbered headings in stereotyped form looked so out of keeping with the whole ethos of Lowmeadow and the more I tried to convey in words the work and endeavours of both the staff and children the more difficult it became.

   I felt as if I were a parent writing down the aims and objectives for bringing up her children, and a cold calculated definition of what we are trying to achieve in our school cannot do justice to the work carried out; it bypasses the all-important family atmosphere. Our school was built as the first community centre in the country, and it still remains a community in the truest sense of the word.

(Lowmeadow School)

A Good School (a statement for staff)
A good school is one where the staff share a clear sense of direction and work together to make the stated philosophy a reality . . . takes as its starting point the child as he is and strives to help him develop his full potential . . . is constantly questioning and evaluating its work. The teachers are concerned for their own professional development and demonstrate this by reading, attending courses and by spending time discussing their philosophy and the best way of implementing it. They are not afraid to learn from each other and use their individual expertise for the good of the school . . . work together to find solutions, supporting and helping one another. By working together these teachers have recognized the value of sharing the ideas and enthusiasms of colleagues . . .

   The good school . . . sees itself as part of the local community.

(Extracts from *Hutton CE Junior School Educational Aims, Philosophy, Objectives and Organisation*, 1986)

Discipline (in the preface to the school's curriculum policy statement for social education)

The happy atmosphere in this school does not happen by accident. . . . Children's activities in and around the school are governed by the use of common sense and a regard for others. Consequently there are very few 'school rules'. In fact there is really only one school rule, and this is embodied in the school motto — 'Think of Others.'

(Greenfields School)

These written statements matched the sentiments of the heads when they talked about their schools and how they saw them developing:

It all goes back to me really, in the sense that I think that the school should — I don't mean everybody do the same thing – but I think they've got to all follow the same pattern. I think that's got to be the underlying philosophy.

(Head, Hutton)

They also echoed remarks made by the teachers:

Miss Proctor likes to plan the general policy so to speak. I think anyone who didn't have similar thoughts about her philosophies would probably find they would have to comply. But at the moment our strength is that on the whole we share the same philosophy . . .

(Teacher, Lowmeadow)

Two points can now be made. First, heads hold two sets of complementary beliefs which appear to operate at the same time. The first are beliefs about ends and means in education with particular reference to its moral and social purposes (e.g., community, concern for others) and to the outcomes and methods of effective educational practice (e.g., high academic results, professional development, teachers who work together). The second beliefs are managerial: how heads believe it is best to run the school in order to achieve their educational ends (e.g., how heads should lead, how staff should work together). Clearly the two overlap and reinforce each other; 'working together', for instance, can be legitimated by reference to either educational or managerial beliefs or to both. The second point is that these five heads appear to match what Coulson (1976) has called the 'traditional concept of headship', where the head is generally presumed to be the pivot and focus of the school through a blend of moral authority and personal control.

Owners of the School

The close association between head and school appeared to be so strong that it is possible to describe the head as the 'owner' of the school. Moreover, this sense of ownership was perceived by staff and heads alike:

This is Miss Proctor's school, this is the school that she developed from a very, very different school with very different staff. So, I say, this is her school and we fit in and we know this is what we have to do.

(Teacher, Lowmeadow)

We've all got one aim and that's to do it (teach) to the best of our ability, in the way that Miss Proctor would like it to be. Obviously we must agree with the way she does it or we wouldn't be able to stay here.

(Teacher, Lowmeadow)

I think any one of us could leave and the place would stay roughly the same. It's changed a lot in the time I've been here. Each lot of people who've been here have been good in their own way, but I think the school could stand to lose any of us, but it certainly wouldn't be the same if Graham wasn't here.

(Teacher, Greenfields)

Graham has these beliefs that have filtered through the whole school, the whole staff.

(Teacher, Greenfields)

Int: Why do you think the staff are so friendly?
Ancillary: I think mainly because of Graham, I think he brings it out. No matter who comes in, everybody is drawn into things. I think the head's got to be like that, don't you?

(Greenfields)

I think the head really is the most important member of staff in that it is she who brings everybody together and helps everybody to work and I think she has a knack of bringing out the best in her staff and I admire her for that.

(Teacher, Sedgemoor)

17 October 1985. The day of the tenth anniversary of the school's opening. The anniversary is marked first of all at lunchtime — a surprise bottle of sherry was brought out by Dennis in honour, not so much of the school's tenth birthday, but of Isobel's tenth birthday as head of the school.

(Fieldnote, October, Sedgemoor)

I would say he (the head) is the school.

(Teacher, Hutton)

I think she (the head) feels it's more her school now. She's been here nearly three years. She came in the January. It's taken a while.

(Teacher, Lavender Way)

They are certainly all involved in a certain way but I feel that I, as the head, have a different role to play to link the school together and to lead really. I do see the head as a leader whether you are leading from behind or what, but I think the head is the leader and having had a year of visiting schools, I still think however much people belittle, all schools have certain atmospheres and I think the charisma of the head is very important and the school reflects that. I don't think there is any harm in thinking of it as my school. I think Sedgemoor is my school but other people have helped to make it as it is. I just feel I take the ultimate responsibility for it — if it's failing then I am the one who should get rapped over the knuckles, not the staff.

(Head, Sedgemoor)

A number of other points follow from the notion that heads owned 'their' schools. As the last quotation suggests, heads felt a deep personal commitment to their schools and were ready to admit to a sense of ownership:

Int: You've been here three years, three at Christmas, is it? Do you feel — my words, not yours — it's 'your school'?
Head: Just about. Coming back in September I began to feel it. Having had a break from the situation you come back and see it in a fresh light and other people have been saying that to me. I feel really for the first time, I am beginning to feel it is more 'my school'. Nobody now makes reference to 'we used to do it like this', and it is nice to be able to say 'Last year, do you remember, we did something like this.' I know the school, not through my eyes, but other people's eyes, has changed from comments parents have made coming into school; 'You don't do it that way now' and 'It's changed.'

(Lavender Way)

Notions of ownership are also related to headteacher succession. This head had been in post for five terms at the time of the interview. In that time the school was beginning to be more like 'hers' which implies it was less like the school she inherited from her predecessor. With the exception of Sedgemoor (which was a new school and opened by Isobel) all the heads referred to their predecessors' 'regimes' as ones from which they inherited something (or someone) which was 'unsatisfactory', or not congruent with their beliefs. Richard (head of Hutton) spoke of the staff being slow or poor at coming forward with ideas when he first arrived. Also, he claimed there was 'nothing much happening in the school', by which he meant that little curriculum change or review was being undertaken. Graham (head of Greenfields) talked about the changes he made in the staff because he wanted the 'right' sort of staff in order to have the particular kind of school he envisaged. Catherine spoke of the difficulties of trying to find out and understand what things had been like before she arrived. It took her some time to find out, despite stories to the contrary, that relationships inside the school had not always been healthy, staff felt they had always been told what to do and some were unhappy. This is how one of the longer-serving teachers spoke of Catherine's arrival:

> I can remember thinking 'when we get a new head everything will get on an even keel again', and we were very glad to have Catherine, even though we knew it would bring a lot of physical changes. It brought a lot of changes in the atmosphere of the school. Catherine prefers a proper entrance hall and a library to be central and this kind of thing, a lot of physical changes, which we actually did like because the drawback of — I won't say it was because he was a man — she made immense efforts that first two terms to get things moving, to get paintwork done and things tidied up, because there were lots of things that we felt aggrieved about. Things like tiles loose on the ceiling, which we were so pleased to see somebody really getting to grips with. It might sound very insignificant but at the time I can remember that it was very important . . . I think Catherine being so different from (the previous head) even though she has a lot of the same values educationally, her personal approach is very different.
>
> (Teacher, Lavender Way)

Quite clearly the departure of one head and the arrival of another creates discontinuities. This is only to be expected given the assumption that the head will articulate the school's philosophy and lead through personal example (see also Southworth, 1987a). The evidence collected on headteacher succession in the project schools corresponds with other research into leadership succession in school settings:

> Changing leaders can represent a psychological impact of a new personal style, a new definition of the situation, a new communication network with the environment, or a jolt to the system that opens its members' minds.
>
> (Miskel and Cosgrove, 1985, p. 88)

'Ownership' also implicitly conferred the right to act as change agents, a role particularly prominent when heads first took up their jobs. The heads of Hutton and Lavender Way were very active in stimulating and supporting changes and it was apparent that at Greenfields, Lowmeadow and Sedgemoor the heads had been the main agents of change in the past. They spoke of developments now accomplished and of the considerable amounts of change they had engineered.

Founders of the Culture

The heads' sense of mission and feelings of ownership indicate that they are the founders of their school's culture, and this viewpoint is consistent with Schein's work on organizational culture and leadership (1985).

According to Schein, organizational cultures are created by leaders, and three of the most crucial functions of leadership may be the creation, the sustaining and — if and when that may become necessary — the destruction of culture (Schein, 1985). Greenfields, Lowmeadow and Sedgemoor were schools where the culture had been created and was then being sustained. Hutton and Lavender Way were schools where a previous culture had been destroyed, or was being dismantled because of the discontinuities brought about by headteacher succession, and a new culture was being created (see also Chapter 7).

Schein also argues that leaders shape and develop culture. Interestingly, he talks about leaders at the stage of creation needing 'the ability to articulate and enforce a vision' (*ibid*., p. 317), which is the same as our notion of mission. What emerges from Schein's work, from studies on leadership and primary headship cited earlier, and from what we saw in the project schools, is the idea that:

> a dynamic analysis of organizational culture makes it clear that leadership is interwined with culture formation, evolution, transformation and destruction. Culture is created in the first instance by the actions of the leaders; culture is embedded and strengthened by leaders.
>
> (Schein, 1985, pp. 316-7)

Although notions of mission and of heads 'providing an underlying philosophy' appear in Hoyle (1986) and Coulson (1986), the idea of the head acting as founder and leader of the school's culture is scarcely to be found in the literature on primary school leadership, organization or management. Other writers have discussed organizational culture and leadership (e.g., Handy, 1981; Sergiovanni and Corbally, 1984; Schein, 1985) and some have applied these discussions to secondary schools (e.g., Jones, 1981; Handy, 1984) but only Handy (1984) and Coulson (1986) have previously attempted to link school culture with primary school organization and leadership, and then only in brief and limited ways. The recognition in this chapter and elsewhere (see Chapters 4, 5 and 7) of the primary head's involvement with the school's culture supports Schein's (1985) assertion that culture and leadership, when examined closely, are two sides of the same coin, and neither can be understood by itself.

The Head as Exemplar

Hoyle (1986) suggests that embedding and strengthening both the school's mission and its culture are diffuse activities based upon the leader's educational beliefs 'and conveyed via language and actions of a symbolic kind rather than through clearly identifiable tasks' (Hoyle, 1986, p. 101). Whilst it is important to discuss the heads' guiding beliefs and their ownership of the schools, and all that that implies for the schools' cultures, it is also necessary to consider how the heads conveyed their beliefs through actions. Heads appear to set great store by leading through example

(Coulson, 1978) and all the heads of the project schools were aware of the power of example. Each head consciously expected to influence staff through his/her example. Yet their actions may also have been symbolic of the values they tried to represent. For instance four of the five heads took assemblies:

> I think from my point of view, from the school as a whole's point of view, the assembly is probably the most important part of the day and I try to engender that sort of feeling, that that's the time when the whole school family are together and we can share things, which is why I don't try as much as some heads, though I'm very much tempted sometimes, to get out of them, as I do feel it's a very important part of the job, it's the only time when you can talk to all the children and enjoy things together . . .
>
> (Head, Hutton)

> When the head told me she didn't take a class, I asked her if this had ever raised the question of her credibility? Her reply was that this must surely come through in her assemblies and in the way that she reacts to the children and deals with them.
>
> (Fieldnote, January, Lowmeadow)

> The head considers assembly: 'A sharing time . . . I don't want them to see me as this great authoritarian figure. It's bad enough when occasionally you have to have them in the hall and do a little laying down of the law act . . . I would hate them to think I was like that all the time.'
>
> (Head, Sedgemoor)

Fieldnotes record one of the head's many assemblies which conveyed in style and content that the relationship between children and adults should be consistent with that shown to exist between adults in the school.

> The children and staff come in quietly and sit equally quietly. The head sits quietly at the front. There is a hymn, and a story read by the head in a quiet voice. It is about a child and a headteacher who have both come to a new school, are feeling lonely and wish they could go back to the place they had come from. They go out by coach on a day to the sea when everything goes wrong — it rains, the lunch is left behind. Everyone searches their pockets and finds odd bits to eat — packets of crisps, chocolate — and offers these around. Soon everyone is chatting and sharing, the day is transformed, and loneliness vanishes. By sharing they have come to know and like each other.
>
> (Fieldnote, November, Sedgemoor)

The fifth head rarely took assembly, leaving it to the teachers to take them in turn. Nevertheless, at the end of each assembly the head would stand up and thank the teacher and the children for their contribution:

> After each of the assemblies I have so far witnessed, the head teacher makes a small informal address to the gathered company. Today Graham talked about the entrance of the pupils. Graham was saying that the entrance was very good and noted the fact that as some of the very youngest children were coming into the hall they stopped so that they could exchange berries and haws that they had been collecting on their way to school. This created something of a queue from the other children coming in behind them but Graham noted how there was a lack of impatience from those behind, who were older, and who waited until the young children had concluded their business, as it were, and then could move into the hall in an orderly fashion. There was no crush, there was no protest. There was no frustration by those who had to wait.
>
> Graham seized upon this as an opportunity to congratulate the children on their co-operative spirit and their awareness of others, particularly the older ones being very aware of the younger ones.
>
> (Fieldnote, October, Greenfields)

In short, the heads used assemblies to convey their beliefs symbolically. They also used their classroom practice as an example to others. It is clear from all five case studies that each head enjoyed teaching. Miss Proctor did not engage in planned teaching activities but was recognized by her staff as a highly competent teacher. The other heads were timetabled to teach specific sessions each week. As one said:

> I do it [teach] deliberately so that staff do become aware of the sort of standards I expect. I think it's so important and I've always felt that, to go in and show by example.
> (Head, Lavender Way)

The heads of Hutton and Lavender Way, who were still trying to make educational changes in their schools, appeared to be more active than the other three heads in demonstrating the kinds of approach and activities they believed in. Richard, the head of Hutton, joined two of the teachers to form a team-teaching trio:

> It was generally acknowledged that the two teachers had an effective working partnership, and so he joined them in a team-teaching trio for the term — at his suggestion. This had two purposes. Firstly, it could influence the ideas of the second year pair. Secondly, it was a demonstration for the whole staff of what Richard meant by his documented ideas on the integrated day in general and the appearance of classrooms in particular.
> (Yeomans, 1987a)

Heads also used displays of children's work:

> The entrance hall has changed and been added to since I was here last. There's new trellis work with new parts. A piece of material draped carefully and a display of buds, almost certainly this is Catherine's contribution, for creating the school image is as important as creating a class image is for the teachers.
> (Fieldnote, January, Lavender Way)

But teaching did not always go smoothly. When the teaching was challenging, one head admitted to experiencing difficulty and 'exhaustion' and did not set unrealistic standards:

> At the end of the afternoon Isobel staggers into the staffroom itself — parody. She has had the reception/middle class for the day and is shattered. I asked her if she would like a cup of tea and she says she'd rather I get the bottle out, which she proceeds to do. Part of the head–staff relationship at Sedgemoor is in Isobel's openness. She makes no pretence of having found the class anything other than difficult. She says to everybody that comes in: 'You can't talk to them, they always want to tell you about themselves.' As staff arrive she tells them the story of what had happened during the day. A child complained to her that her nose hurt, that she thought she had got something up her nose. Isobel had sent the child to the secretary and the child had returned with a bead that had been stuck up her nose. Here is the security of being able to allow others to laugh at you, and offering them the chance. You share your success and your disasters.
> (Fieldnote, February, Sedgemoor)

For their part the teachers appreciated not only the heads' direct involvement in teaching but also their skills and effectiveness as practitioners. As one teacher said:

> The fact is everybody here probably knows that she can do your job just as well as you can and is quite happy to do it and not say 'I'm head now, I don't have to do that kind of thing any more, I'll just sit in my office all day and push the paperwork around.'
> (Teacher, Lavender Way)

Clearly these teachers perceived effective classroom practice as a prerequisite for leadership.

The heads further provided examples of their beliefs in action through their day-to-day dealings with staff. All the heads encouraged, praised and thanked their colleagues:

> He [Graham] will never say 'Oh, that's wrong, don't do that.' He encourages you (as a teacher) to use whatever abilities you have. He's very good at praising his staff as well, to parents and governors, or whatever, which is obviously nice, to be thought that you're appreciated. Everyone likes a pat on the back from time to time.
>
> (Teacher, Greenfields)

> I notice the staff are habitually thanked by the head for every service, however small or unobtrusive. Nothing is ever taken for granted. She seems to thank people as naturally as she breathes and about as often . . . She also marks the special contributions and departures of volunteers, dinner supervisors, students etc. with small, personally chosen gifts. No one is ever forgotten.
>
> (Fieldnote, December, Lowmeadow)

> During the morning Sally's class perform a play to the rest of the school and a few visiting parents. At the end Isobel goes up and quietly thanks the children privately and thanks Sheila too. Peter mouths compliments to Sally across the hall.
>
> (Fieldnote, January, Sedgemoor

All three collaborative schools were characterized by positive reinforcement. It was clear that the heads put much faith in praise as a strategy for developing a supportive climate which built up teachers' and other staff's confidence and self-esteem. Staff were almost always welcomed, thanked and praised either directly or by reference to the children's work or behaviour. The frequency, consistency and quality of these acts of appreciation demonstrated that mutual consideration among colleagues stemmed in part from, and/or is reinforced by, the heads' behaviour. Moreover, the heads played an important part in establishing an atmosphere in which allowance was made for the health and personal commitments of staff. Heads were quick to comfort those staff who faced family sickness or problems and did what they could to accommodate unexpected events in the personal lives of staff.

By the way they acted the heads fostered teamwork and a positive climate which was infused with consideration for others. They did not simply subscribe to certain beliefs at a rhetorical level, they actively and consistently demonstrated those beliefs in their deeds. Indeed, the heads lived the beliefs underlying the culture (see Chapter 4). Whether this was conscious or not is unclear, but what actually mattered in these schools was the head's behaviour, and this was noted by the staff:

> I don't think he ever has consciously told people without giving them the option to question or respond to them first. It's never existed that way.
>
> (Teacher, Hutton)

> From one o'clock onwards Victoria and I were on our own in the staffroom. She asked me what my observations were about the staff group so far. I said I was interested in the fact that there was some divergence in classroom practice but that it didn't seem to have an adverse effect on staff relations, and she asked 'Would I be interested in hearing her views on it?' Victoria then began to explain why she felt that the divergence in practice from teacher to teacher in the school didn't cause problems. The reasons were, she felt, directly attributable to the way Graham operated as headteacher. She described

Graham as being a person who creates a climate which is not competitive from teacher to teacher. Graham deals individually with teachers and in dealing individually with them rarely brings into the talk any other teacher. It could be described as a lack of comparison of one against another. Furthermore, she felt, not only does he deal individually with teachers, but he also praises people, sometimes, a little too much, but generally in a very healthy and supportive fashion.

(Fieldnote, October, Greenfields)

Staff also noticed the personal qualities of their headteachers:

Miss Proctor's a very understanding person. She's got a knack of being able to be a good listener. Whether it's staff, or parents or our families, whatever it is she takes a genuine interest and she's a sympathetic person. My mother said she thought she was one of the most sympathetic persons she'd ever met, she felt she could instantly understand what your problem was and be able to hit just the right note when she was speaking to you about it.

(Teacher, Lowmeadow)

I think Isobel's very open as a person. . . .

(Teacher, Sedgemoor)

The heads themselves were aware that how they behaved as people mattered:

Sometimes when I have done things I've regretted, it's when I've been in a bad mood, but I don't think I'm the sort of person who bears a grudge. I've had one or two arguments with people but once it's over, it's over and I can carry on. I think that's something you've got to be like as head, but I think I just am anyway . . . I think this is something that has a relationship with parents as well as staff. I don't see that the head is anybody particularly special, he's just somebody doing a job as best they can. So I just try to be the person I am.

(Head, Hutton)

They also demonstrated great commitment to joining in and being members of the staff group:

She doesn't see herself as the head and we're the staff, we're a team working together, she just happens to have the title of head. I think it's a team working situation which is why everybody's aware of what's going on.

(Teacher, Sedgemoor)

None of the heads was aloof or isolated from their respective staff group. They joined in, particularly in the staffroom, where they were frequently to be found drinking coffee, chatting, listening and laughing.

She [the head] comes into the staffroom and chats. . . . Not necessarily as head. . . . Sometimes, but then she has to. Other times it's just general chat and a laugh. She's part of it.

(Teacher, Lavender Way)

Breaktime talk in the staffroom — Isobel on giving up drink for Lent: 'I found it really hard.' Peter: '*You* found it hard, how do you think the rest of us found it!' with a laugh. He then said, 'No, I'm only joking.' Isobel can be an equal amongst the staff rather than the superior.

(Fieldnote, April, Sedgemoor)

The head was enjoying all this laughter and playing his part too. However forthright he may be, he is very much a relaxed part of the staff group.

(Fieldnote, September, Hutton)

Membership has been discussed in Chapter 5, yet it would be a distortion of headship to omit it from this account. All five heads were members of the staff group. Whilst it was accepted by almost all staff that their heads performed a dual role — leader and member — the quality of the heads' behaviour as members appears to have added to their credibility as leaders.

The heads' membership of the staff groups exemplified the importance they attached to interdependence. Indeed, without the head's membership there could be no 'common bond' because:

> What each of us does in a classroom is in the knowledge that we all share this common bond. Our ideas about the care of the children and the teaching of the children and their behaviour, everything, all falls into the same slot, because we all have basically the same philosophy, it's difficult to express precisely . . . it's more of a feeling really.
>
> (Teacher, Lowmeadow)

All in all the heads earned considerable respect from their staffs, as the latter made clear in interviews:

> The reason why I think people are hard-working in this school is because I think they are basically hard-working people. There's a tradition for hard work in this school and they do respect the hard work that Richard does and follow his lead in that way.
>
> (Teacher, Hutton)

> I came here and saw this massive great folder and all of these policy documents and everything. I thought 'my goodness, this is somebody who's willing to work' and I admire people who work hard . . . I can't stand laziness and I think I felt from the start that he was a person willing to work for his ideal.
>
> (Teacher, Hutton)

> Although we are encouraged to change and grow, you know there is a standard to reach. It does make you think twice, but it doesn't stop you.
>
> (Teacher, Lowmeadow)

Apart from the connection between primary headship and school culture, little that we have said so far in this chapter is new. However, previous work on primary heads does not cover for all our findings. Two further findings need to be considered: awareness and educative leadership.

Awareness

Successful leaders have extensive communication 'networks' and gather in all sorts of 'intelligence' (Whitaker, 1983; Day, Johnson and Whitaker, 1985). What characterized the heads in the project schools was not simply that they had established ways of communicating with others, but that the communications were subtle and based on sensitivity to individuals, areas of the school, and the whole school. The heads worked very hard at not forgetting people, whether teachers, ancillary staff or children:

> I think what I'm saying is that I actually do consciously see good relationships amongst the staff as important. I see it as part of my job to maintain these good relationships and I consciously and positively work towards it, and that's not just the teaching staff. I mentioned Norma a moment ago. Norma and Natalie are very important parts of that network.
>
> (Head, Greenfields)

> Miss Proctor's art is keeping people happy. Her tact, sensitivity and memory for personal detail are universally admired.
>
> (Teacher, Lowmeadow)

> As she went out to lunch Miss Proctor quickly read the letter that Rosemary had deposited on her desk during the morning while she was busy with a phone call. She caught Rosemary's attention during the lunch break and said, 'What a nice letter from Mrs. R.' In the same way she singled out in the lunch queue a child whom she had had to turn away from 'showing' at assembly this morning and had a word with her about the object that she'd brought and urged her to show it to her class.
>
> (Teacher, Lowmeadow)

Much of this awareness was made possible because the heads were constantly around the school and visited everyone or were around when staff gathered together. In Greenfields there was a ritual of coffee before and after school, with all the staff joining in. At Lowmeadow the head (and deputy) visited all parts of the school either before assembly or, in the head's case, as soon as she could after it. These visits were brief, but supportive, with the head often smiling and encouraging the discussion of classroom or personal matters:

> I am prepared to spend a great deal of time talking with staff, I'm prepared for them to come and see me and just talk, about anything really. Because I think you can learn to be quite a good listener if you can get them to open up and chat.
>
> (Head, Lavender Way)

> I feel it is my role to respond to people, and as a head you are responding to all sorts of people not just teachers, but your canteen staff, your caretaker, your parents, reps, you know, you are totally responding . . . plumbers, you've got to be around to do it, otherwise it becomes easy to shut yourself away.
>
> (Head, Sedgemoor)

The implicit message in much of this is the head's accessibility. The heads were not only approachable but available. They did not simply wait to hear about things; by touring the school, being in the staffroom and visiting teachers in their classrooms or class areas they actively sought out news and information. The heads were expert at noticing all sorts of seemingly small matters:

> She knows a great deal more about us than we think. She's very observant, she notices little things that perhaps others don't, because she can stand back and look.
>
> (Teacher, Lowmeadow)

And from these observations the heads could piece together the details and begin to detect patterns. For example, of one teacher who was experiencing difficulty, the head said:

> It's little things, she borrows things and never returns them. She'll take a staple gun and it never goes back where it should go. It just lies in her room. Similarly you can't cut paper because she takes the paper cutter and that stays in her room.
>
> (Fieldnote, January, Greenfields)

Similarly, heads could sense moods and feelings:

> Graham sees himself as pulling together people, taking away any kind of friction that may occur between individuals and also keeping a weather eye out for how individuals are particularly feeling.
>
> (Fieldnote, September, Greenfields)

Through all their various activities the heads saw, heard and learned much about 'their' schools and in turn had much to reflect on:

> I can sit around and appear to be doing absolutely nothing, in fact I am not, I'm not doing anything if I am honest, but thinking. I do think a lot about what is happening in the school and I wander about a lot thinking — that's the way I work.
>
> (Head, Sedgemoor)

Indeed, a feature common to the heads was how fascinated they were with 'their' schools. They were interested and concerned with every post and person in the school. Moreover, out of all these details the heads began to see the 'whole school' and ask such questions as 'where are we?' and 'how are we doing?' In other words, most of the time they were gathering evidence, checking, organizing and making sense of it in order to learn more about their schools.

It has been recognized for some time that leaders 'tour' their organizations (Mintzberg, 1973) in order to find out what is happening. More recently the notion of 'management by wandering about' or MBWA, has been proposed as a formula for listening, empathizing and staying in touch (Peters and Austin, 1985). In effect all the heads in the project schools did MBWA. In so doing they could use their tours of the school to monitor the school's culture. At the same time their tours also placed them in a better position to negotiate with staff, because they came to know much of what was happening in the school and this knowledge was a powerful resource (see also Coulson, 1986, and Chapter 8). Furthermore, whilst on their tours, they could negotiate with individuals on a one-to-one basis. MBWA enabled the head to act as a 'disturbance handler' not only in the sense of day-to-day crisis management but also in terms of seeking stability for the school as an organization. In this sense the heads' awareness contributed to the development and maintenance of the schools' culture (see Chapter 7).

Saying that the heads devoted time to being aware of the schools' culture does not imply that other things were ignored. The heads all played their part in dealing with the outside world (e.g., parents, educational officers and advisers, salespersons, psychologists, social workers, governors, nurses and medical officers, to name but a few of those we saw coming into school, or with whom the heads met outside school). The heads' constant interaction with their staff should be seen against a background not only of teaching commitments and other tasks but also of continual demands on their attention from people and agencies outside the school.

Educative Leaders

As a result of all these activities the heads were greatly respected, and were described by their staffs in warm and positive ways:

> *Int*: Can I ask you how you find Graham as head?
> *Teacher*: Absolutely marvellous! I can't really say I've ever worked for a better head. I think as long as you're doing your job and getting on and giving of your best, I think Graham is quite happy. I think he knows what's going on but he's not heavy-handed, he doesn't come round laying the law down. And he's very approachable, he's just fine. No problems with Graham.
>
> (Greenfields)

> She is very helpful, very fair. You can go and talk to her, which is more than you can to some heads. You can chat to her. She's available and if she's not, then she'll make herself available to you and I would have said she was interested in her staff. As staff, as teachers and as people, human beings.
>
> (Teacher, Lavender Way)

> I think it is partly because I've got great respect for her as a teacher and I know that she wouldn't ask you to undertake anything that she wouldn't be prepared to do herself. You know that she could do anything, that she would never expect anything of you that she couldn't even demonstrate to you.
>
> (Teacher, Lavender Way)

> Miss Proctor's a good team leader in that she leads from the front, but she doesn't dictate. I suppose if anything went drastically wrong she would have to put an overall pattern on what you were doing. But it's her school and she loves it and she does a wonderful job.
>
> (Teacher, Lowmeadow)

Indeed, so positive were these expressions of respect that it became clear that many of the staff had a strong affection, even love, for their head.

> She is always available, and if you feel that you needed to discuss something with her you could always ring her up and you know she'd be supportive, whenever. I think she's a friend rather than 'the leader'. I think that's important.
>
> (Teacher, Lavender Way)

> I think she's quietly supportive and that is a marvellous position to be in if you've got her support and she's there as an absolutely marvellous resource and I admire the way that she can help people without taking over . . . we've all got a lot to learn from her.
>
> (Teacher, Sedgemoor)

> Miss Proctor brings love, really. Caring with a capital C.
>
> (Teacher, Lowmeadow)

Such respect enhanced the heads' authority and influence. The section on heads as exemplars demonstrated that the heads deliberately used themselves as role models, teachers and coaches. This is consistent with the view that founders and new leaders of organizations generally seem to know that their own visible behaviour has great value for communicating assumptions and values to other members, especially new-comers (Schein, 1985). Certainly heads often claimed they had developed 'their' schools and talked of the need to create opportunities for individuals to grow:

> All my previous deputies have become heads, no doubt Dennis will be shortly and I feel I've got to give him the opportunities whilst he's here before he's thrown into a school himself . . . I mean after all a school is a training ground in a way, it's a training ground for teachers, isn't it, for their career and prospects.
>
> (Head, Sedgemoor)

Similarly, teachers talked of learning from their heads:

> I would say that of all the schools I have ever worked in this is the one I've learnt most in and I have only been here just over a year.
>
> (Teacher, Hutton)

> We come back to this sense of specialness and excellence which we feel about this place which of course Graham has instilled in us and it's something he feels. . . . Those of us that have been here for some time don't actually like something that isn't very good.
>
> (Teacher, Greenfields)

In these statements it is possible to detect notions of learning, 'goodness' and excellence. Also, the teachers felt they were working in the 'right way' because their work matched the head's expectations. Duignan and Macpherson (1987) say that 'educative leadership' involves, in part, the negotiation and determining of what is to count as important in education and what will count as morally right. We have seen that these heads had a mission of this sort and that they sought to educate the staff to secure their commitment to it. Educative leadership was, therefore, one way in which the heads tried to reconcile the dual demands of their personal commitment to their mission and their dependence upon the staff to subscribe to that mission.

OTHER LEADERS

It would be a misrepresentation of leadership in the project schools to suggest that only heads were leading and influencing, and that everyone else was merely following and adapting. There were many other leaders, and the heads relied on these leaders because mutual dependence and respect for the individual were part of the culture. Within each of the project schools there were many instances of leadership and these will be discussed here under the headings of deputies, pastoral leaders, secretaries and curriculum co-ordinators.

Deputies

Surprisingly little is known about the role of the deputy head. Much of the available work has been conducted by questionnaire (e.g., Coulson and Cox, 1975). Only Nias (1987b), in a study based on the deputy head in one of the project schools, appears to have looked ethnographically at the deputy head. In some ways the picture which emerges is consistent with the generalization in other studies made about the deputy's position, namely that it lacks role definition (see Open University, 1981; Whitaker, 1983; Open University, 1988). However, role definitions are usually concerned with mapping the allocation of formal tasks whereas, Nias suggests, the significance of the deputy heads' work may lie in their informal actions. The evidence on the deputy heads in four of the project schools supports this (in the fifth school, Greenfields, the deputy head was frequently absent, being a union representative and engaged on Education Committee duties).

All the deputies performed an important communication function. They felt it was their job to keep everyone (teachers and ancillary staff) informed:

> If somebody doesn't know about something, you know, I feel responsible and people usually moan at me if they don't know about something. But I do feel responsible, and I do try, through little notes and things like that, to see that stuff's going round. Or by flitting from classroom to classroom, appearing, I try to make things go on.
> (Deputy, Sedgemoor)

As Sedgemoor's deputy says, two approaches were commonly used: written notes passed round the staff, or informal visits. The visits took place at any time, whenever the deputy was 'free' or momentarily released from class supervision (e.g., playtimes, lunchtimes, before and after school, as the school was mustering at assembly). Before school started was a popular time and one deputy performed a regular 'morning round':

> Julia's 'morning round' is very helpful. She memorizes every move and things that are coming up and it's very useful. It ensures that this aspect of the communication is kept open, and we all know exactly what's happening.
>
> (Teacher, Lowmeadow)

These morning tours of the school enabled the deputy to check that everyone was not only present but feeling well. Fieldnotes of these visits record how astute the deputy was in noting the feelings of the staff; her extensive memory for personal detail; how laughter accompanied her, and the way in which she reminded staff of every kind of administrative point from apparatus in the hall to visitors and staff meetings:

> I developed this way of trying to make sure people remembered because I know everybody isn't as good at remembering. . . .
>
> (Deputy, Lowmeadow)

All the deputy heads were frequently present in the staffroom, because they saw it as important to be both there and around the school:

> I do think that's part of my brief, to be in the staffroom. I try not to spend my time in my room. It makes it harder in a lot of ways but I do think it's important. For the same reason I have dinner with the staff always . . . I also count on the fact that the staff will talk to me so I can do my job as communicator. They'll often come and talk to me about something they would like me to raise with Miss Proctor but they don't want to make a formal approach to her, like the cleaners, for example. So I listen a lot and say things like: 'Well, I'll mention it to Miss Proctor', which is what people actually want me to do because they obviously think I can cope without making a big scene. It's not that it's anonymous, people are quite happy for me to say 'so-and-so's worried about this, did you notice so-and-so?' It's just that if it comes through me, it's less formal. A deputy is someone who will keep the head informed, make sure they're not missing out on any of the grass roots side.
>
> (Deputy, Lowmeadow)

This deputy makes a number of additional points about her part in communications. First, whilst it is part of the deputy's job to transmit and receive communications, listening appears to be a key skill. Second, she acted as a supplementary channel of communication to the head. Third, the deputy kept the head informed. It appeared to be part of the deputy's role informally to act as the head's 'intelligence agent'. Fourth, as with the heads, it was the deputy's behaviour that mattered. She was appreciated by staff and head alike for what she did rather than simply for what she said. Fifth, since deputies were around the school, and spent much time in the staffroom, they needed to be able to manage the demands of both school communication and their class teaching duties. The fact that all the deputies could do this should not detract from the pressures they felt and the kind of skill and experience which enabled them to cope with the multiple demands of their role.

Because deputies developed an eye for detail they sometimes heard about, or saw, things which few others did. Consequently they ended up doing things which either no one else wanted to do, or no one had thought about:

> At the end of the day Ben is tidying away bits of paper in the staffroom. He says to me 'I do the sorting out of notices because no one else seems to.'
>
> (Fieldnote, March, Lavender Way)

This sometimes resulted in the deputy having an unenviable task load:

> At breaktime I discover that Ben is really rather overworked on TV recording. I ask him 'Have you got a lot to do?' and he replies 'Yes,' with feeling.
>
> (Fieldnote, October, Lavender Way)

Yet, as this deputy said:

> I do all these menial tasks to do with the video and the radio recordings, because it does make other people's jobs easier.
>
> (Deputy, Lavender Way)

In other words, they saw it as part of their work to support their colleagues in any manner of small ways. One of these was to praise them:

> (at the end of class assembly) Dennis fed back immediately his approval to Peter by gesture and by mouthing across the hall — 'that was super' and he turns to Isobel and says how much he enjoyed it.
>
> (Fieldnote, November, Sedgemoor)

> I try to convey to people when they seem to be effective . . . I keep praise and encouragement for the things that if I were in there doing that, I would think 'that's good' and I would enjoy being involved in.
>
> (Deputy, Lavender Way)

Support also took the form of pastoral care. This typical example highlights the small and immediate nature of much of the help they gave to others:

> In the hall at dinnertime Julia noticed I looked cold and went to fetch a spare sweater which she keeps in her room. I was extremely grateful for it.
>
> (Fieldnote, May, Lowmeadow)

Deputies also acted as curricular leaders. For example, the deputy at Lavender Way was seen as an important source of information on science, whilst the deputy at Greenfields played a prominent part in the history curriculum. Their curricular strengths and responsibilities led to their being seen as professional exemplars and their class teaching influenced other teachers. They also took more direct forms of curriculum leadership:

> Dennis shows a video to the rest of the staff, acting as a teacher. He gives a duplicated set of sheets to staff and asks them to deal with particular questions that he has written on them. Throughout the staff meeting Isobel, the head, says nothing and allows him to chair proceedings, though she pops out from time to time to deal with telephone calls as they arise. The purpose of the video is to show how insights into children's mathematical difficulties can be gained by listening to them talking and watching them operating. From the meeting emerges an agreement that staff will try some of Dennis's ideas and he will be free to work with them.
>
> (Fieldnote, September, Sedgemoor)

Central to every aspect of their work was their partnership with the head. Heads found it valuable to learn from the deputy's insights and knowledge of the school, and the heads enjoyed their deputies' support in terms of both the school's mission and the day-to-day processes of the school (e.g. communication, pastoral care, curriculum development). Partnership was most evident at Lowmeadow, where head and deputy had been together for the longest period amongst the project schools. They complemented one another:

> The deputy said that the fact that the head shouldered so much of the overall responsibility gave her a lot of freedom — she could look more broadly at the educational scene.
>
> (Fieldnote, February, Lowmeadow)

> Julia and I work so well together. . . . If I can't do something, I ask her and usually if I can't manage it, she can, and vice versa. . . . You can't put what we do into little pigeonholes.
>
> (Head, Lowmeadow)

There were also times when the heads confided in their deputies and shared concerns, problems or ideas with them.

This partnership was based on some basic premises. First, the school was regarded as the head's:

> I feel that it's Miss Proctor's school and while she's away I'm not going to turn it into my school.
>
> (Deputy, Lowmeadow)

Second, the deputy was expected to be loyal to the head:

> She supports Miss Proctor totally and her loyalty is superb. I'm sure it must make Miss Proctor's job easier to know that she's got such an efficient deputy head.
>
> (Teacher, Lowmeadow)

> She sees her role as deputy head as very much an endorsing of Miss Proctor's ideas, rather than sort of a spokesperson for the staff. . . . Every now and again she disagrees with the head though there've only been one or two examples when she's felt strongly enough about something to make an issue of it.
>
> (Teacher, Lowmeadow)

Third, the partnership was seen as reciprocal. The head and deputy exchanged information, kept each other up to date with news, supported each other and could not be prised apart:

> Commenting on the action taken by a parent in the absence of the head from school today, Julia said, with evident satisfaction, 'She's sussed out that she can't play one of us off against the other. It's finally dawned on her that Miss Proctor and I do tell each other what's going on.'
>
> (Fieldnote, May, Lowmeadow)

> I went into the head's office and joined her and Julia. They seemed to be having three types of conversation simultaneously, (1) Julia telling Miss Proctor about her difficulties with particular children, especially S., (2) discussing jointly the necessity of adapting to a new kind of parental role in school government, and (3) Miss Proctor talking to Julia about her problems.
>
> (Fieldnote, March, Lowmeadow)

Yet whilst this head and deputy developed a strong friendship as well as a productive professional relationship, the partnership was not exclusive. The fact that both were members of the staff group and that the deputy worked hard at maintaining that membership meant that this partnership avoided creating divisions between the head, deputy and staff.

The partnership at Lowmeadow School has been highlighted because it offers the most sharply focused picture. But the data from the other schools is consistent with this picture. At Sedgemoor the head and deputy knew each other out of school as well as working closely together in school:

> It's quite funny really because Isobel saw a primary management thing on the role of the deputy and we laughed about it. It was just sheets of expectations of the deputy. I think I'm close with Isobel and I think I'm involved with Isobel on the whole school issues. You know, we have a sit every Friday, don't we? Where we have a bottle of wine and we sit and talk, you know, about just general things really, you know, being fed up with being head, or being fed up with being deputy head . . . we discuss every aspect of things that have happened.
>
> (Deputy, Sedgemoor)

and:

> There are all sorts of things that you could reel off about what deputies are meant to do, but I see it partly to do with the relationship with Isobel the head and partly to do with the relationship with other people.
>
> (Deputy, Sedgemoor)

In describing his job as being concerned with these two sets of relationships this deputy is saying that his job is contingent upon them. The deputy's work is strongly influenced by the nature of these relationships, yet it has been argued elsewhere that what deputies do generally rests upon what heads allow them to do (Whitaker, 1983; Waters, 1987; Southworth, 1987a; Open University, 1988). Therefore, although the deputies' job is contingent on both relationships, they are unequal in weight, since the head exercises greater control and deputies have to operate within parameters determined by their heads.

At Lavender Way and Hutton, where two newly appointed deputies were in post, the deputies' dependence upon their heads was particularly marked. At Lavender Way head and deputy arrived in post at the same time and the deputy experienced some uncertainty about what his job was, because the head had not yet established her position:

> I think we are both still confused about what our roles are, I haven't explicitly defined what my role should be. So consequently it is a bit difficult for me to define what his role is. So then of course it makes it more difficult for the staff to realize and I'm aware that that is not helping Ben to develop possibly the right sort of role with staff.
>
> (Head, Lavender Way)

Furthermore, in all of the schools there were times when the heads were absent and the deputies became acting heads (although the single longest period was three weeks). The deputies were accepted as the schools' leaders during those times, yet they themselves regarded their job as that of 'caretaker':

> I feel that it's Miss Proctor's school and while she's away I'm not going to turn it into my school. Therefore what decisions I make I will try and make as I think she would want them. If she's well enough I shall contact her over any big decision, because I do see that as my job: a caretaker, not to start making radical changes, just to be able to say, 'Well, I've done this.'
>
> (Deputy, Lowmeadow)

In acting as caretakers, the deputies were careful to 'stop short of usurpation' (Nias, 1987b, p. 52). By trying to avoid radical changes and to act in ways which reflected the heads' preferences, the deputies ensured that even in the heads' temporary absence continuity was maintained and the schools' culture was not disturbed (see Chapter 7).

To summarize then, although deputies sometimes acted as formal leaders, much of the significance of their leadership lies in their informal actions. Their ability to act as communicators was especially important. Their attention to detail lubricated the life of the school and reduced the likelihood of things going wrong because no one had thought to check or to carry out menial chores. Moreover, the deputy supported the head and kept him/her informed. The fact that the deputies and the heads both supported staff doubled the amount of praise and pastoral care within the school. Similarly, their ability to get around the school and listen to staff supplemented the heads' awareness.

During all this activity deputies not only complemented their heads; they were also mirroring them. Just as the heads led through example, listened, praised and joined in, so too did their deputies. The combined effect of the head's and deputy's behaviour was a powerful dual leadership, based on example and action rather than rhetoric. Yet the dynamism of this dual leadership relied on deputies accepting that the school 'belonged' to the head and that the deputy should be loyal to the head.

These findings add to our understanding of the work of the deputy head, particularly with reference to school culture. The heads of the five project schools have been depicted as the founders of the culture, because of their beliefs and sense of mission. Yet we have also said that the heads were dependent upon staff to join with them and subscribe to the mission. In terms of securing the staff's commitment to the mission it appears that the heads looked to their deputies and expected them to act as 'culture bearers'. This expectation is consistent with Whitaker (1983), who says that most heads appoint deputies on the basis of the closest possible match to their own philosophy, in the hope that a doubling of the driving forces will help to bring about the changes that the head wishes to see. It is also consistent with the belief, strongly held by many heads, that it is a major advantage to school management to appoint one's 'own' deputy. Interestingly, all five heads in the project schools had appointed their deputies. Moreover, when the head of Hutton appointed Teresa during the year of our fieldwork (see Chapter 7), he felt the school entered a new phase in its development. We would claim that implicit to his notion of development was cultural development.

Although our evidence points towards cultural development being enhanced when a head can appoint his/her deputy, it should also be noted that when Julia was appointed as deputy head of Lowmeadow the head actually wanted to choose another candidate, but the governors chose Julia (Nias, 1987b). In other words it is not a necessary condition of cultural development that heads should appoint 'their' deputies. But however the partnership comes about, when a head and deputy do work productively together the school's culture is developed and maintained, because the deputy acts as the leading 'culture bearer'.

Pastoral Leaders

Consideration has been noted as a dimension of both the heads' and deputies' leadership. But consideration was not the sole preserve of senior staff. Other staff (teaching and ancillary) demonstrated concern and support for others; where they regularly acted in these ways we have called them pastoral leaders. All teams need people concerned with process and people rather than with task accomplishment (Handy and Aitken, 1986) and, in the sense that these individuals are concerned with people rather than production, they are leaders (Blake and Mouton, 1978). In the project schools, such people led because their personal qualities enabled them to do so, rather than because of allocated responsibilities or job descriptions. Hence their roles were informal.

Their consideration for others appeared in various guises:

> I have a lot to do with Carol because of the ages of the children [we teach] and she's been marvellous too. She's helped me out with the computer and she had the class a couple of times in my first week to let me have a breather, that sort of thing, which is good. And she's had problem children, or children who she felt had special needs and she's tried to ease the load for me. So she's been a great help. She's done lots.
>
> (Teacher, Greenfields)

> Polly seems an important source of information on family background, she's asked about children's families in Sheila's class and she provides the information on one and says she doesn't know the other. But it seems she's the one who is looked to as the expert.
>
> (Fieldnote, May, Sedgemoor)

> Marion's extrovert personality makes her always prominent in the staffroom, in words, or in actions. On Monday she had been reading out horoscopes from the Chinese New Year and asking various staff when their date of birth was, and then reading out with great relish what were their prospects. Today, she's handing round chocolates. Alison follows shortly afterwards with a tin of biscuits.
>
> (Fieldnote, February, Hutton)

> It was usually Marion who took the initiative in making and handing round coffee on the days when there was a staff meeting.
>
> (Fieldnote, June, Hutton)

Such support is small-scale, seemingly ordinary and may appear to be trivial; yet it was significant. Nor was support always a case of accentuating the positive. In this extract the deputy, Jim, was in need of support because he was feeling low:

> The day before Jim had seen the school's adviser who explained that his applications for promotive posts were not receiving support from the authority because 'his management values were in question.' Jim and I were talking about a suggestion from the LEA that he attend some management course as a demonstration that he was keen on promotion, but Jim is currently thinking about whether this is a challenge to his whole philosophy and I think he feels somewhat hurt by the implicit criticism that he's not sufficiently organized. He was telling me this when Carol came in and he started saying that really he had had a rotten week and that this comment was the final straw. Carol leapt on this, but with some tact, by saying 'Well Jim, what else has gone wrong?' And Jim said that he hadn't enjoyed the day before, the same adviser coming into school to discuss Julie's competence in the classroom. 'Oh!,' said Carol, 'Why is that?' And Jim said 'Well, clearly she is still not satisfactory in the eyes of the authority.' He had been upset and affected by the fact that the adviser thought Julie hadn't made sufficient improvement and that her position was still extremely tenuous.

Throughout this he signalled a sense of failure because he felt it was his brief to provide support for Julie, that he and she had shared a class with 50 per cent responsibility on each side. Graham had come in at this point and while Carol was still counselling Jim she said 'Was that part of your brief?', to which Graham, who was being very quiet throughout this conversation, simply said 'yes, it was.' Graham looked serious and tired, it being late Friday afternoon then. Victoria also came in. 'I suppose,' said Jim, 'I feel guilty.' To which Carol said, 'You shouldn't feel guilty.' Jim said, 'No, I don't feel guilty, that's not the right word. It's more . . .' The sentence was left hanging and Victoria moved in on that, saying 'The only thing you might feel guilty about is that we decided as a staff in the summer to take advantage of Julie's presence and we would at some point use you as a floater.'

Jim went on to say he felt he hadn't provided sufficient support for Julie, that when he decided to leave Julie to her own devices that was not an appropriate timing. Carol talked at some length about the problems of Julie as a learner, the fact that she seemed to be unable to focus on a number of things at once. She seemed always to have a narrow plan and would stick to it. There was perhaps an inability to cope with many things all at once?

(Fieldnote, January, Greenfields)

Two points can be taken from this cameo. First, Carol and Victoria offered Jim support. They listened, were sympathetic and helped him to ventilate his frustrations and concerns at the end of what had been a miserable week for him. Second, this discussion began at 4.00 p.m. and ended just after 5.30 p.m.; pastoral care sometimes involved spending quite a lot of time with others.

When all the case examples are reviewed in this section, two teachers, Carol and Marion, seem particularly prominent. Yet this is in fact a distortion, since there were many other teaching and ancillary staff who also figure in our fieldnotes. Altogether there were many pastoral leaders in the project schools, since consideration was a feature of all the schools and played an important part in the culture of collaboration, as Isobel, the head of Sedgemoor, had intended:

Isobel encouraged staff to look to key colleagues for information, support and guidance. Whilst this often meant head of infants or deputy, it might equally mean the teacher who knew the children or the classroom best or whose area was closest.

(Yeomans, 1986c)

Secretaries

Secretaries played a part in the school's leadership even though their titles (secretary or clerical assistant) suggested that their job was administrative and subordinate to others. Whilst there is some truth in such a perspective, it underestimates the way in which school secretaries enabled others, particularly heads, to perform their leadership functions.

As you know, I've got a very good secretary who is ultra-efficient. It's just her nature. She is just a very efficient lady is Molly and so I am lucky because she takes a heck of the load off me, I am sure I am the sort of person who drives Molly absolutely balmy because she does things instantly, when I am very much a 'put off until tomorrow' person and she does push in front of me things that are really urgent, and she makes sure I get those out of the way.

(Head, Sedgemoor)

I see my role as making the kind of trivia less onerous for the head and other things I can do in the school that, occasionally the staff will come in or somebody will come in, 'I've got to try and arrange for a party of school children to go to Alford' and I say 'shall I arrange it?', and 'oh, would you?', and I see that as something I can do. I'm no good at teaching them about Roman history but I see that as something I can do to make life a little bit easier for them.

(Secretary, Sedgemoor)

Just as the head of Sedgemoor admitted to being gently 'pressured' by her secretary, so too secretaries in other schools took administrative initiatives:

[The secretary's] very efficient. She keeps everything in order and keeps everybody on their toes. She's marvellous.

(Teacher, Lowmeadow)

Often, then, the secretaries appeared to maintain the administrative side of the school, perhaps because the heads were busy elsewhere or sometimes were less efficient than their secretaries. Primary schools may appear informal organizations but, nevertheless, they have formal, bureaucratic tasks to fulfil and in these the secretary takes the lead.

Secretaries also played an important part in the communication network. They answered the telephone, made outgoing calls, passed on messages, visited all classes, dealt with all staff and received many of the school's visitors. As a result:

I think there are things that I will hear about or get to know or deal with that everybody else doesn't but I see that as part of my job. . . .

(Secretary, Sedgemoor)

In all of this the secretaries saw themselves as complementing their heads' work: The secretary . . . has always been around to make better the performance of her boss (Secretary, Sedgemoor). So it is not surprising that secretaries worked closely with their headteachers.

Int: Working with Isobel [the head] is a very important area?
Secretary: Oh yes, I mean it's everything . . . there might be times when she will say she is perhaps worried about something or someone, 'I think such and such looks tired, don't you, what do you think?'

(Sedgemoor)

In Lowmeadow where the head was 'shadowed' by the researcher for a week it was noted that when the head was in her office she was constantly in touch with her secretary, Sandra, in either her own room or the latter's, and that the head obviously valued Sandra's reliable and efficient help. The head accepted suggestions on the wording and layout of written communications, shared many problems with her, and they worked together in an easy and fluid way:

After break the head returned to clerical work, involving extensive discussion and collaboration with Sandra, so that action and talk on the nursery outing, the school photograph, letters for the summer fair and reports on the students were interspersed with references to the head's weekend in York and enquiries about Sandra's family. All of this was interrupted three times by children (always given priority), the parent governors and two phone calls.

(Fieldnote, May, Lowmeadow)

Another way of interpreting these characteristics of the secretaries' work is to say that their leadership on administrative matters took the form of initiating bureaucratic structures which would maintain the school's efficiency (in respect of returns, records, finance and communications). In acting in this way they became exemplars of efficiency, a fact which the heads and staff recognized and appreciated. They dealt with all members of staff and were supportive and considerate towards them. In turn, much of the secretaries' work was contingent on the staff's co-operation (e.g., in completing registers). Whilst secretaries worked with all members of staff their work was strongly influenced by their relationship with the head. The fact that a healthy relationship, and mutual respect, existed in all the schools between secretary and head should not disguise the fact that the secretaries' freedom to take initiatives depended upon a negotiated pattern of responsibilities and leadership between themselves and their heads. As a result the heads were happy that their secretaries should be bureaucratic leaders.

Curriculum Co-ordinators

The picture regarding curriculum co-ordinators as leaders is unclear. This is chiefly attributable to the union action which took place in some of the project schools during the period of data collection. Nevertheless a number of points can be made.

First, the teachers' use of time appears to be consistent with that recorded by Campbell (1985), who classified time into 'non-contact', 'group', 'snatched', and 'personal'. There was little, if any, non-contact time for the teachers. Co-ordinators exercised leadership during 'group time' (if they and colleagues were not taking union action), when working parties would meet to discuss plans and to review work in progress. Some of these meetings took place as staff meetings, some took place in time manufactured by someone, usually the head:

> Catherine's playing an important enabling role by taking the school. In so doing she shows her confidence in Stella and in the staff, by leaving them alone.
>
> (Fieldnote, September, Lavender Way)

Much of the co-ordinators' work was performed in 'snatched time'. Curriculum leadership took place at breaktimes and lunchtimes and involved discussions which were often brief or rushed. Sometimes it was supportive and informative, as in this case of a new teacher seeking help:

> I think everybody helped in their official role of maths co-ordinator, language co-ordinator. Really, it was a case of if you went in the staffroom and said 'What shall I do about this, or this, or where is such a thing kept?' everybody would say, 'It's there, or send along and I'll give you paintbrushes' or whatever.
>
> (Teacher, Greenfields)

Furthermore, a great amount of such leadership was informal. Discussions, curricular planning and decision-making were often conversational in tone. Whilst co-ordinators held formal positions in the school (e.g., co-ordinator for language or for display), they exercised their responsibilities in informal ways:

> Isobel tells me that collaborative work is frequently organized in a very informal way. 'An example is the large hall picture. It had become very tatty, we usually leave it up and we do it once a year, so we were talking about what to do about it at the staff meeting. Sally said "What about . . . ?", and she could obviously see the whole thing

quite clearly, so we said "right, you're in charge" (by the way, nobody's allowed to get out of that). Later in the day Sally said to Isobel 'can we have a quick meeting one lunchtime so that we can make sure everybody knows what they're doing for the hall picture'. Isobel agreed, in fact I know the meeting took place the following day because by Thursday three-quarters of the picture is already there.

(Fieldnote, November, Sedgemoor)

Lastly, co-ordinators, indeed all teachers, used their 'personal time' by working and planning at home and attending INSET courses after school, in the evenings and/or at the weekend.

Second, the co-ordinators displayed some ambivalence concerning the nature of their expertise and their authority:

Int: You appear to be defining maths co-ordinator as being to do with showing other people. I was going to say telling, but showing other people what to do?
Teacher: No, no. I definitely don't think that, because there are people in this school who probably know a heck of a lot more about maths than I do. I don't see that as the role of somebody who is a maths co-ordinator. You could be any kind of co-ordinator actually, it could be literacy, it could be anything, it's really getting it all together, it's not telling people what to do, I know that.

(Lavender Way)

The co-ordinators aimed at influence rather than direction or control and this required certain interpersonal skills. Co-ordinators worked with colleagues, leading discussions and advising (see Campbell, 1985), but as Goodacre (1984) has recorded, such work can create a sense of insecurity:

I'm kind of feeling my way along now, because I'm working a new maths scheme, so I've got to find out what people feel and I think one of the most difficult things is getting people to say what they really feel about things, that they're not just saying it on that surface and thinking something else, and not to be afraid of saying what they feel about things, because then we can discuss things and there's nothing wrong in saying 'I don't agree with that', so I've had to work my way into that a little bit and I know I've got a lot more working away to do at that. I'm a bit reticent about some things but I know I've got to come out a bit.

(Teacher, Lavender Way)

One explanation for these characteristics of the co-ordinators' work is to say they are caught between being leaders in their own right, in the sense that they initiate structure and provide an example, and working within the heads' and schools' structures. They had initiated structure (e.g., curriculum guidelines, reviews, meetings to co-ordinate organizational and curriculum work) and did show consideration since they supported colleagues' plans and offered advice. Also, they were aware of themselves as exemplars (e.g., the maths co-ordinator at Greenfields frequently talked about her maths classwork, recent in-service courses and her reading and current thinking). All of this occurred in the context of an individual school's particular circumstances (e.g., no non-contact time, individual colleagues' attitudes to the co-ordinator's area of responsibility or the co-ordinator as a person and a professional). Moreover, the co-ordinators' structures were constrained by their heads' behaviour along the decision-centralization dimension, but this fact was often unclear to colleagues and/or to the co-ordinators. Finally, and perhaps crucially, because of the lack of formalized contact with colleagues, the co-ordinators had little time in which to negotiate their leadership with others, and the pressure of union action in some of the project schools further reduced opportunities for such negotiation.

Altogether, then, their leadership was a product of the dimensions and functions noted at the start of this chapter. Further, whilst these dimensions impinged on the co-ordinators' leadership, lack of sufficient opportunities to negotiate, define and share their understanding of their role with others left them unclear and uncertain about it and therefore feeling ambivalent about their leadership.

CONCLUSION

The picture which emerges from each of these groups of leaders is one of complex and dynamic leadership. Headteachers were the significant figures; all the other leaders were dependent upon them. They provided their schools with a mission based on their educational beliefs which, in turn, helped to develop or sustain the schools' culture (notably, in our research, the culture of collaboration). Yet it was the heads' personal and professional example that was fundamental to the realization of their missions. The heads' behaviour was often informal, easy and fluid, yet they were sensitive when dealing with people, skilled in negotiating with staff and able to manage simultaneously many demands on their attention and time. Moreover, their example created respect and affection and served to coach and 'educate' their staff. As Coulson (1986, p. 84) puts it:

> Primary school headship hinges less upon some *thing* called 'leadership' or 'management' than on the *process* of leading — of the head's exerting influence in the school setting. Thus, personal influence processes, especially leading by example, occupy a dominant place within the head's management behaviour. His/her prime task is to create and nurture an organizational culture which is aligned with his/her vision for his/her particular school. (author's italics)

It is also important to recognize that the obligation both to provide a mission and to set an example meant that heads, like leaders in other organizations, needed to operate at two levels: a high level of abstraction (e.g., defining their beliefs about the social and moral purposes of education); and at the level of their day-to-day actions, even those at the most mundane and detailed level (see Peters and Waterman, 1982; Coulson, 1986). At the same time, they needed to ensure that work at one level was consistent with the other. Our evidence shows that the heads of the project schools did behave consistently.

Whilst the heads were key persons, other staff undertook important leadership functions which supported and complemented the head's work and the school's mission. Deputies and secretaries are the two most obvious groups, since each performed vital communication functions, freed the head from certain tasks and ensured that colleagues were not forgotten or left out. Each school's network of pastoral leaders also played a part. They were quick to support others and were models of personal co-operation and collaboration. Indeed, all the leaders overlapped and mutually reinforced each other, especially as personal and professional examples of culturally appropriate behaviour.

Another characteristic of leadership in the project schools was the ability of those who were leaders also to be members of the staff group. Heads and deputies did not feel they should be distant from those they sought to lead and influence. Rather, the fact that they were staff members meant that they were more effective leaders and members than if they had remained apart. However, there is some evidence for saying that whilst curriculum co-ordinators acted as leaders and members they experienced feelings of ambivalence about, and lacked the time to develop, their leadership.

Lastly, having noted at the beginning of this chapter that leadership is contingent, in part, upon context, we need to recognize that one feature of the schools' contexts was change. Although at a number of points this chapter has mentioned change, the picture we have presented has conveyed neither the extent nor the kinds of change that occurred. Nor has the chapter shown how the impact of change was balanced by actions promoting continuity. The next chapter explores these two ideas.

Chapter 7

Change and Continuity

So far we may have portrayed the schools, especially Greenfields, Lowmeadow and Sedgemoor with their long-serving heads and a core of established staff, as if they were static, even stagnant institutions. Yet this is very far from the truth. Teachers' classroom lives were changing, almost by the minute, numbers of adults (teaching, ancillary and support, visiting, part-time volunteer, full-time) daily came and went from the head's office, the staffroom and the school, their mood and their numbers affected by predictable events (such as in-service courses) and unpredictable ones (such as illness or vandalism), the tempo, rhythm and content of school life altered with the seasons and in response to recurrent events (such as medical inspections and fire drills). The feelings and the energy levels of headteachers and staff rose and fell, following the dictates of their personal lives as well as of events in school. More dramatically, staff left, requiring the attention of those who remained to be focused upon replacing them, upon the subsequent socialization of newcomers and upon their own accommodation to new colleagues and fresh ideas. These constant modifications to the personnel, tasks, climate and feelings of the staff created an endemic potential for disequilibrium within each school. This was, in turn, balanced by ways of thinking, speaking and behaving which encouraged continuity rather than change. The schools' histories were recreated and retold, contacts were fostered with past and present members of staff, inside and outside school, routines were preserved, rituals treasured. In all of this, the schools' leaders (especially but not exclusively their heads) took a leading part in both practical and symbolic ways.

Change was not only endemic and, often, unpredictable; it also affected staff at different levels. They found it relatively easy, for example, to adjust to a new routine for the end of playtimes, but when adaptations which seemed to threaten or affect the foundations of the individual school's culture were experienced these were profoundly disturbing. Change could have emotional as well as practical consequences and the pressures for continuity and stability that existed in all the schools must be understood in this light. They often safeguarded not so much habits as ways of working and living that were themselves embedded in deeply held beliefs.

This chapter will look at particular examples, first of change and then of continuity. It will also show that the two were sometimes inseparably connected.

EXAMPLES OF CHANGE

Part-time Workers

A feature common to all the project schools was the employment of several teaching and ancillary staff on a part-time basis. Whilst in each school the majority of teachers were employed full-time there were one or more teachers who worked in the schools for only a part of each day or week. This was exaggerated during our period of fieldwork because we also were part-time teachers. Ancillary workers too were typically part-time workers. Most caretakers, cleaners, nursery nurses, lunchtime supervisors, classroom ancillary assistants and secretaries were absent from the school site for part of each day or week. This reduced a part-time worker's opportunity for full membership of the staff group. In some cases the timing of a part-time worker's presence/absence further restricted his/her opportunities for membership. For example, the caretaker at Greenfields school was on site before school started and then from the middle of the afternoon until the evening. Consequently, his work was phased in such a way that his presence coincided with that of the teaching staff for only two hours each day. The following extracts provide other examples of how infrequently or briefly one might see colleagues:

> I only occasionally see the temporary special needs teacher as she only works a couple of days a week . . . the music teacher comes in for one morning a week . . .
>
> (Fieldnote, October, Sedgemoor)

> Mary isn't in on Fridays, therefore Graham teaches all day, and the absence of one is, in many ways, noticed. However, Natalie (the secretary) is in on Fridays whilst the ancillary, Norma, is in every day.
>
> (Fieldnote, October, Greenfields)

> The cleaner-in-charge, known always as Mrs Allerton, spends relatively little time on the premises during the school day, though she comes in at the beginning of every afternoon to clear the dining area.
>
> (Fieldnote, September, Sedgemoor)

Absence

The fact that it was not always easy to gather all the staff together, because of work patterns and attendance, was further exacerbated by a variety of 'absences'. The need to prepare work in classrooms, undertake playground duties, supervise lunches or after-school and lunchtime clubs, attend INSET courses and out-of-school meetings all added to fluctuations in the membership of the staff group.

> At no point in the day were all the staff in the staffroom. At some point throughout the day a member of staff was absent either working in his/her classroom preparing for work, or on playground duty.
>
> (Fieldnote, September, Greenfields)

Break duties, the tendency to spend time with music groups in breaks, and preparing for the next teaching session were some of the reasons why all the staff seldom gathered together.

(Fieldnote, October, Lavender Way)

I haven't been to the staffroom today because . . . I haven't been in all week, not because I want to miss anything particularly, but I had duty twice so that was two days out, and then I've got a gym display going on, that's tomorrow and the day after and we practise in playtimes and that's only morning break. There is not an afternoon break, so that's the time gone as we are out at dinnertimes anyway. That's the week gone, so I haven't been in.

(Teacher, Hutton)

Additionally, ill-health and accidents causing time off work further contributed to variations in attendance.

The combined effect of part-time work and absence was to reduce considerably the potential number of occasions when the whole staff group could be gathered together for a meeting. Indeed, in the course of some weeks there were no times when all the staff were available or even on site for a whole staff meeting. Change, then, even in this most obvious sense of presence and absence was ever-present; or, expressed another way, one constancy was the perpetual change in the membership of the staff group.

Life Circumstances

Another kind of change, bringing its own demands and pressures, arose from each individual's life circumstances. In the course of our fieldwork staff experienced bereavements, problems or pressures associated with ageing relatives, periods in hospital, health scares, marriage plans for children or themselves, anxieties concerning their own children's examination results, worries for their children recently beginning college or university life and anxieties about employment prospects for family or self (since some staff were employed on temporary contracts):

Victoria and Mary were talking about their children at college and how they were getting on with courses.

(Fieldnote, March, Greenfields)

As the deputy went into the hall, Mr Richmond asked, 'How's your mother, Julia?'

(Fieldnote, January, Lowmeadow)

Jean started her temporary post in September 1985. A new job coincided with a new home and husband, she had moved to the area to marry. She had previously worked in nursery education.

(Fieldnote, November, Hutton)

At lunchtime Josie, Dennis and I became involved in a conversation about the pressures of working for outside qualifications and of teaching upon family life — whilst Dennis is working at his PhD, Josie is doing her part-time advanced diploma and is finding the commitment a considerable call on her time. They both agreed that the extra work involved puts considerable additional demands upon the partners. Josie says that her husband spent all Sunday looking after the children and cooking, whilst she did her course work. They share a concern about the difficulties of being a second wage earner in a household with two full-time workers. For Josie it arises in terms of who should stay home if her children are ill. She feels her job is particularly important to her, but as her husband points out it's his salary that they depend on since he is a bank manager.

Dennis says that he and his wife work on a basis of equality in terms of sharing responsibility for their daughter, that they will take it in turn to stay at home but he too is aware that it is his salary they could do without if they had to, since his wife is particularly well paid.

(Fieldnote, March, Sedgemoor)

Such pressures and role conflicts obviously affected individuals' attitudes to work and to colleagues, and their receptivity to other challenges and changes.

Children

Children in each teacher's class, or in the school generally, created changes. Concerns for individual children ebbed and flowed bringing different emphases and foci to the teachers' talk, perceptions, worries and feelings of success. The very job of teaching — of caring for and sustaining the child's self-image, of developing each child and enabling him/her to progress through successive 'stages' of learning, while overcoming setbacks and challenges — led to teachers, and often ancillary staff too, experiencing feelings of concern and success. These resulted in moments of self-analysis, puzzlement, quiet satisfaction, euphoria, anger, in *ad hoc* 'case conferences', or in exhaustion:

Lunchtime was almost entirely taken up discussing a child, A., who has particular learning difficulties. This child is in Julie's class and he is a child in need of encouragement and attention. However, the discussion with the teachers roamed across whether the child was autistic, whether his behaviour was attention-seeking, whether he needed individual attention, did he work best with men, that the boy had actually missed his first year of schooling because he went to the US where children don't start school until they are six, so when he returned at the age of six he was effectively a year behind in England. Because of this late start in his first school (which was not Greenfields) he'd been a special case and had enjoyed special status. Now, at Greenfields, he was often unpopular with his peer group and he sometimes needed a firm hand. There was agreement that since he was well into his third Junior year, he needed to be shown that his level of working was unacceptable, particularly for a boy soon to be in his fourth year and thereafter preparing to transfer to secondary school. Victoria in particular felt that he was not going to be able to cope with secondary school.

(Fieldnote, January, Greenfields)

Margaret to Veronica and Sue in Sue's room after school: 'Ian did great this afternoon, he's learned all the words he needs for his reading book.' She said this with a delighted grin, sharing his success.

(Fieldnote, May, Sedgemoor)

Union Action

One important feature of our period of fieldwork was the presence and effect of union action. Potentially divisive differences were introduced to the school or brought to the surface because of individual allegiances to union, school, colleagues or principles. One of the schools (Lowmeadow) was barely affected whilst in the other four some staff took some action. Each school appeared to respond in an individual way (see Chapter 8) because those teachers who were members of unions taking action sometimes followed the instructions of their union to the letter or, more commonly, interpreted the advice in their own way and in the light of the school's circumstances. For example, at Hutton five teachers were in a union which was taking action:

> They wanted to support their union, but decided they would not take action which would seriously damage the school. In practice this meant that the five would not attend after-school staff meetings (which thus ceased), after-school clubs or participate in evening activities such as Christmas Plays. They decided that they would vacate the premises at lunchtime. However, they would not strike. They did continue to attend parents' evenings and to spend time after school on preparing displays and classwork.
>
> (Yeomans, 1987a)

When union action took place, staff described its effects thus:

> There have been a lot of times when we have needed to come together, and I think missing out on the staff meetings and not being here at lunchtimes, you have missed meeting together in the staffroom. You go up there and there's nobody there which I think is an awful shame.
>
> (Teacher, Hutton)

> It's a pity you're in school this year, really, because you're not seeing us developing.
>
> (Teacher, Greenfields)

> At lunchtime Richard said that he felt the industrial action was making a lot of difficulties especially not having staff meetings and after-school activities — the Christmas parties were going to be in the afternoons and they were going to have only a very curtailed carol service — as an extended Friday morning assembly. The Christmas play in the pre-term plan has disappeared.
>
> (Fieldnote, December, Hutton)

Whilst all members of staff were aware of and felt the effects of action, the heads appeared to be more keenly aware:

> There've been times when it's been difficult to keep my cool, particularly as term's gone on. They [the staff] think school's getting off lightly, but I reckon strikes would do far less damage. We're not having any staff meetings except when I have to have one, say during assembly, and even then we can't do any curriculum business.
>
> (Head, Hutton)

These feelings are consistent with the heads' sense of ownership of the school (see Chapter 6). But others too experienced the effects of action. The union representative at Greenfields, for example, followed his union's instructions to the letter and this left him isolated:

> I was quite relieved when the action was over vis-à-vis the staff because I ceased to be an outsider . . . Although the staff accepted the reason why I had to leave the premises at lunchtimes they appreciated that it did isolate me somewhat.
>
> (Teacher, Greenfields)

There were also instances of some other changes in relationships because staff belonged to different unions and associations which were themselves reacting differently (e.g., the single PAT member in Greenfields school, where everyone else was NUT or NAS/UWT; see Chapter 8). This affected each staff group's sense of interdependence and solidarity. Also, as the action wore on (it lasted for two out of the three terms of our fieldwork), attitudes altered and feelings of frustration and bitterness towards the government, unions or the LEA increased. Indeed, union action revealed that change has an emotional content; changes brought about by union action were deeply felt and experienced. Moreover, whilst union action revealed most clearly the emotional side of change, many other kinds of change also affected people's feelings, as the following examples show.

'Projects'

Change, we have so far suggested, can occur in two ways. It is either unplanned, resulting from unexpected events (accidents, ill-health) or planned (e.g., union action). 'Projects' is used to describe a different kind of planned event such as educational visits, dramatic productions, exhibitions, curricular projects and those Christmas activities which survived union action. Such projects are a feature of many primary schools, and all the schools undertook at least one during the 1985–6 academic year.

The significance of projects is twofold. First, they altered the rhythm of either the whole school, or part of the school. They modified work patterns and in some instances the nature of work — particularly for ancillary workers who switched from routine tasks to, say, making costumes or preparing tables for parties. Secondly, projects increased pressure upon staff. Rehearsals, dress rehearsals, and opening nights created their own special tensions, whilst the 'final curtain' simultaneously brought exhilaration and exhaustion.

Crises

The schools also experienced crises. To take Greenfields as an example: first, there was a theft:

> A talking point before school was the fact that last week Carol had her handbag stolen from the staffroom . . . It transpires from what had been pieced together, that a child who was waiting outside Graham's room saw a man come in, who despatched this child to go on to the field and look for the caretaker, whilst this person, having asked the child if the head's office and staffroom were empty went straight into the staffroom and picked up Carol's bag. Carol's bag was discovered in Branfield and the Branfield police still have it. Police have visited the school, talked to the boy who was outside Graham's office and also talked to others and a CID officer came in today to talk a little more to Carol.
>
> (Fieldwork, July 1986, Greenfields)

Second, during the autumn and spring terms, a teacher, Julie, who was working full-time in the school although on an annual temporary contract basis, was trying to demonstrate to both the LEA and the school her competence as a teacher. Unfortunately she experienced difficulties with children (e.g., discipline, organization), and the head with worried parents and governors. By Easter of that academic year she had failed to meet the LEA's requirements and, following a summer term when she was relieved of class teaching responsibilities, she left the profession. Julie's problems created, for the staff, considerable worry, concern, tension, frustration and guilt:

> *Int*: How do you now feel about Julie? Because you spoke about feeling quite guilty about it all.
> *Teacher*: Yes. One learns to live with one's guilt. I think, on reflection, perhaps we were too fair. The guilt still remains but perhaps it's one where we had to bend over backwards to try to be fair and perhaps it was misplaced. I'm a bit worried because she's only got four weeks to the end of term and I don't think she's got anything lined up yet. It's in her nature that she'll probably get a job the day before the pay runs out.
>
> (Greenfields)

Third, the school was broken into and vandalized:

> The vandals, having got into the staffroom, had sprayed orange juice over the room, poured fluid into pieces of equipment such as the photocopier, ruined the typewriter, broken some windows, smashed a lot of crockery, upset Graham's room and all his files and some of his personal papers. It was a terrible disturbance. It was discovered on Sunday. Displays had been ruined, including Victoria's corridor display of children's constructions of space vehicles and space habitats. Graham was obviously busy . . . Norma and Natalie were working hard to get things ready for the collection of dinner money and one of the parents, the PTA secretary, was already in, doing an assessment of the damage that had occurred and equipment that would need to be replaced. Norma was undoubtedly upset about the damage to the school and both she and Natalie had lots of things to sort out.
>
> (Fieldnote, March, Greenfields)

Additionally, during the year, the staff at Greenfields coped with encounters with angry or dissatisfied parents, building alterations and repairs which dislocated teaching, and accidents to staff or children. Although each crisis brought its own particular problems, all of them challenged tacit beliefs (e.g., that everyone is secure within the culture of collaboration; the school's view of effective educational practice). Each crisis was, to varying degrees, a shock to the culture. Therefore, each crisis was felt; it affected individuals emotionally, making them feel guilty, unfairly treated (by the angry parent) or upset and often, as a result, very tired.

Fatigue and Mood

One of the more obvious changes that occurred incrementally each term was the onset of tiredness, which became fatigue and then exhaustion. The staff not only worked under the pressure created by many of the aforementioned changes, they also worked long hours:

> Although my life here finishes at five, I take all the work and the books and things home, but then I give my children till nine and then I start my school work again after that.
>
> (Teacher, Sedgemoor)

> Ben says that he and Catherine had been in all Sunday getting ready for the play, doing the lighting etc. He left at half past five yesterday, that was the earliest he had left for some time. In spite of supposed industrial action NUT members are working throughout the lunchtime and are still there at half past four. At lunchtime the staffroom is empty apart from Sandy getting her brief moment of peace, then Ben snatching ten minutes

before the afternoon starts. Ben says 'the tiring thing is having so many different things to think about', Catherine comes in and says 'we have got all next week to sort out yet.' During the lunchtime Rita and Julie have been in the hall dealing with final play preparations, refining props and checking.

(Fieldnote, December, Lavender Way)

June (secretary) on my arrival 'Everyone's a bit fraught.' It's been a heavy week — one thing following the other. Bill says he feels as if he hasn't been home before ten, including the weekend. Richard in the hall, surrounded by all the school maths equipment, with dark shadows under his eyes, his hair slightly dishevelled, looking fed-up. He raised a tired smile when he saw me.

   Richard's programme had been Monday — clearing up after the village gala; Tuesday — speaking to Young Wives; today — governors' meeting after sports in the afternoon; Thursday — cricket match and barbecue with Education Department. Next week: Monday — parents' evening and open evening. 'All things I wouldn't be involved in if it wasn't for the school.' Also school contributed to the church festival last week, disco previous Friday. Exhibition next week. Bill at lunchtime looked equally tired and sat in the staffroom saying barely a word, also dark tiredness patches under his eyes.

(Fieldnote, June, Hutton)

Obviously some feelings arose from fatigue, but often during the period of our fieldwork union action and the teachers' pay dispute also affected the staffs' moods. There were moments of anger — especially when a politician had made comments, unsympathetic to teachers, on TV, the radio or in a newspaper. Sometimes there were outbursts of frustration directed against union action:

The head said: 'If I thought teacher action was going to last for the rest of my career I'd get out now' and Victoria said 'well, actually I'm pig sick of not having staff meetings.' There was some eye contact with Jim at this, to see how Jim, in his union representation role, felt about the potential role conflict between union member and teacher in the school.

(Fieldnote, April, Greenfields)

There were also signs of a 'siege mentality' when the 'enemy' was seen to be outside the school (see Chapter 3), often in the guise of government, the press, the LEA, governors, parents or some combination of these. Staffs' expressions of anger, exasperation or frustration at these enemies were also tinged with bitterness, not least because their long hours, personal commitment, investment of energy and resulting fatigue appeared to have little or no effect upon the industrial dispute.

Climate

The notion of organizational climate is well established (see Halpin, 1966; Mortimore *et al.*, 1988). According to Hoyle (1986), climate is essentially concerned with the quality of relationships between pupils, between pupils and teachers, between teachers, and between head and teachers. Hoyle's definition must be modified for our purpose because we did not study pupils, and because Hoyle, rather surprisingly, does not include relationships with and amongst ancillary staff.

   Since climate, in the sense that we use it, refers to the quality of inter-adult relationships, it follows that a school's climate is not a fixed or permanent condition. Rather, it is always altering as relationships change in response to planned and unplanned events, fatigue and mood. Indeed, climate is a useful metaphor since the schools experienced periods of high and low pressure, suffered bouts of depression, encountered periods of storm or drought, turbulence and calm. In turn, climatic changes threatened the stability of the school culture. For example, when Greenfields experienced a large number of 'crises' and other changes in the course of a half-term (e.g., failing teacher, absence, vandalism, union action, fatigue, promotion of one teacher and thus impending change of staff) the climate was 'turbulent', and even 'stormy'. Consequently, staff felt less secure and this was compounded by the fact that union action prevented them from meeting formally. Therefore, the staff decided to meet at one staff member's house on a Sunday evening, ostensibly to talk but also to reaffirm the culture of collaboration. The relative ordinariness of some of the changes we have described should not lead us to underestimate their impact on the schools' cultures.

Headteacher Succession

Change also occurred at different levels (for example, union action at Hutton and Greenfields changed the schools more than the temporary absence of individual staff did). As a consequence, some changes were more difficult to adjust to than others; coming to terms with the failing teacher took longer to adjust to than did the absence of a part-time worker. In other words, having acknowledged that change is a felt experience we also need to recognize that the emotional effects of change were determined by the perceived depth of the change and the scale of adjustment needed to cope with it.

Perhaps the most potent example of this is a change of headteacher (and sometimes of deputy head; see Chapter 6), since such a change is both deep and difficult to adjust to. Chapter 6 demonstrated the heads' ownership of their schools, in that they were closely associated with their school's beliefs, provided it with a sense of mission and felt a deep commitment to it. It follows that a change of head is analogous to a change of 'owner'. Moreover, because the head is the founder of the school's culture, a new head will change the culture.

As a result the departure of one headteacher and the arrival of the successor is a time of uncertainty:

> We were very apprehensive about a new head but we also looked forward to it in a strange way and I think we'd had a very strained time because the deputy head and the head left at the same time.
>
> (Teacher, Lavender Way)

Also, the length of each teacher's association with the previous head was strongly associated with the extent of his/her identification with the former 'regime':

> A couple of staff who had been here a long time found it difficult. They didn't really want any changes as they were so used to doing things their way. It didn't worry me in the least as I hadn't been here long enough to get into the swing of doing this anyway. I think most of the changes have been for the better personally. I think Catherine and Ben were very aware that people had been here for quite a long time, and were not

going to change things overnight. I didn't feel any more pressure to produce things, or
that I would have to change my routine or do anything really differently.

(Teacher, Lavender Way)

Engrained in these comments is the tacit understanding both that the newly arrived
head will initiate change, and that individual heads will want particular kinds of
change. The head of Greenfields, for example, had returned from a year's secondment. During the year of his absence an acting head was appointed from another
school in the LEA. Although the acting head was a temporary appointment and
avoided any major curriculum changes he did alter certain procedures, in particular
how children moved around the school. When the seconded head, Graham, returned,
he reverted to the original pattern. But many parents evidently preferred the acting
head's way of moving children into and around school and told both Graham and
the school governors of this. Graham responded by defending his beliefs:

> Yesterday there had been an extraordinary governors' meeting, a meeting when Graham
> had been presenting his views on self-discipline . . . there have been some comparisons
> made by parents and governors as to the discipline policy adopted during the inter-
> regnum (when Graham was on secondment) since the acting head had promoted a more
> regimented scheme of movement around the school. Graham believes in self-discipline
> and the freedom of children to move as they see fit, since that allows the pupils freedom
> to discover from experience the kind of consideration for others needed in order to
> make any system work effectively. This he put to the governors.
>
> (Fieldnote, December, Greenfields)

> There were things which my 'stand-in' had done, which parents saw as good and which
> I didn't see as good and which I was going to change and which parents resented. I
> think they've come to terms with them now and see it my way, I was determined to do
> it though, and I had an awful lot of problems with some parents, heated arguments and
> so on. I think we've come through that period, I hope so. But I think 're-entry' is
> difficult.
>
> (Head, Greenfields)

Lavender Way provides another example of change resulting from the arrival of a
new head. In this case, Catherine expected a different approach to responsibility and
leadership from her infant co-ordinator and because so much in these schools rested
upon the professional and personal preferences of their heads (see Chapters 6 and
8) she was able to ask for the change:

> When I first took over I asked about her Scale 3 and she wanted to know what I expected
> of a Scale 3 Head of Infants, and I told her, and she was prepared to take on board all
> the things that I'd expect from a Scale 3. That wasn't how she worked before, I mean,
> she literally had the position but she wasn't really a leader as such.
>
> (Head, Lavender Way)

Heads also played a central role in defining what constituted 'work'. For example,
when Richard arrived at Hutton he made a series of changes. First, he stated that
the integrated day was the preferred way of working. Second, he determined how
regularly displays should be changed:

> Staff were told (by the head) that the classroom displays should be changed regularly,
> and every fortnight a year group was responsible for a new set of displays in the entrance
> hall, whilst the rest of the staff shared the responsibility for changing the display boards
> in the hall.
>
> (Fieldnote, November, Hutton)

Third, he did not want staff to order resources for their own classes:

> When Mr Smith [previous head] was here . . . you had your own allowance and you ordered your own books which did mean we ended up with a hotch-potch of all sorts of things . . . we don't do any ordering at all now.
>
> (Teacher, Hutton)

Fourth, he felt that children should be allowed greater involvement and choice during classwork:

> There was a totally different approach to the curriculum because there was this new element in the curriculum. There was the idea of giving the children freedom of choice.
>
> (Teacher, Hutton)

Lastly, he altered the way the decisions were taken:

> I think it was pretty obvious at one stage, that it was 'this is the way I want it done and you will do it'.
>
> (Teacher, Hutton)

The following accounts raise four points: that these headteachers perceived themselves to be central figures in changing 'their' schools; that they significantly affected the direction of 'their schools' development; that they were keenly aware of the pace of change which they required their colleagues to experience; and that longevity for a head does not equate with stagnation.

Graham, head of Greenfields, talked about his eighteen years as head of the school:

> I've changed the school considerably. I had to change the school considerably to start with because my predecessor was not a primary school teacher, had never been in primary schools. It was ultra-formal, a secondary modern with 11-year-old children. So there had to be drastic changes when I first came, which included actually getting rid of staff . . . I tried to do it humanely, but it was obvious that there had to be drastic changes . . . The children had been brought up on what I considered to be spoon-fed education. They'd been spoon-fed facts and then asked to regurgitate them, which is not education to me. So my approach was completely different, particularly in areas such as mathematics, because as a mathematics teacher the new initiatives in primary mathematics were one of the reasons why I came from secondary teaching. It was exciting as well as difficult and gradually I got a good staff together . . . within two years the [pupil] numbers had risen considerably. Then it became obvious as more and more of what you might call 'upwardly mobile' middle-class parents brought their children in and some of the more settled land-owning parents brought their children in, that there was a great gulf between the social classes and that there was a need for integration so I saw that as part of my job. I began to bring into the school activities which hopefully would get the two classes together. So from about 1968, I suppose, we were moving very closely towards a community school. I saw the attitudes of children towards their school change, as they saw their parents involved in the school . . . So we moved towards involving all kinds of adults, not just parents . . . In 1970 the CEO [Chief Education Officer] and his senior adviser decided that community education should be extended into the primary sector and they invited six heads to discuss it and look into possible ways of doing it and we spent about two years, off and on, discussing it and then the Authority set up six community primary schools in 1972, of which Greenfields was one.
>
> I'd gone through the exciting period of changing the school from the formal pseudo-secondary modern, into a live, village primary school . . . I'd integrated, to a large extent, the communities within the village and I think I can say that's a success. And then we got the excitement of the community schools. You can see why I stayed on, and on, and on. I didn't want to leave all that excitement . . .

We're now actually going through a period in the school of reassessing, not so much the philosophy, but I think we need to stabilize and really look carefully at what we're doing and try and make sure that it becomes a school thing and not a series of things from individuals. This is what we've been doing with such schemes as GRIDS, probably that's the most important thing at the moment, really to make sure that the staff look closely at what they're doing, look at their practices, look at their thoughts and ideas and get a consensus, so we can look at it and say 'Yes, this is where we think we're going.'

I think we've been moving in that direction for some time and I really don't see any really drastic change of direction.

(Head, Greenfields)

And, of course, there would not be a 'drastic change of direction' until Graham left and a successor arrived. Richard, who had been head of Hutton School for five years, saw it this way:

When I first came, and everything was completely different from how it is now, I was prepared to wait a year before saying anything about what I wanted to do but in actual fact it never worked because it was demanded by the staff that I set out what I thought, so we did. We had long talks, which were not always completely amicable, on how I saw the school, what they should do in school, and we did evolve a way of working . . . At that time they recognized that the school needed a change, which they got and they probably got more than they bargained for, in a shorter time.

However, the school, since January, has taken on a new sort of phase which has coincided with Teresa coming. But only because she was chosen as deputy head for this particular reason; that the school we had for the first years when I was here, was not necessarily the school that I wanted ultimately.

(Head, Hutton)

Catherine, the head at Lavender Way, provides a further explanation for discontinuity at the time of headteacher succession. Newly appointed heads know so little about what has gone on before their arrival that it is difficult for them to understand the legacy of their predecessor, or to know precisely what they have 'inherited' (see Myer, 1987; Myer and Southworth, 1988). Consequently, new heads may be working in the dark, trying to understand what is presently happening in the school, what this means in terms of the past, and where the school might 'go' in the future. Unless heads are able to learn about their predecessors (e.g., their educational beliefs, notions of effective practice, preferred ways of decision-making and leading) it is likely that they will create discontinuities in the culture because they will not know enough to be able to continue those practices of their predecessors which they find acceptable:

It's interesting because you come in with certain set ideas about a place, but, it's only when it's actually yours that you realize that there's very little in common with your previous school . . . you get talking to the previous head, you think you're going to come into this very smooth-running school and no problems and it's been running very smoothly, fantastic relationship with staff and head and parents, all that sort of thing. You think 'marvellous, not going to have to do anything, just come in and do my own thing and everybody's going to be happy'. But, it doesn't work in that way at all . . . I thought I can come in and it would be a case of, obviously getting to know the staff before you build up a relationship with the parents and the children. It wasn't an easy task, it took me longer than I thought it was going to do, for all members of staff were initially very loyal to the previous head and I can understand that. They were trying to find out what I was going to be like and what my policies were going to be and if they were going to be any different or the same or what-have-you. It took towards the end of the first year for people to open up, longer than I expected. And it was only then that I began to find out what the school had really been like, and there hadn't been a good relationship. I can say that now because so many have said it to me and I can tell.

(Head, Lavender Way)

The sum total of all of these points concerning headteacher succession is both simple and profound. Because a head is the leading agent of change, when one leaves and another comes the school faces a period of potential alteration. In essence since heads are perceived to have the right to alter the basis of the school's culture, a new 'culture founder' arrives.

But headteacher succession does not simply highlight issues concerning cultural change, it also provides insights into continuity. At the root of the discussion is the idea that where schools have not had a recent change of head, continuity exists. Yet, by itself, this is too simple a view. The head will certainly ensure continuity in terms of mission and beliefs but, nevertheless, there is scope within the school for other changes in, for example, curriculum, teaching approach, use of time and space and so on. A head may provide continuity at one level (e.g., beliefs) while also making changes at other levels (e.g., curriculum content, planning). Hence, although a head may work in a school for a long time it does not follow that there will be little or no change, as Graham's account, cited above, demonstrates. Rather, change will occur only at certain levels; the most resistant is that of belief.

Staff Selection

If a new headteacher was a 'deep' change, so too was the arrival of a fresh staff member, something that took place several times during our year of fieldwork. The greatest number of staff changes occurred at Hutton, but staff also left or joined at Greenfields, Lavender Way and Lowmeadow. Altogether we witnessed the appointment of a deputy head, teaching staff, and ancillary staff, including a caretaker.

The appointment of new members of staff can involve both change and continuity. The departure of a member of staff is often a loss and the arrival of a successor always a change, but in appointing a replacement the school can try to appoint someone who closely matches his/her predecessor in respect of curricular strengths, experience, age, gender, teaching style, and educational philosophy. Heads and staff talked about colleagues 'fitting in', not about whether particular individuals had the right qualifications for the job. Fitting in at Greenfields, Lowmeadow and Sedgemoor meant selecting someone to *sustain* the school's dominant culture, whereas at Hutton and Lavender Way staff were appointed to contribute to the *development* of the school in ways congruent with the head's mission and the school's developing culture. Appointments at the former schools were intended to provide cultural continuity whilst at the latter appointments were aimed at cultural development, that is, they represented the possibility for change at a deeper level than at the other three schools. The 'depth' at which a change of staff member was experienced depended upon the degree of correspondence between predecessor's and successor's values and beliefs, and between the successor's values and beliefs and the appointing school's culture. The most profound changes occurred at Hutton or Lavender Way when a staff member left who had not been contributing to the developing culture and when his/her successor was someone who did contribute to that culture.

Whether heads wished to develop or maintain the culture, they all saw the selection of staff as a vital task. Much of the selection process therefore relied upon their personal perceptions of candidates:

> I have always regarded choosing staff as the most important thing I do and it's possibly the thing I take the most seriously, I spend an awful lot of time on it. I like to meet people before they actually apply, I like them to come and see the school and I like to talk to them at length about the school and tell them how we've got to where we are, the sorts of ways in which people work and that although there is flexibility in the way that they work, that we are all working towards the same end. If you like, I almost put people off really because I let them know that it is hard work, we are looking for people who want something that is a challenge and want to be part of a team, and not just an individual teacher tucked away. Then if I haven't put them off hopefully they will apply, but if I have put them off then I feel fair enough, you know that's probably just as well.
>
> (Head, Sedgemoor)

> So, of the people that we all interviewed, we chose very, very carefully in terms of looking at their educational philosophies and the general approach they have, or they want to have, with regard to classroom organization and the way they like children to learn. We questioned them in great depth about what they felt they wanted. Then that makes it so much easier, that you're not sort of trying to convert people who don't actually believe or who perhaps haven't got the same educational philosophies as you have yourself. I think, when you're trying to build a team, it is important that the members of staff feel committed to that particular way of running it and the particular philosophies that it's trying to enhance . . .
>
> (Head, Hutton)

Because heads felt it was so important to appoint the right person they seldom relied solely on interviews. Individuals already known to the school were less of a risk than strangers, because their capacity to fit in had already been assessed. So it was a common tactic for schools to appoint people they already knew. In all the schools there was evidence of teachers (and other staff) commencing work in the school on a temporary or part-time basis and then after some trial period being made permanent or full-time, or both.

> The school now has a new ancillary named Audrey who was already employed in the school as a cleaner and who some years back had done the job of ancillary in relation to a child with special needs.
>
> (Yeomans, 1987)

> It is the same with Polly, she's been involved with the school because she was originally a parent, one of our first parents with our initial group of children, then she sort of gradually came in as a dinner helper and then eventually as welfare helper. I think she sees herself totally as part of the school, I hope she does, she's very loyal to the school and to everybody in it.
>
> (Teacher, Sedgemoor)

> In general, new staff are people that we've known beforehand so we know that they will fit . . . that's another reason for knowing people before they become part of the establishment.
>
> (Teacher, Lowmeadow)

However, not all staff employed on this basis were successful:

> The two people who had had temporary posts have not been kept on although, as people see it, there was the opportunity that they could have been kept on as, obviously, we've been advertising for people to replace them.
>
> (Head, Hutton)

> We've all been very carefully selected to fit in. Abrasive personalities have either not been appointed, generally speaking, or have not stayed.
>
> (Teacher, Lowmeadow)

When selection involved candidates who were entirely unknown to the staff, the heads arranged opportunities for the candidates to visit the school before the selection interview. These visits were significant occasions, as the head of Sedgemoor intimated above and as the head and staff at Greenfields made clear:

> The staff always have an opportunity of meeting the candidates beforehand. They talk to the candidates and before the interview they will have spoken to them and conveyed some sort of opinion [to me] . . . every conversation is a form of mini-interview. They'll talk about the job, they'll ask pertinent questions about experience and they'll discuss the kind of set-up we have here. I think they [staff] would probe fairly deeply.
>
> (Head, Greenfields)

> There's no doubt about it, one looks at people and says, 'Am I going to be able to work with her?' or 'What type of personality is this? Am I going to like this person, not necessarily work with them, but like?'
>
> (Teacher, Greenfields)

Because 'fitting in' meant being in sympathy with the school's prevailing or developing beliefs, it required the passing of certain membership tests:

> Those who have experience of joining a school's staff may recall the *rites de passage* they endured. Such rites may signal not just a 'getting to know you' phase but, perhaps, a series of 'tests' of the newcomer's ability to fit in. These 'tests' are likely to vary from school to school, as will the criteria employed to make judgements but whatever the tests are, they constitute the staff group's conditions of membership.
>
> Southworth (1987b, p. 108)

Only when the membership tests have been passed will the newcomer be fully accepted into the staff group. Selection therefore appears to be a two-stage process: first, the candidate's acceptability is judged on the basis of perceptions gathered from the school visit and interview; second, s/he is accepted (or rejected) by the staff group.

> It's interesting in this close-knit group though, when a newcomer comes, you're not in straight away . . . it's all very friendly, but you're aware of them waiting to see you work, and what you're made of. Well, that's how I felt, anyway. Maybe I was being over-sensitive, I don't know . . . It's how you cope with the job, how you're seen to cope with the job as well. How you react in the staffroom, too.
>
> (Teacher, Lowmeadow)

This two-stage process served another purpose as well. While newcomers were being inducted into the school and further tested for acceptability, they were also being socialized. In other words the changes which resulted from the newcomer's arrival were offset by a conscious attempt to provide continuity. Socialization took several forms, including support, assistance, and advice. Its purpose and effect was to 'gentle' the newcomer into the school's ways of operating. The process was subtle and in a way 'soft' but for all that there was no mistaking the fact that the newcomers were unmistakably nudged in the 'right' direction.

Yes. I did have a lot of support from various groups. The deputy head when I first came here. She helped a lot by recognizing that I needed reassurance. If there was something not quite right, she would very, very gently and tactfully say so, but would come into my room regularly and say 'oh, I like this' or 'oh', that sounds very good, what are you doing now?', 'that sounds very interesting', and then she would talk to me about the educational implications of what I was doing, so she was reinforcing that. She was reassuring me all the time, although I don't know that she was really consciously aware. I never felt that she was coming in to give me a boost chat.

(Teacher, Hutton)

I've been lucky in that I've always had a deputy who has been able to do this [induct new staff], and I think the two of us tend to work on new members of staff and I think the deputy actually plays an even more important role because they've got the classroom contact more, and can wander into the classroom. I mean I do, as you know, but I think when people are very new — I feel that even with me there is a slight 'oh dear, here's the head, am I doing it right?' — there's not so much with the deputy. Therefore I tend to say to Dennis let's make sure that they are working along the same lines and just keep an eye on this or mention that, you know, that we do it this way or that way, and this is what tends to happen and I think there is more influence that way than giving somebody written sheets of paper.

(Head, Sedgemoor)

A number of related points have now been raised but in isolation from one another. In practice, they tended to combine and work together. The following extracts from Hutton are put together as a cameo, to illustrate the complexity of the staff selection and socialization process. The cameo also shows that socialization is not 'one-way'; that is, socialization is not simply about the successful candidate (Teresa) being accepted or not by the staff. The evidence suggests that Teresa also modified her behaviour to present an image which was acceptable to the group she had now joined.

These extracts also indicate that the selection of a new deputy head raised many feelings, demonstrating once again that change is a felt experience. In part the emotional side of the appointment relates to the context in which it occurred. For one thing, there were sub-cultures at Hutton (see Chapter 3). For another, the head wanted to appoint someone who would help him develop the school. Lastly, the departing deputy represented an important piece of continuity with the past.

Cameo of Selection and Socialization

The existing deputy at Hutton who had been at the school for several years left at Christmas. During the autumn term the post for her replacement was advertised, applications flowed in and interview candidates were invited to visit the school:

The Newssheet appears — the head says: 'I would welcome your comments (serious) after they have departed.' (This refers to the candidates for the deputy headship.)

The deputy headship candidates are about to arrive. The tour is today, interviews tomorrow. The head is restless and wanders up and down the staffroom, not feeling able to settle down, but not wanting to go to his office, where he has one of the candidates sitting, waiting for him. We laugh at an imitation of 'The Woodentops', anything will do as a release.

The head had suggested that he intended to seek staff opinions on the deputy headship candidates but said that it was particularly difficult now because of the lack of staff meetings, so he would have to discuss it with people individually. His view seems to be that he would like to be aware of what the staff think, but he wouldn't be prepared to regard it as in any way binding on what he would do.

This is the day of the deputy headship interviews. I'd been unable to attend an after-school discussion of the candidates and asked one of the staff about it. 'It's like an unexploded bomb this morning.' She went on to explain that the staff had been equally divided and that things had quite heated and she had in fact left because she found it rather embarrassing.

(Fieldnotes, October)

One of the difficulties which emerged was that one of the strongest candidates (Teresa) came from a neighbouring school which some staff disliked because of its reputation as a show school (see Chapter 5). Then:

> At lunchtime one of the staff comes into the staffroom, looks at Rachel and says 'Who got it?' Rachel — 'Teresa'. A little later she comes back in but there is no further reference to the interview and to the candidates. The atmosphere is subdued and there are silences for almost the first time I can remember in the school. One teacher feels the effects of the morning: 'Have you ever had one of those headaches when you can't see?' Later, after school I sit down and have a cup of coffee expecting references to the interview to begin. Only after half an hour is there a brief reference to the interviews. Nobody seems to want to talk about them.
>
> Richard, after school, 'I will organize these football matches. I feel more like going home and putting my head in a bucket of ice.' Looking weary.

(Fieldnote, October)

It had been a long and tense day. A difficult decision was made. The head, whilst exhausted, felt the right appointment had been made even though not all the staff were satisfied with the choice:

> I had no doubts really, if I'm honest, from the very first time she came to visit the school. I thought that in her visits prior to the interview she had a good feel for the school and put her finger on some of the problems.

(Head)

> I think things will probably change in January to a degree because Teresa is coming in from outside and I think she is bound to have an effect, hopefully a good one, on staff relationships because she won't be aware of all these little ins and outs of things, that I am terribly aware and very very conscious of.

(Teacher)

> I think one or two members of the staff have their backs up already so they are not going to accept her which I think would be a shame, because they are not going to give her a fair chance, are they?

(Teacher)

Teresa started her job as deputy head at Hutton in January. She had been attracted to the school both by the job, since it was a promotion for her, and by the head's desire for the school's development to continue. Richard had conveyed the idea that the school was ready for the next stage in its development and Teresa felt she could contribute. However, she was aware of the dangers of overwhelming her colleagues so, at first, she adopted a low profile. During the spring term some staff developed a favourable opinion of her, whilst others felt her behaviour confirmed their initial judgements:

> I suppose if Teresa had come in here saying 'everyone should do the drapes like I'm doing mine and this, that and the other', I suppose people would have ignored her, but I think she has kept quite a low profile and that's probably why it's worked. I mean anybody coming into a new situation with any sense doesn't say much, just listens and watches, and notices and I think Teresa has tried to do that really. I think she had summed up the situation fairly realistically before she came and then thought out a way of getting round it. That's probably why it's worked out quite well.
>
> (Teacher)

> I think she's a jolly nice person. I thought she was when she came. When I watched her with the children I thought she was a very caring, sensitive sort of person, and that is what I find her to be. She communicates so well, she reasons things out all the time with everybody. I mean she's put herself out to get to know the staff. I think she's won me over anyway . . .
>
> (Teacher)

For her part Teresa said:

> I feel now, people have warmed a little more. There was an interesting situation at the beginning of term where I took a parent into the staffroom and in fact parents are not invited into the staffroom, they have coffee in the classrooms, and at that time I was told categorically by one member of staff that we didn't do that in this school and, perhaps rather stupidly in a way, I had bristled at that slightly and said 'Oh well, we'll see about that' and in some way perhaps it was just as well to lose that first battle, from a tactical point of view, perhaps it was a good thing to lose over that, rather than something that was a policy type of situation . . .
>
> Obviously I felt people would be sceptical and understandably so. I think I actually said to Richard in an informal interview, perhaps because of the nature of the school that I had come from, that it might make them feel more sceptical and there was initially a feeling of slight distance which is absolutely understandable. I deliberately tried not to push and press ideas that I had brought from my last school.
>
> I felt when I came here I had to not do a hard-sell job otherwise I would, I am sure, have alienated people, so I played a fairly low profile and just used my own classroom as an example of the direction I would like to see the school moving.
>
> (Deputy)

At the end of the year Teresa looked back on her first term as deputy head and said:

> I consciously placed myself in a partnership with Richard, working with a team of teachers, not against a team of teachers [so] . . . that people felt we were working altogether as a partnership, with senior management people leading that team but very much that we were members of that team and we want to be.
>
> (Deputy)

The evidence from the head, staff and Teresa showed that whilst it took time for the new deputy head to settle into both the school and the role, the change proved to be helpful to Richard's, and now Teresa's, desire to develop a new culture.

EXAMPLES OF CONTINUITY

The co-existence of change and continuity has already been noted. To separate the two, in the way this chapter does, is misleading for it presents too straightforward a picture of each and of how they interrelate. Nevertheless, our account of the schools would be incomplete without further discussion of the notion of continuity and of the ways in which heads and staff sought to ensure that it was maintained.

History

Each school had its own history and historians, as the stories relating to headteacher succession have suggested. The retelling of the school's history served a number of purposes for its staff. 'History' was accounts of 'what we do well', and 'why we are special'. It demonstrated how the school had developed and explained why some things were as they were and how the school had previously experienced changes and developments:

> When the school first opened it had been very small, with only me, two other teachers, and 26 children. Both teachers subsequently became deputy head of the school in turn and moved on to headships in the same county.
> I didn't have a class the first year although I taught groups as the children moved in and the two classes got fairly large. But the second year we had one more member of staff which made two infant classes, but the junior class was rather large and the children were from seven to eleven, so I made a class of third- and fourth-year juniors for myself. It wasn't very big, it was only about 18, but I did actually teach, because again as the village head this is where you actually influence staff if you're teaching yourself, and it was very helpful at that stage to do that.
> We were four classes in the second year and then it sort of grew a class a year . . . It's the same also with staffing, only having to look for one teacher each year I could really concentrate on that person and choose the next person I felt would fit into the team and was able to think, 'Well, what do we need now, yes, I've got some good basic teachers and I'm looking for somebody who can offer a bit more, something different.'
> (Head, Sedgemoor)

> Then three years ago, when Isobel was away for a year as advisory head, there was a sudden staff exodus, largely for promotion. It was at that moment that Dennis became acting, then permanent, deputy head, and Sally, Veronica and Peter joined the staff. At the same time Isobel returned to rebuild the staff that had begun to disperse in her absence. Dennis had been a critical link between the 'old' and the 'new' school, and was now the only remaining full-time teacher from the 'old'.
> (Yeomans, 1986c)

and:

> The school's history was alive in the memory of the head (in particular) and many of the staff (some of the welfare helpers, for example, had known the school as pupils, mothers, volunteers and/or dining room helpers). The development of the school under the present head who has held the post for 20 years has affected her thinking and practice and those of her teachers. So too have significant incidents (such as the rebuilding programme, the head's visit to Buckingham Palace in recognition of her services to multi-cultural education, and particular community celebrations).
> (Nias, 1986)

History reinforced a sense of common pride, by affirming the way in which staff had endured and survived difficult times:

> Margaret and I used to shove newspapers in the cracks round the windows to try and keep the cold out. Well again you see, all those things give you common ground, common understanding. When Kath touched the drainpipe it fell off in her hand and she went flying — all those sorts of things. . . . We kept one another going.
>
> (Deputy, Lowmeadow)

> Julia and I were over there when we had a very, very bad winter. And the only heating we had was overhead gas heating on concrete floors. And so consequently you used to end the day feeling your brain was a jelly and that your legs were icicles. Julia and I have the same sense of humour so we made a joke of it. Really that was the only way we survived over there. . . . As I say we both helped each other, we could pop our heads round and say 'Gosh look at this, you know, it's raining in here' . . . I think perhaps that did more than anything to make us get on so well because we shared that time together under very difficult circumstances.
>
> (Teacher, Lowmeadow)

Historical tales also helped newcomers to make sense of their new staff group for they explained not only 'the way we were' but also why things today are as they are. For example, explanations as to why children entered assembly as they did at Greenfields revealed that current patterns of behaviour had sprung from past negotiations and agreements among the staff.

Routines and Rituals

Two other obvious ways of maintaining continuity were established routines and rituals. On the face of it, routines are relatively superficial devices used to keep the organization working smoothly but they play an important part in ensuring continuity. Each school appeared to have located at least one regular supply teacher to cover for absent staff and these, when available, reduced the school's sense that it was experiencing change. In turn, one reason why these supply teachers were willing to keep returning was because they found the schools' routines predictable:

> It's so organized, everybody's so helpful. Miss Proctor sets such a wonderful example and everybody just follows on. Some schools are so disorganized you don't really know what's going on and it's really hard to follow in somebody's footsteps. You tend to do your own thing. But not here.
>
> (Temporary teacher, Lowmeadow)

Other examples were arrangements for registers and children bringing money into school, and habits over communications (e.g., notes and written messages). Together, the smooth operation of these administrative details gave staff a sense of security. Moreover, this sense of security was a felt experience: the school felt stable because familiar, unchanging patterns continued. In Chapter 4 we argued that predictability helped to establish trust; routines contributed towards creating the conditions in which trust could develop.

Also, routines demonstrated that values were consistent right through the organization (Peters and Waterman, 1982) so that, for example, routines to do with collecting registers, displays, sending messages, showed the same concern for individuals and interdependence as major rituals did. Routines should not therefore be seen as trivial or irrelevant details, but as important clues to a school's culture.

Assemblies

It was also important for a school to have rituals which were predictable in form and content. Because these occasions had a symbolic as well as practical dimension, they reaffirmed for members those aspects of institutional life to which particular importance was attached (see Chapters 3 and 4). Assemblies were particularly significant in this respect.

The importance of assemblies has been stressed at a number of points in the book (Chapters 3, 4 and 5), yet it would be a serious omission to exclude them here for they contributed to the school's sense of continuity in a number of ways. They brought the whole school together and kept staff in touch with one another. They were at one and the same time a demonstration of the continuing potency of the school's or head's guiding beliefs and a further reinforcement of them. Perhaps more than any other single aspect of school life assemblies assured staff and head that the school, and all it stood for, was still there:

> Sometimes when I sit and watch a class assembly I feel I'm watching the school which is perhaps a peculiar thing to say. I don't want to say every single time but there are times when I can watch it and think, this is what we are all about. . . . And sometimes Dennis and I will say, that's become quite a Sedgemoor Assembly.
>
> (Head, Sedgemoor)

Keeping in Touch

When one member of the team left, the rest coped with their loss by keeping in touch (e.g., by letters, telephone, meetings on in-service courses). Also, since staff saw each other every day and were used to working closely together, some saw holidays as interrupting the contact between them, and wanted to continue the links during the breaks:

> A few of [the staff] actually said 'Look, don't worry about things in the holidays. Here's my phone number', and I was given their phone numbers to contact them if I had got any worries.
>
> (Teacher, Hutton)

> We got together in the summer holiday with Phyl and Stella for some reason and we spent a long time pushing things around and we just came to the decision together.
>
> (Teacher, Lavender Way)

In short, keeping in touch meant that, for some, relationships were constantly and actively maintained, and in the process the idea of the staff group was kept alive.

Leadership

Heads and deputies worked hard at maintaining the culture of their schools as several of the characteristics of leadership discussed in Chapter 6 suggest (e.g., educative leadership, example, membership, the deputies' capacity to become acting heads without causing discontinuity). Apart from anything else the presence of the three long-serving heads of Greenfields, Lowmeadow and Sedgemoor added greatly to cultural continuity in these schools because, as the founders of their schools' cultures, they represented in themselves the ability of the culture to survive over time. They ensured continuity in other ways too.

First, they had the capacity to absorb many of the unplanned, unexpected and urgent demands which occurred in the schools:

> As usual Catherine is thoroughly organized. It's crisis management that she is taking one of the classes whilst the visiting teacher is taking the other spare class. When new parents visit, the head sets the infant class to work with an ancillary supervisor while she shows the parents round. She organizes me for the afternoon to take Amanda's class because she isn't working afternoons. Thus everything runs smoothly without any supply teaching.
>
> (Fieldnote, February, Lavender Way)

Such 'crisis management' was also aided, in part, by the head's awareness and sensitivity to individual or organizational needs:

> Co-ordination is the key skill and it is always somebody's job to ensure that individual efforts are co-ordinated. This is principally Catherine's role. She seems to spend time checking where needs exist, and then helping to fill them.
>
> (Fieldnote, December, Lavender Way)

All this meant that heads had to have the stamina to cope with an unenviable workload:

> Everybody's tired, I'm very tired. The staff have been saying 'Don't know how you're managing to get through all this', and being very sympathetic. I know at one point I had two advisers at different ends of the school at the same time, trying to talk to me. We were having a lot of complaints from the kitchen staff about their hours, and so on. Jim and I had to do all that dining furniture ourselves. Lots of little things which you quite happily do, but they all seem to have come at once. Then there are the staffroom meetings and this burglary business and the accident yesterday to a kitchen lady.
>
> (Head, Greenfields)

Second, the heads and others set up an organization which worked even when circumstances altered or when staff were absent or changing. Third, the heads' sensitivity meant that they could empathize with others and foresee changes in individual staff:

> I think it is very important to put yourself in other people's positions. Very, very often, all day long, I think 'What are the staff doing?' (so I can be more aware of what their problems are).
>
> (Head, Lowmeadow)

In other words heads (and deputies) managed to anticipate and absorb many of the changes which could potentially have disturbed their schools. In so doing they maintained a greater degree of organizational stability than might otherwise have been the case and in the process protected their colleagues from undue emotional and organizational disturbance. At the same time, because the heads' behaviour was consistent with their beliefs (see Chapter 5) they made continuity manifest in the ways in which they coped with change.

SUMMARY

Even the most apparently stable of these schools was full of change. It took place at different levels and in varying and overlapping ways, since several kinds of change occurred simultaneously. The culture of the schools was therefore under constant threat.

Faced with such a degree of change the heads and their staffs consciously cultivated continuity. The heads established an organization which was resilient, willingly absorbed demands and anticipated changes before they became too disturbing. Their deputies also minimized disturbances, particularly when the head was absent. Other staff contributed to continuity through the retelling of historical tales, keeping in touch with one another and partaking in rituals and routines.

The co-existence of change and continuity meant that neither was ever total. In the daily dynamic of life in these schools both were simultaneously present. Yet, although they co-existed, they did not necessarily do so in equal or unalterable measure. At any moment in the day there could be greater or smaller amounts of change or continuity, each affecting the culture of the school in more or less fundamental ways.

Change and continuity not only co-existed but were linked, each acting as a counterbalance to the other. Given their interconnection and the potential each had for affecting school culture, we can portray the latter as being in a state of dynamic equilibrium: that is, involved in a constant process of balancing the forces of change and continuity. Furthermore, this dynamic equilibrium can be seen as cultural stability. Stability does not suggest a fixed and permanent state, rather it indicates a temporary position of balance in the midst of change and movement.

Lastly, we should recognize that change and continuity had an emotional content. Each was both experienced and felt. Changes in life circumstances, in children's development, in staff or brought about by a crisis were not perceived as external affairs, objectively noted and dealt with. They were felt experiences expressed as relief, pressure, delight, anger and happiness. Similarly, continuity was described in terms of friendship, affection, empathy, community and family. As organizations of adults and children these were places infected with feelings.

Yet notions of change and continuity could also be applied to matters of school policy. So far we have paid little attention to how policies were made and implemented, and differences resolved. Chapter 8 will therefore consider these matters.

Chapter 8

Implementing Policy and Resolving Differences

In our discussion of leadership, and elsewhere, we have made mention of school policies but have so far paid little attention to the ways in which these were decided upon or implemented. Similarly, we have pointed out that in two schools in particular differences existed between individuals or sub-groups or between one or more of these and the headteacher, but we have not examined how such differences were confronted and resolved. We may also have given the impression that no interpersonal or inter-professional differences existed in the other three schools, a state of affairs which is far from the truth. So in this chapter we look, in respect of all the schools, at how policies were made and carried out and how the staff dealt with differences. We examine the widespread reliance upon negotiation and compromise which characterized day-to-day decision-making, especially in the collaborative schools, and the associated preference for informal rather than formal types of decision-making.

POWER, AUTHORITY AND INFLUENCE

Our analysis rests upon distinctions we wish to make between three related concepts — power, authority and influence. Schools are, by common consent, places in which control is a central issue. The question is not whether teachers feel the need to control children but how this is done. One answer has been given by Waller (1932; 1961 edn, p. 9) who, over fifty years ago, argued that within schools the interests of teachers and children are constantly and inexorably in conflict and that in consequence schools have a 'despotic political structure'. This, he claimed, 'seems to hold true for nearly all types of school and for all about equally' (*ibid.*). In the project schools we did not find this to be the case and suggest that Waller's generalization needs modifying in two ways: to take account of the differences between power and authority, and to allow for the use of influence. The first two concepts describe in different ways one person's capacity to make others do something which they otherwise would not do. The third indicates a state in which people can dispose others favourably towards a particular thought or action without possessing the ability to make them behave or act in specific ways.

Power implies the use of force, whether in coercive or other forms (Etzioni, 1964). It is often associated with a strategy which Pollard (1985, p. 189), in a study of teacher–pupil relationships, calls 'domination'. In classrooms, domination is most obviously exemplified by coercive displays such as threats, sarcasm, verbal abuse or humiliation, as well as, sometimes, by physical violence or restraint. Pollard comments that it is unusual to find domination in routine use in primary schools and we would argue that it is even more rare to encounter it in staffrooms. Although it can occur (Nias, 1980), we did not record any instances of its use among adults in the project schools.

In their dealings with children, teachers also sometimes use normative power (Etzioni, 1964), that is, they make appeals to conscience or manipulate affective rewards such as smiles, or symbolic ones such as stars. This form of domination is also found in some staffrooms. Its effectiveness depends on the existence of a close personal relationship between leader and led, or upon the latter's identification with the school as a reified institution (as in the well-known admonition 'not to bring the name of the school into disrepute'). As is often the case with the use of normative power in families it can lead to feelings, on the part of the dominated, of resentment, frustration and guilt. In the project schools we sometimes saw headteachers, in particular, using what looked like normative power, but from the reaction of the staff we judged it to be an appeal, by symbolic means, to authority rather than a subtle form of domination. The line between power and authority is not objective, but resides in the mind of those who obey.

The distinction we draw between the two terms follows Weber's claim (Gerth and Mills, 1946) that authority is 'legitimated power', that is, power exercised in accordance with rights which participants accept. We have not used Weber's typology of the bases of authority (traditional, bureaucratic, charismatic) because within the 'culture of collaboration' it is difficult to make, let alone sustain, a distinction between the personal and the professional, the charismatic and the bureaucratic. Occasionally however, we use the term 'formal' to describe authority which is vested in the role rather than the person and which is, therefore, essentially bureaucratic in origin.

Now it will be clear from much that we have written so far, in particular in Chapter 6, that in the project schools the heads had a good deal of authority. The fact that they generally led from within the staff group or team should not be misinterpreted as meaning that they lacked 'legitimated power'; collaborative schools were certainly not institutions which felt that they could dispense with their formal leaders.

Some of the heads' authority was bureaucratic in origin. In addition, as Chapter 6 makes clear, much of their legitimated power derived from their position as 'culture founders' and from the associated tradition that they were the 'owners' of their schools, especially when they had been in post for a long time. Further, they all had considerable personal authority, based on their professional credibility as teachers, their standards of conduct as persons and professionals, their accessibility, willingness to listen, reliability, predictability and the affection in which they were held. Moreover the standing of the heads was enhanced by the fact that deputies and curriculum co-ordinators relied heavily on delegated authority, in carrying out many aspects of their jobs, although these postholders also earned the respect and affection of their colleagues through their own personal and professional behaviour.

The distinction we have drawn between power and authority makes it possible for us to accept Waller's contention that schools are hierarchical institutions without agreeing that they are necessarily therefore despotic. It also enables us to reinterpret his view (1961 edn, p. 10) that a school exists in a state of 'perilous equilibrium' because it is 'a despotism constantly threatened . . . capable of being overturned in a moment, exposed to the instant loss of its stability and its prestige' (*ibid.*). We would agree (Chapters 7 and 9) that the notion of balance is central to an understanding of the project schools. But we find the metaphor more positive than he does because, in the collaborative schools in particular, it encompassed a complex but flexible set of relationships which made the institutions resilient and internally responsive rather than insecure and vulnerable.

These relationships resulted from the mutual dependence which is one characteristic of the culture of collaboration (see Chapter 4). Each member simultaneously controlled and was controlled by all the others. Power was therefore distributed in such a way that even the exercise of legitimated power was offset by the tacit understanding that individuals could, if they felt the need, challenge or negotiate within it. In other words, individuals generally shaped one another's behaviour through influence rather than power and authority. Notwithstanding a greater accretion of authority to some individuals, and at some times rather than others, the staffs of the collaborative schools could not in general force one another to fall into line over particular or general issues.

There is one major exception to this generalization. As Chapters 4 and 6 make plain, the main policy directions relating to the curriculum, teaching methods and discipline within each school were laid down by its head. In this respect alone his/her authority was neither challenged nor counterbalanced by that of other staff members. Yet it could be argued that the equilibrium of the school depended upon and stemmed from these policies and was therefore very vulnerable to changes in them. In this sense, primary schools and the staff within them are 'perilously' balanced, a fact which may account for the profoundly unsettling effects of a change in headteacher (see Chapter 7).

IMPLEMENTING POLICY: USING AUTHORITY

The headteachers of the project schools were conscious of possessing a great deal of authority:

> If it really came to it in the end — making a decision between their views and mine and we'd really thoroughly discussed it — they would in the end say, 'Yes, we'll do it your way because you're the head.' Because although they're very strong, I think that underneath they have got a respect that I'm the head and it's as simple as that.
>
> (Head, Lowmeadow)

> They feel free in staff meetings or discussions with me, to make their opinions known quite clearly. They know that I'm going to accept their opinions, but that there is no one on the staff who is going to express an opinion which will push me in a way that I don't want to go.
>
> (Head, Greenfields)

Their awareness was mirrored by that of their staff:

> As for sitting down at a full staff meeting and chewing over the concept of doing an integrated day, I don't think those of us who were there when Mr Handley came would have dared say that we didn't like it. We got the feeling that this was going to be done and we jolly well had got to try and make it work. And let's face it, if a head says it will, it will, and that's the way it's done, isn't it?
>
> (Teacher, Hutton)

> *Int*: Would one have to accept the Christian basis of this school to work here?
> *Teacher*: I don't think you have to believe it; I think you have to accept it. . . . But you mustn't oppose it or I think life could be difficult. I am not saying it would be but it might be.
>
> (Lowmeadow)

Teachers and ancillaries generally accepted, or came to accept, their heads' authority, even when it was not exerted in an openly assertive fashion:

> Isobel's a very definite lady. . . . If it's something that she disapproves of, then you know there's no way it's worth your doing it here, because it's going to be frowned upon. . . . She does it very carefully. I did a display once and I left a great gap at the bottom and I knew it didn't look right, but I'd spent hours doing it and I thought 'No way I'm going to change it now'. And Isobel very quietly said to me when it had been up a couple of days, 'Did you mean to leave a big gap at the bottom? Why did you leave a big gap?' And I thought 'Down it comes. I'll take the gaps off.' You are made aware of whether it's right or it's wrong, but it's not done nastily. It's just done and you're left then. I don't know what she'd do about it, or whether she'd do anything.
>
> (Teacher, Sedgemoor)

> At break, one of the students asked Miss Proctor, 'Do you mind if I pop out for a few minutes and collect my car, because Mummy's got it and I need it this evening to get to the dentist?' She responded with a long pause and then said, 'Well, it's not the sort of thing the staff do. I'm not going to stop you . . .'. The student countered, 'Don't you want me to go then?' and was answered with, 'I'm not going to stop you going' — and so on. In the end, she did go out but it was made sufficiently awkward for her that she realized that this was unacceptable behaviour. I shall be surprised if she does it again.
>
> (Fieldnote, May, Lowmeadow)

There were occasions when individual staff members were not prepared to conform or felt unable to do so. In these circumstances heads used the full weight of their authority to persuade them to leave the school:

> You've got to be fairly ruthless. If you want a particular kind of school, you've got to have a particular kind of staff and if the staff you've got are not like that, you've either got to persuade them to become like that or you've got to get rid of them . . . I actually did get rid of all the staff, except one — she was an absolute gem. . . . But with the others, their attitudes were all wrong so I had to get rid of them . . . I haven't got any great sympathy for heads who spend years complaining about staff they've inherited. They've got to do something. It sounds unlike me, but I think that underneath you've got to be fairly hard.
>
> (Head, Greenfields)

To achieve similar ends they were also ready to invoke their formal authority. At Hutton, for instance, the head terminated the temporary contracts of two teachers because he did not feel they 'fitted in' with his educational policies, and at Lavender Way the head instituted disciplinary procedures against the caretaker for breach of contract. There was historical evidence of similar events in some of the other schools. Significantly, the exception was Sedgemoor, to which, as a new school, the head had been able to appoint all the staff.

IMPLEMENTING POLICY: USING INFLUENCE

But although headteachers could and did encourage or, in the last resort, require staff to leave their schools, they and the schools' other formal leaders found it much harder to alter the practice of those who remained. It is, in particular, notoriously difficult for anyone other than teachers themselves to change the ways in which they behave or to modify their pupils' learning experiences. This account of a Lavender Way staff meeting, run by the science co-ordinator (who was also the deputy), makes clear the relative impotence of the schools' formal leaders in relation to the pedagogic practice of individuals:

> For most of the time Ben is talking there is absolute silence, as there is at the end . . . Catherine spends some time talking about why the boxes would be useful with infants and saying that it wouldn't be necessary to follow them with a work card — that they could be used in any way. Eventually Ben says 'You may like to look at them, or not, and try things out. I take it that I can leave them in the science area where you can take them to your classrooms or not as you choose.'
> There is no response from the staff to Ben until after the meeting proper is finished and though he says 'I take it then that you'd be happy to use the boxes' it's clear that the silence doesn't imply consent. Rita says not a word throughout and towards the end very carefully folds the sheets Ben has provided, and then proceeds to play with her pen. Her body language seems to say that she really doesn't want to know at all. . . . When the meeting has officially finished, Sandy and Phyl talk together about some of the things they've done, but I'm left with the feeling that some staff will do nothing about it at all and so I suspect is Ben. At the end of school he and I talk about the lunchtime events. I ask if he thinks anything will happen. He shrugs and says that it's a way of trying to get science done and trying to get people to think about how science could be tackled . . . [Yet] without the staff deciding actively to engage themselves in the issues Ben is raising, they are not aired at all, we simply sidestep them by not talking about them. Those who felt science was not necessary or didn't want to change, didn't make that statement. Theirs are legitimate views and ones that ought to have been discussed. In fact Ben deliberately goes out of his way not to be prescriptive and insist what people should do or even whether they should do anything at all. The message of Catherine quietly sitting and her supportive comments afterwards is that she does support Ben's innovation, but that she's not going to insist that they take particular initiatives in science.

(Fieldnote, September, Lavender Way)

Four of the heads realized that they could not easily change the way in which teachers behaved in their classrooms. Instead they relied on their capacity to influence teachers' educational beliefs in what they perceived to be the 'right' directions. The fifth, at Hutton, moved during the year along this path, seeming to become increasingly aware that open displays of authority were, in this respect, not only ineffectual but counterproductive; he could not modify teachers' practice simply by telling them what they 'should' be doing and his efforts to do so confused some and alienated others.

The success of heads' attempts, and those of other formal leaders, to influence their colleagues depend on a number of factors. One was visibility. Staff expected their heads, and often deputies, to be exemplars of the schools' professed policies. In the project schools, the heads fulfilled this expectation not only through assembly but also by interacting informally with all the staff as often as they could throughout the school day (see Chapter 6). Deputies, being closely tied to their teaching areas, had a more difficult task in being 'conspicuous' (Deputy, Lavender Way) as professional examples but they all succeeded by one means or another, not least of which was, once again, assembly:

> [After listening to a staff conversation arising out of the deputy's assembly that morning] Obviously this is one of the main ways in which curriculum development takes place. Staff enjoyed what she and her class did, several have mentioned how many ideas are fed into them through this kind of assembly and they often seem to develop them.
> (Fieldnote, March, Lowmeadow)

Of all the formal school leaders, curriculum co-ordinators found it the hardest to exercise influence through example, partly because union action reduced, or eliminated, opportunities for staff workshops and partly because there was almost no time in which they could work alongside their colleagues (Chapter 6; see also Campbell, 1985; Taylor, 1986).

A second major factor was communication. Leaders who communicated their wishes and expectations directly and in unambiguous terms helped staff to understand exactly what they wanted:

> Jane quoted Miss Proctor as having said that it was no good being cross with the welfare helper if the children were swinging from the coathooks in the cloakroom. It was up to the class teacher to see that the helper knew exactly what standards the class teacher required, and how to meet them.
> (Fieldnote, March, Lowmeadow)

> He came in full of this integrated day but quite honestly even after four years nobody really knows exactly what he wants. That's our biggest problem as a whole staff. . . . We are all trying different things, and he'll never come down and say 'No, that's not right, try it this way.'
> (Teacher, Hutton)

> I've been trying for five years to talk to Richard and find out what activities he would really like to be happening in this school. . . . The one way that made it work was him coming into the classroom, me being totally open about what was happening and then letting him constructively criticize what was happening, and make suggestions.
> (Teacher, Hutton)

The manner in which communication took place was also crucial in determining how much attention individuals paid to it. Several factors were operating here. As has often been pointed out (e.g., Lortie, 1975; King, 1978; Alexander, 1984), the occupational culture of primary teachers does not attach much importance to the force of abstract ideas, preferring the practical and pragmatic to the theoretical. By association, it is an oral rather than a literary culture. In none of the schools did teachers refer spontaneously to school documents such as curriculum guidelines, and when these did exist they appeared to influence specific aspects of classroom organization rather than educational beliefs. As Yeomans (1986c) noted after discussion with the head during his first visit to Sedgemoor, 'This is obviously not a school in which paper is an important energy source.' Similarly, only at Greenfields and Hutton did staff meetings regularly have written agenda or minutes, and at Hutton where the head had put an enormous amount of effort into written guidelines and statements of aims, teachers tended to be dismissive of them. For example:

> You are told it is all in the book, but you are not quite sure that you are interpreting the book right and . . . you haven't got time to keep going back to the book and re-reading it.
>
> (Teacher, Hutton)

Tone was important too. When written communications were used, those which were perceived by their receivers as being in tune with the culture of the school were heeded a good deal more than those which were not. So, in the collaborative schools, notes generally had the informal quality of personal conversation:

> 'I'll put the apparatus up unless anybody particularly doesn't want to use it.'
> 'Ta very much.'
> 'Are you free this dinnertime, Dennis, for buying plants?' (Margaret).
>
> (Extract from deputy head's 'Notice Book', Sedgemoor)

By contrast, at Hutton, the following notes were more typical:

> *General Notes*
> 1. With reference to my comment about tidiness earlier — I am becoming concerned about the general untidiness of the classrooms, particularly art areas. Children should be capable (or made to be so) of keeping areas tidy as they use them and cleaning up waste materials after themselves. Worktops should be left tidy at the end of each day so that they can be cleaned.
> 2. Please ensure that apparatus such as tape recorders is not left in classrooms overnight.
>
> (Extract from 'Staff Newsletter', November, Hutton)

Similarly, within the project schools staff implicitly distinguished between the use of authority and authoritarianism. When they detected the latter, as at Hutton they sometimes did in the manner of their head, particularly towards the start of the year, their response was grudging. As the head of Sedgemoor said, 'The "do you think?" approach is better . . .'. Accordingly all the heads, with the exception of Hutton, tended to phrase demands as requests, directions as questions. Their example was generally followed by their deputies and curriculum co-ordinators:

> [The new deputy] took things head on but not in a stroppy way — which is what people were expecting. She'd be apologizing for putting things forward, saying, 'I didn't want to come in and change everything all at once.'
>
> (Teacher, Hutton)

> So I think perhaps next half term I shall suggest that . . . but I wouldn't say 'Tell you what, Phyl, let's do this', I think that is the wrong approach. I would say, 'Well, how do you feel about doing that, do you feel OK about doing that?' or I hope I would. . . .
>
> (Teacher, Lavender Way)

> Catherine said, 'Could you get people to stay after school?' so I said 'OK' . . . I was a bit dubious, so I said, 'Look, are you happy to stay after school?' not 'There will be a meeting after school' and everybody did and there didn't seem to be a problem.
>
> (Teacher, Lavender Way)

Heads, and sometimes deputies, were particularly skilled at expressing disapproval in subtle ways:

> She wouldn't make a point of saying 'I want to see you today for a particular reason.' A chat would perhaps occur and things that she's thought would come into the conversation naturally so you wouldn't feel as though you were being told off, are you with me?
>
> (Teacher, Sedgemoor)

> [After watching an incident] Julia seldom draws attention to things that people have done wrong, and never in a way that makes them feel ashamed, threatened or under-valued. But the message is clear.
>
> (Fieldnote, January, Lowmeadow)

In this context, humour (see Chapter 5) was particularly important in all the schools, often being used to soften reprimands and obliquely to draw individuals' attention to minor deviations from school policy or from accepted standards of behaviour. Here too, as Chapter 6 makes clear, deputies tended to be prominent, perhaps because their authority was delegated and they therefore had to rely even more than their heads did upon influence.

The importance which was evidently attached to the tone of oral and written communications in turn draws attention to individuals' capacity to read between the lines, that is, to the extent to which they attached the same meanings as others did to words, phrases and actions (Chapter 4). Yet to learn the subtleties conveyed by shared understandings took time and cultural sensitivity:

> I found that it took a while to develop the sensitivity to what was expected of me. Sometimes I didn't pick up the vibes as it were, and it was a very hard time, I must say. It has sometimes happened in the past that people haven't realized that what could be a directive can be put in a fairly pleasant, observing sort of way but is meant to be followed through. They haven't taken that hint.
>
> (Teacher, Lowmeadow)

A third way in which heads could indirectly influence their staffs was by determining opportunities for interaction between them. Appreciating the effect which proximity has upon patterns of interaction, and so upon staff learning, they often did their best to ensure that organization or buildings brought together staff members who were likely to have a beneficial effect upon one another's practice or attitudes. Particular types of interaction were often carefully devised:

> When you get down to the nuts and bolts of curriculum planning [in staff discussion], all that stuff comes into the open. . . . Some of the underlying things that shape the way teachers work with children come to the surface. You don't have to threaten them and say 'I want it done this way or that way.'
>
> (Deputy, Lavender Way)

> From the start I've been aware that my progression round the school, week by week, has been very carefully planned by the head. Though I can't yet judge why I am being placed with particular teachers at specific times, I am aware that her choice is not random.
>
> (Fieldnote, December, Lowmeadow)

Finally, heads could exercise another form of indirect influence, through the staff group. Once the majority of the staff shared their beliefs about the purposes of education and how these could best be achieved, they did not often have to act overtly or alone. As a staff became a group, its normative influence reduced the need for displays of overt authority by the schools' formal leaders:

So partly it's us actually . . . we just have this standard. It's all of us, it's ourselves, we're all part of it. . . . Anyone who didn't hold those opinions would probably not fit in.

(Secretary, Lowmeadow)

CONFLICTS OF INTEREST

No matter how effective heads were in communicating their expectations to their staffs and in securing the latter's acquiescence in carrying out their policies, disagreements sometimes occurred. In all the schools there were people who did not always or in all respects agree with their heads or with each other, so the apparent cohesion of the staff group sometimes concealed unresolved and apparently unresolvable differences of belief, value or practice:

Everything in the garden isn't always lovely. You're not always seeing eye to eye a hundred per cent with everybody, because you're not realistic if you think that's going to happen.

(Teacher, Sedgemoor)

We have a meeting and everybody has their say and then we feel that everyone's agreed. Because people have agreed they will do so-and-so, we do, or most people do. We all know some people won't or not all of the time. We realize we can't change them, but there is no reason why we should join them, or let them think we approve. We just agree to differ.

(Teacher, Lowmeadow)

The existence of latent disagreements even within collaborative staffs should not surprise us. In the first place, all staff were simultaneously members of several different sub-cultures which could be in conflict with one another — when, for instance, teachers with a personal commitment to children felt they had to take industrial action out of loyalty to principles of union solidarity, or when a male caretaker was asked to undertake cleaning tasks hitherto carried out by women. Secondly, in every social group, however closely knit, individuals have their own 'interests-at-hand' (Pollard, 1985, p. 24) which will unavoidably run counter to one another at some point. Pollard suggests that teachers' chief interest-at-hand is the preservation of their self-image (see also Woods, 1981; Nias, 1984), and Nias (1989b) argues that because this self-image includes individuals' most deeply held and closely defended self-defining values, it is closely associated with their sense of personal worth. Long before they enter their profession, teachers are people rooted in their own reference groups and sub-cultures (e.g., family, ethnic group, church, political party). They carry these 'selves' into their work. In consequence they have alternative lives and commitments out of school which sometimes conflict with their professional responsibilities. More fundamentally, they also have beliefs about the way the world is and should be which are an integral part of their self-image and therefore of their self-esteem. Moreover, many appear to choose teaching because they want to propagate or live consistently with these beliefs and the values associated with them (Nias, 1989b) so their self-concept is particularly closely involved with their work. If we accept these hypotheses, that teachers seek to preserve their sense of personal identity, that this incorporates deeply internalized beliefs and values and that it is closely linked to a sense of self-worth, it is inevitable that clashes will occur within school staffs. Indeed, the more teachers identify with their work, the more they feel it is imbued with values that they see as important, and the more closely they are expected to work together, the less likely it is that they will be able to avoid intermittent conflict.

Although no systematic attempt similar to those by Woods, Pollard and Nias has been made to identify heads' 'interests-at-hand' there is evidence in this study to suggest that these too are self-referential. All the heads were conscious of their educative function; though no longer full-time in the classroom they had a powerful instinct to teach. As teachers, they were aware of their own beliefs and values; they all had a 'mission' or 'vision' which they wished to realize in their schools. Moreover they were encouraged to identify closely with their work by the general assumption, in which they shared, that they were the 'owners' of their schools (see Chapter 6 for elaboration of all these points). In other words, heads have even more incentive than teachers to preserve through their work their self-image and sense of self-esteem. Their 'selves' are heavily invested in 'their' schools, particularly in the form of the mission which they wish to accomplish. The ways in which they perceive their schools to be developing reflect strongly upon their self-concept and can radically affect their feelings of personal worth.

Now headteachers can accomplish their 'mission' only with the co-operation of their staffs. They are in this sense heavily dependent upon them, just as the latter depend in large measure on their heads for the opportunities and resources to work in ways which preserve their sense of self. Even in schools where teachers operate with considerable autonomy they and their headteachers are locked into a situation in which both need the other, if either is to achieve their goals. Further, the more committed heads are to involving their staff in decision-making, to working closely with them and to encouraging them to work together, the more likely it is they will from time to time be faced with conflicts of interest.

Disagreement is then an inescapable phenomenon in school staffrooms, as it is to a greater or lesser extent in all social groups. Our concern should not be that it exists but to discover the strategies which were used in the project schools to contain it or turn it to constructive ends.

Preventing Conflict

Three main factors prevented the build-up of lasting conflict. First, the culture of the collaborative schools made it possible for differences to be defined as normal and seen as capable of easy assimilation by the group. Indeed it was necessary for the survival of the culture that this should be so, for the values to which most of the staff subscribed stressed the importance of interdependence, of the team and the group as well as the individual. The less open disagreement there was, the easier it was for everyone to sustain these values. So membership of a common culture, resulting as this did in shared definitions of reality (see Chapter 1), enabled staff to perceive disagreements, even quite powerful ones, as everyday, non-disruptive occurrences. To be sure, as Chapter 3 makes clear, the notion of what constituted 'normal' was differently construed by members of each school staff, but the underlying trend in Greenfields, Lowmeadow and Sedgemoor was the same. In all three schools it was towards the legitimation of individual differences and the assumption that their existence did not threaten the cohesion of the team or the group.

The tendency for disagreements to be perceived and therefore treated as a natural part of human intercourse showed itself in several ways. Incidents which in other schools might have caused lasting resentments were dismissed as personal idiosyncrasies or, more positively, were treated with kindness and tolerance. Headteachers, teachers and ancillaries were aware that they were all liable to behave irritably or unreasonably when suffering from tension, and they made allowances accordingly:

> They are able to see that things you normally cope with, if you've got personal stress or anxiety for any reason, you just don't cope with. So things don't flare up out of proportion.
>
> (Teacher, Lowmeadow)

In this context, it was important that people knew one another well and could therefore recognize and deal appropriately with one another's bad temper, frustration or lack of sensitivity. Affection also played a part. Staff members in Greenfields, Lowmeadow and Sedgemoor were unashamedly fond of one another; some spoke of loving each other (see Chapter 4). They were therefore additionally willing to forgive or to make amends, that is to behave as if inconsiderate or abrasive words or actions were temporary deviations from a generally accepted norm of interpersonal consideration and tolerance.

In this respect, much was due to the school's 'pastoral leaders' (Chapter 6) who displayed a marked capacity to listen, to see other people's point of view, to respond constructively but sensitively to it and to help others to do so too. Several people paid tribute, in this context in particular, to the ancillaries, but 'peace-makers' could be found throughout the staff group. Significantly, at Lavender Way and Hutton, the part such people played in relation to the rest of the staff became more important as the year went on:

> I know now that you've somehow got to stand apart from [a disagreement] and yet be involved in it. Do you understand what I mean? You can't take somebody's side on an issue when you've got your own different ideas on it. So you've got to try and put those across, but not to be saying, 'I think that's quite wrong, you should be doing so-and-so.'
>
> (Teacher, Lavender Way)

> That's how I see my role — it's one of uniting people. Probably the key factor in the personal relationship side is trying to help people to understand somebody else's perception of the particular thing that has caused whatever it is.
>
> (Deputy, Hutton)

'Pastoral leaders' also played an important part in lowering the emotional temperature of interpersonal encounters or highly charged situations by the deliberate use of humour (see Chapters 5 and 6; and Nias, 1987b).

So far the capacity of the staff in the collaborative schools to perceive potentially divisive actions as non-threatening to the solidarity of the group may have appeared to trivialize the differences which existed between them. That this was not the case becomes apparent when one considers the way in which they dealt with the divisions caused by union action. During 1985–6 many primary school staffs faced the necessity

of deciding what stance they would take on this matter. The decision they made
threw into relief among staff groups issues of principle that they could not escape,
yet which they were ill-equipped by training or tradition to resolve. Participation in
the culture of collaboration had a noticeable effect upon the way in which staff in
different schools dealt with this harsh reality. Where the culture was dominant,
headteachers and teachers tacitly defined their own actions and those of their colleagues as non-disruptive. Differences which had within them the seeds of interpersonal conflict were treated not as if they did not exist but as if they would not be
allowed to fracture staff cohesion. To put it another way, the three collaborative
staffs were obviously determined from the start to 'frame' union action in ways which
would not endanger their close social and working relationships. At Lowmeadow, it
was ignored. Not only did everything proceed as normal, but the topic was seldom
mentioned in the staffroom. Only two teachers belonged to one of the unions which
was taking action. Both followed the rest of the staff in taking none and, when asked
how they reconciled this with their NUT membership, they said that the union made
allowance for cases such as theirs, where one or two teachers were in a minority on
a staff. At Sedgemoor, where the deputy spent the Christmas holidays preparing a
musical production with which the staff decided in January not to proceed, there was
an implicit agreement to deal openly but unobtrusively with a situation which nobody
enjoyed:

> People have been aware of how other people feel. I was PAT anyway, and I explained
> the situation to everybody else, I said 'I appreciate the way you feel about it, the same
> way that you appreciate the way I do.' It didn't really cause any friction.
>
> (Teacher, Sedgemoor)

> I remember coming to school with Veronica and we had differences of opinion about
> strike action, Veronica didn't agree with it and I did, and we talked about it. We had
> discussions about it, but we weren't prepared to fall out about it. I didn't agree with
> what she said and she didn't agree with what I said, I could understand her point of
> view, she could understand mine. Obviously somewhere along the line something must
> have influenced us to make us believe what we felt and therefore that was that really.
>
> (Teacher, Sedgemoor)

At Greenfields, the deputy was employed half-time on union (NUT) and Education
Committee duties and was an active supporter of strike action. Four other teachers
were NUT members, taking action, and the head, as a member of NAS/UWT, was
broadly in sympathy with their stance. One teacher, who also taught in the mobile
classroom across the playground, was a PAT member. Such a mixture of attitudes
presented potential opportunities for abrasive encounters, scapegoating or divisive-
ness. Indeed, the PAT member spent increasing amounts of time in her classroom,
alone except for the ancillary worker who also spent much of her day there. On
some occasions the head spent his breaks in the staffroom alone with the secretary
and ancillary, five staff being at a union meeting and one on playground duty. In
addition, the school closed for half-days, even though not everyone believed in
striking, and both NUT members and the PAT member decided not to participate
in the Christmas pantomime which was, by tradition, the headteacher's personal joy
and triumph. Notwithstanding, 'there were no signs of tension, frustration or ill-will'
(Fieldnote, September) and several months later the PAT member said:

> Of course, when the NUT members of staff hold their meetings I'm excluded, which I

accept quite happily, and naturally, being the only PAT member, I don't join in discussions about NUT matters which take place frequently in the staffroom in an informal
way. The staff have been very pleasant to me. I can only remember two occasions when
there has been any unpleasantness, which I think is a record when you think of how
long this action has been going on. Really I've found them very kind.

(Fieldnote, March, Greenfields)

The case study reports one of the occasions to which she refers (an open attack by
one teacher upon union action because of its effect on curriculum development in
the school) and the subsequent exchange between herself and the NUT representative, the obvious intention of which was to prevent the disagreement between them
from becoming a lasting rift. She subsequently reflected:

I'd say we all got on very well . . . I think it's because everybody here wants to get on
very well that we achieve that and we overlook each other's faults and take each other,
warts and all, possibly more than we do in any other aspect of our lives. I mean, I
tolerate things here from other people on the staff that I wouldn't readily tolerate at
home and I'm quite sure that other people say the same things about me.

(Teacher, Greenfields)

The tacit refusal of these three schools to perceive union action as capable of
damaging their social and professional relationships, with the result that it did not,
contrasts with the situation at Hutton. There, staff meetings ceased, and because
informal communication in the school was not well established, latent sub-groups
began to develop. By Christmas one teacher felt:

I think it's developing into the two sides of the school. I hardly see anything of the
people on the other side. Before the action we used to see more of each other, people
used to bring sandwiches in at lunchtime.

(Teacher, Hutton)

In the head's view:

Things have disintegrated a bit over the second half of this term, it's partly the industrial
action and not getting together at staff meetings. The things they're doing are hurting
the fabric of this school. . . . It's not that they haven't been working hard, but it's been
isolated in little pockets.

(Head, December, Hutton)

Indeed, so disruptive was the situation felt to be that, when the head unilaterally re-
started staff meetings in January, all the staff came and admitted they were glad to
do so. In other words, because union action had come to be perceived as potentially
divisive, it had had that effect. Professional dialogue among the staff could not start
again until the head made the decision on behalf of them all that it would.

The second main factor preventing the destructive build-up of tension within the
collaborative schools overlaps with the first. Sub-groups were not part of their social
structure, so it was relatively easy for the whole staff group to share common
perspectives, and because they shared common perspectives they did not easily divide
into sub-groups. This cohesion in turn (see Chapter 3) facilitated the development
and maintenance of a single, dominant culture. But the absence of sub-groups at
Greenfields, Lowmeadow and Sedgemoor was not accidental. In part it was due to
careful selection and socialization of staff. It also stemmed from the fact that they
interacted through a network of overlapping pairs, trios and sub-groups, a network
whose existence was encouraged by headteachers. Moreover, the latter sometimes

consciously inhibited the development of exclusive sub-groups by the ways in which they allotted school responsibilities and arranged the use of space. In this respect, union action was peculiarly damaging because heads could do little to offset, for instance, the informal, off-site 'lunch club' which developed in Hutton or the growing isolation of the teacher at Greenfields.

Lowmeadow offers an example of a complex social structure which helped to inhibit the growth of sub-groups. Two members of staff belonged to the NUT, neither did dinner duty and once a week they ate lunch together in the town. Yet others too absented themselves from the dinner table at which much formal and informal business was transacted, and one of these shared out-of-school interests with one of the NUT pair. The other one of this pair had little social contact with any of the staff outside school, but in the staffroom she was a valued raconteur and humorist. Inside school, the head shared a professional interest with one of these two and the deputy often worked with the other. In addition, their classrooms were physically separated, making it easier for them to meet informally during school hours with other staff members than with one another. And so it went on. Social interaction in this school as in the other two collaborative schools was a complex affair. Those who chose to see a good deal of one another outside school tended to interact with other people at work, and vice versa.

A third, related factor was that many of the staff in all the schools led full lives outside school; they were not just teachers or ancillaries, but also musicians, spouses, gardeners, travellers, church members and the like. These other identities gave them, as they said, alternative outlets for stress or ill-humour and, by ensuring that school was not their only preoccupation, prevented them from brooding too long upon the events of the working day.

Agreeing a Working Consensus

Yet notwithstanding, disagreements sometimes occurred even in the collaborative schools. In this respect, the adults in the project schools faced a similar situation in relation to one another to that described by Pollard (1985) as existing in classrooms. It is in the interests of both teachers and children, Pollard argues, that they should work out ways of co-existing in classrooms that safeguard their respective interests-at-hand. This they do by negotiating a 'working consensus', a set of 'tacit conventions and rules which constrain the behaviour of not only the children but also the teacher' (*ibid.*, p. 160). This consensus becomes 'an assumed, taken-for-granted reality which frames each situation' (p.10) and which therefore allows teachers and children broadly to predict and control one another's behaviour. It is based on the asymmetrical power sources of teacher and pupils and can be unilaterally abrogated by a strategy of 'domination' by the one or 'rebellion' by the other. Either strategy makes the working consensus untenable and it is therefore in the long-term interests of both participants to maintain it and to pursue their interests-at-hand by strategies other than open confrontation. One alternative is 'open negotiation . . . where each party seeks to recognize and respect the interests and concerns of the other, in addition to their own' (p. 185). Within the consensus which governs the conduct of each classroom, teachers and children can therefore use open negotiation to reconcile conflicts of interest.

If one substitutes 'headteacher' for 'teacher' and 'staff' for 'children' in Pollard's account, one has a reasonably accurate description of the social situation facing adults in schools. They too are bound mutually to negotiate 'interdependent ways of coping' which involve 'some degree of accommodation of each other's interests' (p.158). To be sure, adults can escape from one another more easily and more often than teachers and pupils can, but the more committed they are, as the staff in the project schools generally were, to joint decision-making and the implementation of agreed policies, the more difficult this becomes, and the more likely they are to want to evolve a 'working consensus' in which differences are resolved by 'open negotiation'.

In any case, as a strategy for conflict resolution, negotiation was particularly suited to the collaborative schools. Since the mission and therefore the interests-at-hand of the heads included the acceptance by the staff of collaborative ways of working, a policy of 'domination' would have been self-defeating. By the same token, neither 'submission' nor 'rebellion' would have been acceptable to teachers and ancillaries who themselves valued interdependence, with its corollary of mutual influence. As a result, compromise suited all participants, so they were generally disposed to work towards it.

There was another reason why the staffs of these schools were disinclined to fall out professionally with their heads or with each other. For the most part, they enjoyed a high level of job satisfaction, much of which derived from the fact that they found their work self-enhancing. Most importantly their schools' main policies did not conflict with their own educational principles:

> Obviously we must agree with the way Miss Proctor does it or we wouldn't be able to stay here. I mean we wouldn't be able to do a job that was totally against the way we felt was right, so obviously to us it is the right way.
>
> (Ancillary, Lowmeadow)

In particular, they agreed with their heads' determination to put the interests of the children before everything else, even when they themselves were inconvenienced as a result:

> [Of the rehearsals for the Christmas play] I did find myself getting a bit frustrated when rehearsals started. It did start to get me down, because as a teacher you've got plans, you've got things that you want to complete. But then I had to stop and say to myself that I'd got to make a real effort to be flexible. The children do learn so much. . . .
>
> (Teacher, Lowmeadow)

> It was that real concerted effort to make a compromise work that finally pulled me through and it was very successful. I have found that the children were doing the most exciting and interesting things, they were doing things that were coming from their own ideas. They weren't coming from me at all, and I began to realize this is much better, because they are doing something that they've chosen to do . . . I began to see some really good educational work. They were developing so much better this way.
>
> (Teacher, Hutton)

> One has to be ever aware, I think, that a school that is lovely and does really well for the children doesn't just happen. The sort of flowing curriculum, the interconnection, doesn't just happen. It can be at the expense of individuals, but there you go.
>
> (Teacher, Lowmeadow)

Further, active participation in the adult life of the school increased people's sense of self-esteem. Chapter 4 described the ways in which the self-regard of individuals was enhanced by praise and thanks, by public recognition of talents and expertise, by the fact that disapproval was expressed in ways that left their dignity intact. But they also enjoyed and valued the sense that 'everybody's involved and pulling together to a common purpose' (Teacher, Lowmeadow). In other words their sense of professional competence and so of personal worth was heightened by knowing that they were part of an effective team and of a supportive, appreciative group. Indeed, so powerful was the satisfaction to be derived from 'pulling together' that individuals persisted in it even when the going was rough:

> Commenting on last term, she said, 'It was, I think, the most wearing term emotionally we've ever had.' When I asked why they all appeared to survive it so equably she said, more or less in these words, 'I think we've just made up our minds not to get riled by one another. There was the odd harsh word between individuals but on the whole we have a commitment to one another as a team. We value what we've got and we want to keep it.'

> (Fieldnote, April, Lowmeadow)

Similar factors also encouraged the heads in the collaborative schools to work through compromise. They too enjoyed a substantial measure of personal fulfilment and therefore of job satisfaction, both of which derived in part from the fact that they felt they had accomplished their mission (Chapter 6). Although they were not self-satisfied, they were conscious that their most important policies had been accepted by their staffs and that their schools were now running more or less as they wanted them to. They therefore had every incentive to maintain the goodwill and commitment of their teachers and ancillaries by negotiating with them mutually acceptable outcomes to any differences of interest that arose.

Yet such a statement appears to contradict many of the arguments so far advanced in this book. In particular, in Chapters 4 and 5 we suggested that headteachers and staff members actively participated in creating and maintaining a collaborative culture because they held common beliefs about the equal value and interdependence of individuals and groups. Now we are apparently suggesting that they behaved towards one another in the ways that they did because to do so enabled each to satisfy their own interests. Is the culture of collaboration merely a matter, then, of enlightened self-interest, of a negotiated agreement in which all participants make some accommodation to each other's interests in order better to secure their own? Or were members activated by a common desire to create a particular kind of social and moral climate within their schools?

The answer appears to be that both were the case. Heads and the majority of their staffs did indeed believe that individuals should be treated with respect and appreciation and be given the opportunity to develop their potential; at the same time they found that acting in accordance with these beliefs was mutually advantageous. For example, headteachers gave potentially recalcitrant individuals additional time or resources to develop curricular strengths, ensured that they were given status and a share in the limelight, supported their applications for courses, encouraged them in particular pedagogical initiatives or, from time to time, turned a blind eye to specific deviations from school policies as long as others were followed. Typically:

Miss Proctor, as a head, will make a fuss about having support staff in. She doesn't wring her hands and wait for miracles to happen, she'll get people in for individual children or make sure there are enough adults around to enable the teaching staff to give them individual attention.

(Teacher, Lowmeadow)

In return these individuals modified their behaviour, fell into line with school require-ments they found irksome, put themselves out for the benefit of others.

Nor were heads and deputies unaware that in seeking to make individuals feel valued they were acting for reasons of both principle and pragmatism:

I see it as an important thing to joke with dinner ladies because I haven't got time to spend a lot of time talking to them, but it means that you have got some sort of relationship with them, and when it comes to a situation when you need to ask them to do something you know them in a particular way.

(Deputy, Sedgemoor)

They genuinely believed that they should support and appreciate their colleagues but, because they also knew that teachers and ancillaries would give more to the job if they felt it was self-enhancing, they seldom lost an opportunity to bolster the self-confidence and self-image of each staff member. For example:

I think it is very important when you are making policy documents that everybody is involved and has a feeling of ownership, because if people feel their little contribution has been valued and they can actually see a document that contains their contribution — 'Oh that was my little bit' — there is very much more a feeling of wanting to carry that out, rather than just thinking 'This is what the boss wants.'

(Deputy, Hutton)

In the same way, staff did indeed feel as a matter of principle that their relationships should be characterized by mutual consideration and that in this respect, as in others, heads should set an example. At the same time, they undoubtedly appreciated it when the latter bent the rules to allow time off for domestic commitments, rang them up at home to enquire after a sick relative, spent hours listening to their personal troubles. In return, they were the more ready to render the same services to their leaders and to one another.

Similar points can be made about the value which was collectively attached to interdependence. Membership of a staff team was held to be valuable in its own right, but it was also enjoyable, productive and could reduce the difficulty or stress of work. Similarly, individuals appreciated the emotional and social support of a group even though it meant they were heavily subject to the normative influence of their peers, something which in turn reduced heads' necessity to exercise their auth-ority openly. By the same token, heads genuinely believed in the importance of community but they too found a cohesive staff group supportive and self-enhancing.

It is also possible to see love as double-edged. At the start of this chapter we said that we had sometimes seen heads using what could have been normative power in their dealings with their staffs, but that we judged from the latter's reactions that they experienced their leaders' actions not as manipulation but as the exercise of personal authority rooted in affection. Nevertheless, as is always the case in such circumstances, a fine line divides resentful obedience from willing acquiescence. We cannot be absolutely certain that heads and staff members never exploited the affec-tion that others felt for them. The culture which they had created and to whose existence they all daily contributed was full of ambiguities and contradictions. Yet for most people, most of the time, it seemed to satisfy both principle and self-interest in ways that ensured their continuing commitment to it. In this sense, the working consensus in the collaborative schools can be conceived as a tacit agreement among all the staff to maintain both norms and the beliefs which underpinned them.

Negotiation and Compromise

This being the case, negotiation was the strategy best suited to the resolution of difference within the culture of collaboration, and compromise its most acceptable outcome. Yet it will be clear from what has already been said about the authority of the heads, and by extension that of their deputies, that the nature of the working consensus which characterized the collaborative schools limited the extent of possible negotiation:

> Miss Proctor used to have us into the staffroom and say, 'This is what I've thought of. If anybody's got anything that you want to add to it, or you think would be a useful widening of experience, say so.' Much as I do with Rita [the nursery nurse] now. I come in and say, 'This is what I've thought of for this week and we'll follow it through. I want you to do this, this and this. Is there anything else you'd like to do?' Well, Miss Proctor does that on a larger scale with the rest of the staff.
>
> (Nursery teacher, Lowmeadow)

> We [the head and I] say to new staff that every time somebody comes you can't reinvent the wheel, that there are certain things that have been recently evolved and we couldn't start rearranging that. But in anything that we're reviewing at the moment, their say, whatever their position, is as valid as anybody else's and will be heard.
>
> (Deputy, Hutton)

> If I have a frank exchange of views with somebody over something, I am quite prepared to step back. . . . But at the back of my mind is the fact that I'll just have to go another way round instead of the way I went last time.
>
> (Deputy, Lavender Way)

Given acceptance of these parameters, both head and staff members were committed to negotiation and to compromise:

> I decided what things I wanted to make a stand on, what were the important things, and I let the rest go. . . . There have been things that I didn't want to do, there might have been a bit of tough talking over several weeks, but eventually it was hammered out and negotiated to everybody's satisfaction. . . . Both of you can give a little and both of you can take a little, whatever you can work out. I haven't always been like that.
>
> (Teacher, Lowmeadow)

> [During a staff meeting] Miss Proctor requested that objects brought by children into assembly be kept to very special ones and that in general only certificates and awards be brought into the hall. Jane made the point that this favoured the already fortunate and limited those who would like to have awards but couldn't. She very quietly but firmly stuck to this. There wasn't time for a full discussion because the children started to come in, but as the teachers left she went up to the head and said, in effect, 'I wasn't being difficult but . . .'. Miss Proctor responded, equally pacifically and Jane left knowing

there had been a silent compromise, that she could still use her discretion about the objects children brought in, but that she would have to screen them to some extent.

(Fieldnote, May, Lowmeadow)

So Graham said, 'Well, clearly there is a majority view against maths tests.' He then deferred in the light of the staff's views, even though he was obviously keen on the idea. He withdrew it altogether rather than making a unilateral decision and imposing it on the staff.

(Fieldnote, June, Greenfields)

I've got what I think is a realistic view that a school isn't a job that you ever finish. You have to make do with what influences you are managing to have within the limits of your capabilities.

(Deputy, Lavender Way)

There is no way that everybody can achieve their views in any situation, that everybody's thoughts can be carried out. There has got to be some consensus of opinion.

(Teacher, Hutton)

Explicit Negotiation

Sometimes the process of negotiation was open and direct, carried out in ways which suggested a willingness to speak one's mind, to risk professional disagreement with the head and with one's colleagues:

> Victoria was unhappy with the fact that Graham had not carried out what she thought were his headmasterly duties concerning the giving of the leaving present. It transpired that when he was asked to sign the card, a space had been left for a few words to be put in and Graham had said, 'Why do I have to do this? Why don't you do it?' Victoria felt he was ducking out of his responsibilities. As she said, she thought it would have been odd for Vera to receive a card on which some expression from the head wasn't present. She appeared to be troubled by the fact that Graham hadn't organized the signing of the card or very much else, as she thought, and apparently she'd told him so.
>
> (Fieldnote, March, Greenfields)

> Shortly before assembly, Rita [the nursery nurse] came down to the office with a query about the nursery nurse students. Miss Proctor said she was wondering how to fit in the nursery children coming up for the goodbye to the students with the fact that she wanted to finish off the Handel story and it wasn't suitable for little ones. Would it be convenient if Rita brought them up at 9.30? 'No', said Rita, 'it wouldn't', she was going to be cooking with them, though she supposed that she could mix the stuff up and leave it at 9.30 ready to go in the oven. Miss Proctor promptly thought again and suggested, 'Bring them in right at the beginning and I'll start with the goodbye.'
>
> (Fieldnote, May, Lowmeadow)

This kind of open negotiation contrasts with the reluctance of some teachers in Hutton and Lavender Way directly to confront the differences between them. This is illustrated by the long-drawn-out saga of the 'shared area' at Lavender Way. Within the 'infant department' of this semi-open plan 5–9 first school, two pairs of teachers had for several years avoided making any attempt to resolve the long-standing rivalry between one of each pair, a situation compounded by the latter's different pedagogical styles. As a consequence they had increasingly separated their two sets of teaching areas leaving the shared area between them virtually unoccupied.

Their excuses were difficulties of access to this area and the noise created for one pair when children from the other were playing in it. The head recalled that soon after she had arrived 18 months previously, she had begun to work with them on this problem:

> I would say 'Look, I feel this is an issue at this point and it's not appropriate at a whole staff meeting, so could you get the infant staff together?' Or 'when you are getting together would you bring this issue up, because I feel it's got to be sorted out, and get cracking on it.' Finally, I had to intervene and we had several sessions where I had the four of them and we had to thrash things out.
>
> (Head, Lavender Way)

When this strategy failed, she, her husband and the deputy came in one weekend and took down a partition. She then invited the four infant staff to work out together how they could use the opened area.

> They got together and said, 'well it would be nice to have a nice playhouse', and I said what bits did they want in the playhouse? So Ben [the deputy] and I, I think it was a half-term, we came in and we decorated the whole area, painted it from top to bottom, we found some wallpaper and put some wallpaper on and cleaned up the carpet and cleaned up the cookery area and put all the bookcases as they'd said, lugged all those around and left it ready for them. And then over the next couple of weeks all the equipment came and it sat there and it sat there and it wasn't being used.
>
> (Head, Lavender Way)

She felt obliged to push the problem back to the participants:

> So I must admit that by this time I said, 'I'm sorry, I've had enough of this. I have listened to you all, I've listened to you individually, you got together, you decided this is what you wanted and that when you'd been provided with the area and the equipment you would get together and you would work out how you were going to use it. It's not for me to tell you how to work it. You want it, so you need to decide how it can work. If it hasn't worked and you can't do it, you must come and tell me and I shall have everybody together.' And that's what I had to do because it didn't, it still didn't work properly. So I'm afraid I had them all in the staffroom and told them what I thought, then left or took a back seat. It was Sandy and Stella who rescued the situation. They changed actually from that day, I feel. That's when the change began to happen.
>
> (Head, Lavender Way)

However, although greater and more amicable use was made of the area from then on, Catherine still continued to seek situations which would oblige the infant group to co-operate (such as rearranging class groupings for music). In this she was handicapped by the refusal of some 'junior' teachers to see the implications of the problem for the staff as a whole:

> Among the things for which I have no tolerance is unnecessary conflict. . . . So I'm afraid I'm a bit of an ostrich and I put my head in the sand and got on with what I was doing. . . . In that situation you could hide, well, not hide, but claim diminished responsibility, for having to cement relations down there.
>
> (Teacher, Lavender Way)

A willingness to enter into open negotiation with one's head and one's colleagues depended, as Chapter 4 explained, upon a sense of confidence in oneself and in them. A sense of reciprocal security was a hallmark of relationships at Greenfields, Lowmeadow and Sedgemoor:

> After school when Jim entered the staffroom and Victoria was there, Victoria apologized

for pressing him and making him feel uncomfortable. Jim said 'I don't mind, because with you it's benign, but sometimes it is difficult to resolve all the different opinions and beliefs about what my role really is.'

(Fieldnote, January, Greenfields)

By contrast at Hutton and Lavender Way, at the beginning of the year, not all the staff felt secure. Referring to a staff meeting in which no one had expressed dissent to any of the head's curriculum plans, a Hutton teacher said:

> It's people's vulnerability. We talked about it afterwards and we'd all got reasons why we didn't say anything and yet everybody felt they should have said something, so it was the staff's fault as well for not taking things on.

(Teacher, Hutton)

Despite their initial diffidence, the staff in both these schools began to feel noticeably more secure during the year. The new deputies, actively backed by their heads, played a large part in this, working hard among the teachers to encourage professional self-confidence and the habit of open speech:

> The ways of influencing curriculum are first of all to have 'cordial relations' between all the people involved. You need to be working out problems like which people you can have a joke with . . . [so that they don't] feel that if you are going to tackle the curriculum, it is because something has gone wrong, someone has fallen short or isn't living up to expectations or the children aren't succeeding or whatever. I think if you have got an atmosphere where you can do that [admit to failure] and instead of going behind doors and muttering about it, can take it on mutually, then you are getting 'the right sort of atmosphere' in which you are actually going to make changes that affect the children's experience in school. . . . That's one of the things that I, and I'm sure Catherine, has felt. We wish that people would be more open at staff meetings, instead of going along with things and then thinking to themselves 'Oh, I don't really agree with that.' I don't think there's anything that can't be said in the right way, if you see what I mean. You don't have to make it sound contentious, it can still be the truth.

(Deputy, Lavender Way)

> The attitudes that Teresa [the new deputy] appears to be adopting are that people are important and their views are important, so respect their judgements and if you don't agree with them, try and change what you don't agree with in a gentle way.

(Teacher, Hutton)

> I wouldn't speak out at staff meetings until the last couple, and that's through Teresa urging us: 'Don't moan and groan, you've got to bring it out and say' and with her talking about it and saying 'It is reasonable, say it.' I have got this feeling that I'm a bit thick in comparison with the rest of the staff, not that I can't teach, I feel confident about teaching, but I used to have certain reservations about being shouted down, whereas I will speak out now. . . . People have made me relax because they are actually saying 'I've got this problem,' or 'Where are we going with this?'

(Teacher, Hutton)

So in this context it is perhaps significant that at Hutton the growth of public debate about the school's policies was taken by the staff themselves as a sign that they were beginning to feel more at ease with the head and with one another:

> Something has changed in staff meetings — there is more conversation, instead of one person talking. I think it's great — I find it revolutionary, incredible. . . . After the staff meeting last week, I said to Teresa 'Did you realize that all you said was absolutely contrary to what the Boss has always done?'

(Teacher, Hutton)

Jill's comments on curriculum documents: she says that she feels staff need more practical ideas instead of being given thick guidelines full of long words and fine phrases they don't understand. She openly admits failure in a lesson herself, she explains the great complex set of ideas behind the lesson but says 'The lesson was absolutely crap.' This provokes laughter (and approval).

(Fieldnote of staff meeting, February, Hutton)

Interpersonal security did not grow of its own accord. Frequent, open communication was at one and the same time one of its causes and one of its most important outcomes (see Chapter 5). In turn the fact that people felt free to speak openly to one another facilitated the resolution of differences between them. They could often settle disagreements by a forthright statement of opinion or an expression of emotion, instead of grumbling to a third party. It is instructive to compare:

There is very little intrigue here. . . . All right, somebody will come rampaging into the staffroom and say, 'Do you know what such and such has done, I just . . .' and so you have a quick blow up. Everybody else laughs or else they come in and say something and it is sorted out. It never gets to a kind of really troublesome or nasty level. Somebody will have a blow out, or if somebody is worried about something, it seems to come out.

(Teacher, Sedgemoor)

with,

[The staff] know I am not here all the time, so if something does upset them they can come in and talk to me. Then once things have calmed down again I am not here any more so the whole thing to them is finished.

(Part-time secretary, Lavender Way)

Further, where open communication had become a habit, difficulties could be tackled while they were still quite small and therefore relatively easy to sort out:

If we have got something that's very good, we discuss it; if we've got something that's worrying us, we discuss it. And the whole thing is to troubleshoot these things before they get to bursting point, that's the big secret, to see if you can unravel something before it gets into a big ball. It's too late then, it's got to be teased out well before that stage, and I think that's what we attempt to do: talk things out and work them through steadily, and, hopefully, come to a sort of agreement.

(Teacher, Lowmeadow)

If anybody's got anything to say it's not bottled up, they say it. When people do bottle things up inside, when it does come out it's one almighty explosion, isn't it? But because we talk as we do, it doesn't occur. Rather than let something sort of boil inside you, you would say right at the beginning, 'well, I'm not so sure about that, I don't know that I agree with you', before it ever got to the stage where it was going to be a major issue.

(Teacher, Sedgemoor)

Additionally, discussion created mutual understandings which reduced the likelihood of misinterpretations:

Because Miss Proctor talked a lot to me and took me into her confidence . . . it meant that if there were occasions when she made a decision without telling me first, instead of thinking, 'what a silly thing to do' or 'why on earth did she do that?' I became sure in my mind that she would have thought it through, that her reasons would be good ones, even if at the time I didn't know why.

(Deputy, Lowmeadow)

Implicit Negotiation

Often, however, there was neither the time nor the opportunity for extended talk or direct interpersonal negotiation. Nor would the latter have been appropriate on all occasions, since differences were sometimes less potentially disruptive to the team if they were left unspoken. We found that implicit negotiation was most often used when one participant did not wish for whatever reason to state a desire openly or make a request to another (see also Hoyle, 1986). At Lowmeadow, for example, the staff accepted the head's right to suggest which classes individual teachers should take in the forthcoming year. Yet they also had their own preferences and wanted the head to take cognizance of these. A subtle exchange resulted:

> Conversation with Miss Proctor revealed that the proposed class changes had been her idea though Sarah thought she might have suggested it. Apparently in a casual conversation with Miss Proctor she'd mentioned some previous work she'd done with seven year olds, and Miss Proctor had replied, apparently equally casually, 'Do you like working with older children?' Then shortly afterwards Miss Proctor had suggested, again with apparent casualness, that Sarah might like to move up with her class, allowing Margaret to take reception. So Sarah is left feeling the change was her idea even though she knows it may not have been, being well aware that it was probably Miss Proctor's intention all along.
>
> Jane too felt that she had 'floated the idea [of working with an older class] into the air' and then waited to see if her 'seed fell on fertile ground', 'urging it along with little puffs' when she had the opportunity. She was delighted that it had. Margaret, by contrast, had been approached by Miss Proctor and had initially felt that since she hadn't taken reception for years she wasn't all that keen on the change. However, she felt 'in fairness to the others' she had to be prepared to move, and acquiesced quite readily. Like the others she felt her influence was indirect: 'What I would have to do is just say to Miss Proctor, 'If by any chance you want to have a change round this year I would be quite happy to have a different age group' and she would say, 'All right, I'll let you know as soon as there's a chance.'
>
> (Fieldnote, July, Lowmeadow)

The success of this kind of negotiation depended almost entirely on people's ability to 'read' one another's behaviour accurately or to interpret the nuances of gesture, facial expression, body language and single-word utterances. Newcomers to the schools, including ourselves, found this difficult but in time, and given a willingness actively to seek membership of the culture, it was possible to learn its 'languages' (Chapter 3).

Once staff members had learnt the appropriate norms and knew how to convey and to interpret meanings, much could be accomplished in a short time. This fact throws new light on two aspects of headteacher and staff behaviour described in Chapters 4 and 6. First, because the main concerns of heads and of staff members were the preservation of their own values, self-image and self-esteem, negotiations between them frequently depended for their success upon an intimate knowledge of persons. Seen from this perspective headteachers may be viewed as very knowledgeable professionals, an important part of whose skill in staff relationships lay in knowing people, knowing tasks and knowing how to achieve an optimum match between them. They therefore also needed constantly to update this knowledge. Their constant enquiry into their schools was in one sense a ceaseless process of information-gathering and checking, made necessary by their heavy reliance upon implicit negotiation.

Similarly, the better teachers knew one another, the more deftly they could bargain with one another. This too throws a different light on their expressed desire to get to know each other as persons. Once again, the personal and professional interests of individuals appear to be served by means which were also adopted in pursuit of cultural aims:

> The more I got to know her, the more I realized what the way was to approach her and she probably felt the same about me. She was a very strong-minded person . . . I think we were getting to the stage where I was saying what I thought and we were reaching a compromise on some things.
>
> (Teacher, Lavender Way)

Secondly, heads, and sometimes deputies, who were always accessible and frequently on the move about their schools were well placed to engage in informal negotiation. Adjustments could be made to timetables and arrangements, help given, minor problems solved, individual preferences suggested, messages relayed to other people, news exchanged, plans aired; individual staff members had the opportunity to make classroom needs plain, heads to thank, praise, offer assistance — and all this could be achieved without a single planned meeting, public announcement or formal communication. The schools were constantly kept in balance by the movement around them of their formal leaders.

Truces

Notwithstanding heads' desire to maintain the school in a state of equilibrium, their access to information and their skill in both explicit and implicit negotiation, they were not always successful in persuading staff to accept their policies. In all of the project schools except Sedgemoor there was evidence of past disagreements (often, but not always, between the head and a member of staff) as a result of which participants henceforward 'agreed to differ' (Deputy, Lowmeadow). Such 'truces' endured for many years, usually until one or other of the combatants left the school. Often sustained with great courtesy, they became part of the negotiated order of the staff group and for both these reasons were frequently difficult to discern. Yet because defended positions existed behind the 'truces' the latter hampered the development not just of the people directly involved in the dispute but also of those with whom they came in contact. Accordingly, one of the heads' skills appeared to lie in their ability not to see 'truces' as final, but to keep negotiation open so that fresh compromises could be reached as new circumstances developed.

DECISION-MAKING PROCEDURES

It will be clear that formal settings, such as meetings, were less well suited to the conduct of this kind of negotiation, relying as it did on finely tuned interpersonal sensitivities and understandings, than were informal ones. Indeed much business was conducted in all the schools in a manner which might have appeared casual to the uninitiated observer:

> They are so informal about everything. They're very easy-going. Everybody would be in the staffroom including the head and somebody would say 'Oh look, there's a course here, I'd love to go on that, what about you?' and the other one would say 'Oh good, yes I would' and the rest of the staff would say 'Let's have a look. Yes, why don't you?' and the head would say, 'Yes, go if you like.'
>
> (Newly appointed teacher, Greenfields)

> Discussion happens all the time in this school. . . . If something crops up and the person you want to see happens to be there, then you just sit and discuss it wherever you happen to be. It's an on-going thing rather than things happening at certain times of the week.
>
> (Teacher, Sedgemoor)

> Sometimes [consultation] can be quite direct, if one's asked directly for an opinion one can proceed to say it. More often, if one isn't asked an opinion, but one might like another view to be heard, one kind of initiates a conversation in the staffroom . . . partly because it enables other people who may hold similar views to comment as well and make some more general, less personal discussion. That's the way I think is used in this school, because occasionally I can recognize that somebody else is doing it and that I'm implicitly being invited to comment. Perhaps something that I've said I'm invited to repeat before a larger audience and our comments are listened to and some-times change is quite unobtrusive but it happens. Or perhaps something that was going to happen doesn't happen.
>
> (Teacher, Lowmeadow)

Of course, reliance on the informal and interpersonal could lead to lapses in com-munication, especially when discussion took place on the assumption that everyone was present:

> If you don't go into the staffroom, for any reason, you're likely to miss a lot of things that are going on. Then something happens and they say 'Oh well, we discussed it in the staffroom, but you weren't there.' You can miss a lot that way.
>
> (Teacher, Sedgemoor)

> Although we have staff meetings they're not terribly frequent. Most of the smaller things are decided informally and if one wasn't around to make a contribution, the opportunity just wouldn't be there in the more formal sense. . . . As you know, we are often all together in the staffroom at coffee time and lunchtime and we talk about it then.
>
> (Teacher, Lowmeadow)

That such lapses did not cause disruption was due, as staff themselves saw, to the existence of interpersonal trust, born of familiarity (and thus predictability) and to a sense of shared endeavour (see Chapter 4). When either of these was missing, as both were with the 'failing' teacher at Greenfields, the weakness of the predominantly informal communication system became apparent:

> They are good teachers on this staff and I think Julie has found that difficult. The staff here are fairly seasoned campaigners and they are well-seasoned enough to spend a fair part of the day in the staffroom . . . Julie . . . has had to spend a lot of time out of the staffroom and therefore has missed this integrating influence [which helps people] become part of the social unit of the school. . . . A lot of the time she could be spending in the staffroom, she's been spending in her classroom.
>
> (Head, Greenfields)

It is consistent with this reliance upon informal procedures that formal methods of decision-making were not in general particularly efficient. Staff meetings were an essential part of institutional life in most of the schools and were productively used at various times in all of them. In those schools in which meetings ceased during union action, staff missed them and welcomed their return later in the year. Yet despite the fact that they were seen to be important as a forum for discussion of whole-school issues, such meetings were often inefficient and relatively ineffectual, a fact to which several organizational factors contributed. Lack of time was one:

> In the first part of the first term we did it about twice a week formally. We said, 'Right, we need half an hour, we must sort this out, we'll go and sit down for half an hour and do it.' Then after Christmas we had other constraints on us . . . [and] I suppose we felt it was less necessary and we didn't do it as much. So the formal side of interaction dropped off, but we got quite good at sharing ideas and information, less formally. . . . Communicating has been much freer and easier and done in times other than half-hour formal sit downs, which is preferable really, it seems less arduous to people.
>
> (Teacher, Lavender Way)

Group size was another:

> I think people's commitment to [a curriculum policy] would be different if they felt that part of them was invested, that they could personally see their contribution or their ideas in play. I think that comes about better when ones and twos make things happen, rather than sixes and sevens sitting together.
>
> (Deputy, Lavender Way)

Faulty organization was a third:

> Staff meeting (afternoon session begins at 1.10 p.m.): It was scheduled for 12.40, no place given. On the staff dining table at 12.40 Patricia looked meaningfully at the time and gathered her plates together. Julia then noticed the time, told everybody, rose to her feet, saying 'I'll do something about tea.' We all went down to the staffroom where Julia said 'We're all taking it up to Miss Proctor's room. The meeting is up there.' Some time after 12.45 everyone was there except for Jane; there weren't enough chairs because Kath miscounted. We started without Jane who was on dinner duty and who had (I subsequently learned) been told by Miss Proctor to finish her lunch. At 12.50 Miss Proctor did a swift run through the agenda to see which items Patricia, who had to leave at 1.00 p.m., could miss. By 12.53 we had decided the only item for which she was essential was the date of the open evening (there were five items) . . . and Jane had joined us. The date was fixed, taking about two minutes. Patricia left at 1.00 p.m. after five minutes discussion of the next item. That left eight minutes for three items. . . . On one there was discussion but no decision and one was not raised at all.
>
> (Fieldnote, May, Lowmeadow)

SUMMARY

All the headteachers had a strong sense of what they wanted to accomplish in educational terms and none hesitated to use their formal authority if they felt it would be helpful to do so. In particular it was through their authority that they established the school's main aims and the chief means by which staff would attempt to achieve these. But they also knew that persuading teachers to implement school policies was more difficult than laying these down and so they relied heavily on their capacity to influence their staff's practice.

Influence, by heads and others, was most effectively exercised through example and culturally appropriate communication. The latter was generally oral, informal, often humorous in tone and its success depended on other people's ability to pick up implicit meanings. In addition, heads influenced their staffs indirectly, by ensuring that interaction between particular members was facilitated by buildings and organizational arrangements. Further, cohesive staff groups influenced one another; norms and routines were powerful socializing agents. Not surprisingly, therefore, decision-making procedures were generally informal; formal procedures, such as staff meetings, were often inefficient and relatively ineffectual. Yet, paradoxically, they were valued as a forum for whole-staff discussion.

Not all the staff in every school were equally committed to their head's educational policies and some disagreement was therefore inevitable. However, since most people found that membership of the culture of collaboration enabled them to satisfy their 'interests-at-hand', chief among which for both heads and staff were the preservation of self-image and the enhancement of self-esteem, they tacitly agreed to a 'working consensus'. In line with this unspoken agreement sub-groups were discouraged, disagreements were defined as non-disruptive or were defused, by a number of strategies, before they became conflicts. Those which remained were usually resolved by subtle, informal negotiation which continually went on between all participants as, in the course of their frequent daily encounters, each accommodated to the others' needs. Sometimes this kind of negotiation took place openly and directly, sometimes it was tacit. Either way, it was well suited to the culture of collaboration because principle and advantage were equally served by habits of mutual sensitivity and consideration and by a willingness to compromise. But not all differences of opinion or interest were resolved by negotiation, and in two schools in particular longstanding, deeply buried disagreements continued to impede the implementation of whole-school policies.

Chapter 9

Implications for Teacher Education and the Management of Schools

Our immediate aim in undertaking this research was to describe the workings of primary school staff groups, and the case studies we constructed after working in the five project schools satisfied this objective. At the same time they provided us with a wealth of evidence to analyse in our search for ideas and themes which might further professional understanding of primary schools as organizations of adults. In other words, we have been concerned not simply to describe but also to analyse and interpret. It was never our intention to be prescriptive about the ways in which adults work together in school, and certainly not to suggest that the five project schools were 'effective' schools. To make the latter judgement would have involved a very different research project, as school effectiveness studies show (see, for example, Mortimore *et al.*, 1988). Yet, although we wish to make it clear that we stop short of prescription, we nevertheless believe that our work has implications for teachers, headteachers, teacher-educators, INSET providers and co-ordinators, LEA officers and those with an interest in developing primary schools. In this chapter we discuss the most important of these implications.

Since, at the outset, we wanted to add to the very limited number of existing portraits of primary schools as organizations of adults, it is fitting that we take this as our starting point. The most common description of schools is that of the organizational chart which places the head at the top, the deputy beneath and teachers below the deputy. Ancillary staff, caretakers and secretaries are always omitted from such diagrams. The organizational chart is a minimalist device. It is concerned with hierarchy, formal lines of responsibility and utilizes a line management perspective. It tells us nothing about the people as professional practitioners and persons, nor of the school as a living organization. Occasionally, on courses, one encounters descriptions of schools which provide background notes for a simulation or case study exercise but these are no fuller than the pictures with which we began our report (see Chapter 2). The other relatively common descriptions of primary schools are those contained in HM Inspectors' published school inspection reports which are available from the DES. In these, HM Inspectors devote only a little attention to working relationships between adults, comment only briefly on formal organization and not at all on informal relations, and demonstrate no awareness of school culture. In short, it appears that we have not yet developed an adequate way of describing, let alone conceptualizing, primary schools as organizations. As an initial and tentative proposal we offer the idea of the primary school as a mobile.

THE PRIMARY SCHOOL AS A MOBILE

Mobiles are often used by primary teachers as ways of decorating their classrooms. They are usually suspended from the ceiling and typically the children have made colourful, eye-catching shapes to be individually attached to spars, which are then strung together and hung up as a whole. Once suspended the air currents move the individual elements, making them rotate and catch the light. Ambitious mobiles can involve many elements, each linked to a spar which is connected to others. They can be delicate and intricate constructions. We see these constructions as analogous to the primary school as an organization.

Of course, all metaphors have their limitations and before this one is explained it is necessary to ask that the reader resists thinking too literally. In particular, most mobiles are arranged so that at the top they are linked together and hung by a single thread. This thread is usually hung from the classroom ceiling. In order to avoid becoming too elaborate we have not included any account of what the school as a mobile might be suspended from. Nor have we attempted to represent its past, because we feel that this is incorporated into the present. Notwithstanding, we feel the metaphor of the mobile offers three useful ways of perceiving schools: shape, space and movement.

To look first at shape, the school as a mobile will have a vertical dimension. Elements hung at the top might be described as higher (e.g., head, deputy), so the mobile takes account of hierarchy and levels. There is also a horizontal dimension which, unlike the organizational chart, provides a three-dimensional perspective. If staff are represented by the elements, then they can be fitted into the mobile according to buildings or departments or teams. For example, three teachers working along a corridor could be represented as attached to the same spar. Similarly, if one teacher works in a temporary classroom some distance from the main school building, s/he might be depicted by being hung independently. If the school is organized as infant and junior departments then the elements could be so arranged. Ancillary staff could be located according to where and with whom they work; if the nursery nurse spends her time with the reception class teacher, that is where she would be positioned in the mobile. The siting of the secretary sets an interesting challenge: should she be situated by herself but close to the head, or somewhere else? The caretaker might need to be situated adjacent to the cleaning assistants (in large schools) or on his/her own in small schools. The idea of a mobile allows each school to be depicted according to those characteristics (e.g., buildings, departments, teams) which affect most strongly its organizational patterns and relationships and therefore its culture. Also, if informal patterns (e.g., friendships, groups) are stronger than formal ones then these might be the ways in which the elements are hung. Indeed, the mobile helps us to analyse the particular characteristics of each school, and since all schools are different (see Chapter 2), to represent them in individual ways.

Within the mobile, space is an important feature. The distances between elements are significant. For example, when the headteacher is aloof and distant s/he might be represented as an element placed somewhat 'above' the others. In our study the heads of Greenfields, Lowmeadow and Sedgemoor would be depicted as close to all the other elements since their membership of the staff group was a notable feature of their leadership. In the case of Hutton and Lavender Way the heads were close to some, but not all, staff and 'their' mobiles could reflect that too. The same principle of association/disassociation could be used for all other staff.

Whilst space reveals distance and proximity between elements it is, in another sense, invisible. One can see space but not necessarily understand it, rather as one can see the sky as air but not necessarily know about or understand oxygen, carbon dioxide or ozone layers. Space in the mobile will be important because it might represent such invisible things as feelings towards other people, attitudes and beliefs. It could be that it is the feelings or beliefs which account for the distance or proximity between elements. The mobile of the schools with a firmly established 'culture of collaboration' might show the elements quite close together. By contrast, at Hutton or Lavender Way, some elements might be more distant than others since the culture of collaboration was not widely developed there and these two schools were more 'loosely coupled' (Hoyle, 1986) than the other three.

The school-as-a-mobile will also move. For example, each element will be moving, one might say developing. Some will be turning at different rates to others. Some might be in a fast spin, whilst others are rotating, but gently. Indeed all could be moving at their own rates, or the mobile as a whole could move at a uniform rate. Then there is the matter of direction. Not all elements need be moving in the same direction. Some elements might be turning clockwise whilst others rotate anti-clockwise. Moreover, some combination of elements (e.g., the infants) might be turning in one direction whilst the rest of the school, or some other elements of it (e.g., the juniors), turn in a contrary direction. Of course some elements might actually be motionless. In terms of the project schools one could say, for example, that at Sedgemoor the whole mobile (i.e., every element within it) was turning in the same direction, whereas at Greenfields all the permanent staff were turning in the same direction, but the teacher who was failing was moving in a different one.

It is also possible to combine rates of movement with direction. Thus an element in the mobile might be turning very fast in one direction whilst the other elements, or some of them, were moving at a different rate and in the opposite direction. Again the mobile idea is sufficiently flexible to capture each school's particular circumstances.

If the elements were hooked on to the mobile's spars in such a way that they could be lifted off, this would enable the mobile to represent another idea. As part-time staff are absent as well as present, they could be fitted on to and taken out of the mobile at appropriate intervals. As anyone who has suspended a mobile knows, taking away and adding on elements to one affects the whole balance of it. The changes created by part-time staff, and by staff absence and presence (see Chapter 7), could be reflected in the shifts in this balance. Furthermore, as additional staff or new staff arrive they too would need to be fitted into the whole. They might be located somewhere new in the configuration of the school, or be seen as having a different 'weight' (i.e., influence, such as a new deputy or head might have). In either case they would affect the whole kilter of the mobile. Staff movements and changes (e.g., headteacher succession, staff selection) did affect the schools and this the notion of balance would reflect.

Rather than continue to elaborate this metaphor we will highlight three principles it illustrates: perception, wholeness and equilibrium. First, the mobile demonstrates that seeing the school is inherently problematical. For one thing, not all of the school is actually visible since certain of its features are invisible or symbolize something other than themselves (see Chapters 3 and 4). For another, what you see depends upon where you are. Take, for example, the view a head might have of the mobile. S/he might be close to the staff but nevertheless slightly 'above' them and, perhaps, towards the centre of the mobile, whereas a teacher might be on the edge of the mobile and 'below' other colleagues. Even in this crude sense the two individuals do not perceive the same mobile or school because they are in different places, each having a unique vantage point. Moreover, because there is movement in the mobile (both up and down as it balances, and around as it rotates), at different times you might have a different view because things, including perhaps your own position, have literally moved, shifted and altered. You might see less because some element close to you is blocking or obscuring your view; or you might now see more because that element has moved. And not only might you see different things but also the same things differently. This might apply to: job (headteacher, teacher, secretary); the school's climate (fatigue, mood, pressure, see Chapter 7); authority and influence (see Chapter 8) or relationships. In the case of the latter we have shown that in the project schools the personal and the professional were blurred (Chapter 4) and this fact too affected perception. To know that a teacher at Sedgemoor was very worried about her child's secondary schooling or that the mother of the head of Greenfields had recently died affected how you interpreted their behaviour (composed/bearing up/tense/tired) and encouraged you to make allowances for them.

Two other points arise from thinking about perception. As researchers we had to try to 'see' the schools in which we worked. Not only did we find this difficult (Chapter 2) but it also took a long time; we needed long and close acquaintance with the staff. Even as the year of our fieldwork was drawing to a close we still were finding out new facts, and so too were the staff, even those who had been at the school longer than ourselves. In other words, if those who work together and inside a school find it takes time to know the school, it may be difficult for 'outsiders' who spend only a brief period observing in them (e.g., LEA advisers/inspectors, HMI, teacher educators, governors, researchers) to gain little more than a partial perspective. Moreover, unless outsiders can secure the co-operation of the insiders and gain access to staff's views and knowledge, it may be even more problematic for them to 'see' a school.

The second point is to do with bringing all the staff's perceptions together. If everyone possesses a unique perspective on the school, no individual can have an all-encompassing view of it. Even though the heads worked hard to see all the school (Chapter 6) their reliance on their deputies and others for additional information was an implicit acknowledgement that whilst they might have more information than other people it was not, by itself, sufficient. In a sense the heads, indeed many of the staff, appreciated the message of a popular primary school story: 'the blind men and the elephant'. This is the story of a land visited by a hitherto unknown animal, the elephant. Being blind each man relied on touch and each touched only a part of the creature (trunk, tail, leg, ear, flank). Yet he believed he therefore knew the nature of the whole beast, when in truth each needed to add his knowledge to that of the others. In a tacit acknowledgement of this fact, the project staffs tried in a very real sense to embrace everyone's perceptions. Talks, get-togethers, visits, meetings, chats, coffee, mealtimes and so on (see Chapters 4 and 5) were times when perceptions were shared. Participation was not only a matter of joining in; it was also to do with integrating staff perceptions so that collectively all could benefit from the different view of each (Chapters 4 and 8). In turn, staff constantly 'managed' the accretion of knowledge about the school as a whole and this had implications for the second principle: wholeness.

The idea of 'wholeness' has gained currency during the 1980s. Much has been made of the notion that teachers should work together. Indeed, the idealized image is that of a whole or collegial school (Campbell, 1985). Since Coulson (1976) advocated collegiality many others have joined in by promoting mutual accountability (Alexander, 1984); co-ordination and collaboration (DES, 1985; House of Commons Select Committee, 1986); the operation of schools as combined teaching units (DES, 1987); or simply reiterated the call for collegiality (Richards, 1986; Tomlinson, 1986; Thomas, 1987). Only a few writers have attempted to analyse notions of wholeness (Campbell, 1985; Southworth, 1987a; Open University, 1988). Even so, there appears to be little understanding of the scale of the task of developing a 'whole school'. We have raised two difficulties: seeing the whole school and integrating individuals' perceptions. The metaphor of the mobile illustrates other problems too.

A school is not, in fact, a monolithic organization. Rather, it is a composite of many different parts (people, buildings, teams and groups, beliefs and values) which all need to be accommodated or reconciled to one another before they will fit together (see Chapters 4, 5 and 8). The 'whole school' needs to be understood in terms of the complexity and number of its constituent parts. Moreover those who seek wholeness need to recognize the intricacy of the ways in which the parts are arranged, interrelated, balanced and moving. Movement raises a particular problem: schools are not static places (see Chapter 7) and to create a situation in which all the parts (e.g., staff) are moving in the same direction can involve considerable effort, take a long time and rely upon the opportunity to appoint key staff — witness the feelings of the head of Hutton school (Chapter 6) and his expectations that the arrival of a new deputy would help development to take place (Chapter 7). Looked at another way, the potential for fragmentation, rather than wholeness, is considerable. Schools can easily fracture or fall apart because of differences in perception, belief or behaviour.

Since schools are not monolithic, those who seek to develop wholeness need to recognize that whole schools have to be made (Chapter 5). Just as individual perceptions need to be integrated, so too do beliefs. Our analysis shows that the culture of collaborative schools stems from school-wide agreement with, and commitment to, particular beliefs about the nature of human relationships (Chapter 4). This culture has to be made, and needs maintaining (Chapters 4, 5, 6 and 7). Since it is built upon beliefs, any sense of wholeness in a school rests upon the degree to which these beliefs are shared. The socialization of staff is an important corporate activity.

The notion of wholeness implies a sense of cohesion. If whole schools are to 'work', it is important that those who seek to develop them know what will bond them together. Clearly, agreement at the level of beliefs enhances the likelihood of staff cohesion. Yet agreement at this level, whilst necessary, may not be sufficient. In addition to school-wide agreements the collaborative schools also worked hard to keep open all channels of communication. The high number of interactions, the persistence of talk and the sheer multiplicity of communications (see Chapters 3 and 5) suggests that communication was the 'glue' of the schools. In terms of the mobile, communication might be represented by the strings and spars that linked all the pendants together.

The fact that neither 'wholeness' nor culture are 'given' raises a further point. Culture is not immutable, as changes that we have described in Hutton and Lavender Way suggest. Moreover, in the three other schools (Greenfields, Lowmeadow and Sedgemoor) staff worked hard to maintain the culture, and this implies that they were aware that it could change. Indeed the behaviour of the heads and deputies in constantly attending to the culture (e.g., through assemblies, negotiation, resolving differences; see Chapters 6 and 8) suggests that they were aware of this need. This brings us back to the notion of balance and therefore to the importance of equilibrium as a principle. A school needs, for example, to attain a balance of power (Chapter 8). In these schools authority structures did not form tidy, hierarchical pyramids; rather influence was evenly distributed. As a result a great deal of negotiation between staff was needed to maintain the school's equilibrium. The staff also sought to ensure a sense of stability by counterbalancing change with continuity. One limitation of the metaphor of the mobile is that it fails to convey how, whenever a change occurred (e.g., vandalism; a new teacher), staff worked hard to sustain continuity and to maintain the school's poise. As a result of their efforts, the schools were always in a state of dynamic equilibrium; their cultures, while constantly threatened by change, were always adapting to it.

IMPLICATIONS FOR TEACHER EDUCATION

These three principles — of perception, wholeness and equilibrium — lead, in turn, to a range of specific implications for those involved in teacher education and the management of schools. Some of these implications derive from one of these principles in particular, others from some combination of them.

The Headteacher as Cultural Leader

The idea that primary heads are founders of their schools' cultures is not widely recognized, yet, because they are (Chapters 5 and 6), a number of implications follow for them, for their schools and for others.

The expectation that heads and others hold of the job effectively requires heads to have a sense of mission which they can articulate and defend. They therefore need to be able to persuade others to share that sense of mission. This involves securing the commitment of other staff (and parents and governors) to the beliefs and values that the individual head believes to be most important for his/her school. In other words heads need both to be certain of their educational philosophy and skilled in negotiation. Moreover, much of the heads' authority and influence derives from their behaviour and sense of example. Hence they must be able to demonstrate both the ability to put their educational beliefs into action (e.g., through classroom practice, school discipline) and the capacity to operate in several spheres (e.g., interpersonal, leadership, group work) in ways consistent with their beliefs (e.g., by showing consideration and offering support). These demands constitute a formidable challenge for individual heads and suggest that they need support. In the collaborative schools, and to a lesser degree in the two other schools, the heads found support from within the school (deputy, secretary, colleagues). Their membership of the staff group was a great help: it prevented isolation, helped them to share their concerns, and created opportunities for others to lead, which in turn led to a sharing of responsibility.

To acknowledge that part of the head's work involved negotiation (Chapter 8) is to raise the question of how prospective heads might be helped to acquire the skills they need and to learn to deal with differences. The way the project school heads encouraged their deputies to conduct negotiations shows that they provided on-the-job training for them. Such training has regularly been proposed and recommended (Waters, 1986), although the significance of the deputies' work in terms of depth (e.g., values), extent and impact may be less widely realized. Since the heads' responsibility for founding new cultures involves persuading others to accept fresh beliefs and values, and because beliefs are the deepest and most difficult part of a person to change, it follows that the heads' work in this respect is an intensely difficult activity. This may in turn explain both why developing a culture appears to rest significantly upon opportunities to appoint new staff and why heads feel strongly about making such appointments (Chapter 7).

Accepting the right and the responsibility of heads to be 'culture founders' also throws into relief questions about their beliefs. It is interesting to speculate about the origins of these, but it is even more important to consider how heads and deputies might be helped to articulate, modify and develop those beliefs that particularly affect their practice as teachers and as leaders. In this respect, courses of advanced or further study have much to offer, particularly when they provide opportunities for the critical examination of such beliefs. If heads want to feel that they have the authority to establish many of the school's guiding beliefs, then it behoves them to be willing to subject them from time to time to scrutiny. It is also vital to give careful, informed consideration to the selection of headteachers. Given the expectations, obligations and responsibilities of headship, their selection must be thorough and rigorous enough to establish whether or not they have developed the skills the job demands and whether they can articulate and defend their educational values.

One other implication should be addressed. The expectations and obligations of headship place the heads in a position where they need not only a sense of mission but also a sense of deep conviction about it. Such conviction has long been a feature of the traditional role of primary headteachers (Coulson, 1976; Alexander, 1984; Southworth, 1987a) and has existed comfortably alongside the relative autonomy of primary schools (King, 1983; Southworth, 1987a). However, changes in the role of governors (Education Acts 1986 and 1988) and greater centralized control of the curriculum (Education Act 1988) may create conflict for the heads. In the project schools the head of Greenfields, on his return from secondment, and the heads of

Hutton and Lavender Way, in relation to their developments in hand, experienced feelings of pressure and dissatisfaction which arose from their efforts to reinstate or to gain acceptance for their preferred ways of working. A national curriculum and greater governor involvement in many aspects of school life may increase the chances that heads will be asked to put effort into installing in their schools professional practices with which they disagree. If headship was dissatisfying when they were trying to create the kind of institutions they believed to be educationally right, how much more dissatisfying might it be when they are trying to implement someone else's plans, perhaps, indeed, ones with which they are in profound disagreement?

Management as School-Based Enquiry

The difficulty of perceiving the 'whole school' implies that those in management positions should be helped to develop their perceptual skills. Chapter 6 showed how the heads and deputies of the project schools consciously and regularly visited all people and places in their schools. They also ensured that staff met frequently and shared their individual perspectives. The heads talked to staff individually and kept up to date with everyone's views and concerns. But the heads also reflected on all this information and were able to empathize with their staff members. By getting around the school and talking and listening to colleagues the heads and deputies increased their awareness and their perceptual acuity. Above all, they constantly enquired into their schools. They took little for granted, remained forever curious and had an insatiable appetite for information and for the feelings and insights of colleagues. As a result, they knew their schools as organizations and as living organisms.

Their quest for information not only developed their sensitivities, it also enabled them to identify problems and difficulties at an early stage. The heads could anticipate shifts in attitude or behaviour and keep the school and its culture in a state of equilibrium (Chapters 7 and 8). Yet much of their enquiry relied upon them being on-site and sufficiently free of other tasks to 'manage by wandering about'. Local management of schools and the need to spend a greater proportion of time with governors and parents, both of which feature in the Education Act 1988, may not facilitate, let alone promote, these and similar ways of working.

Each School is Different

On a number of occasions (Chapters 2, 3, 4) we have made the claim that each school is different. This is consistent with the contingency theory of leadership (see Chapter 6) which suggests that what leaders do is affected by where and whom they are leading. We have also argued that each school's culture is unique, for although the collaborative schools were similar in fundamental ways they were also markedly dissimilar. Their cultures were influenced by particular sets of circumstances (e.g., buildings, personnel, organizational arrangements) and expressed in special ways (e.g., through language, rituals and symbols).

Because each school is different, new staff need to learn how to participate in the school's culture and therefore have to be included and socialized into it. At present, in many schools, newcomers are left to their own devices, or are at the mercy of the individual school's induction process, if it has one. In the absence of a planned induction programme, or alongside one if it exists, colleagues frequently and informally help newcomers to settle in and to fit in. Notwithstanding, new staff may be unaware of the school's rituals and symbols, and may blunder into the culture. Hoyle (1986) has suggested that each school is a thicket of symbols, and our work supports this view. Perhaps more should be done in initial training and in-service education to help teachers perceive and understand the notion of culture and of how it affects life within schools. Certainly within schools greater attention should be given to helping staff, particularly new ones, to find their way through the institutions and cultures they work in. Induction should be a process which prevents teachers from becoming lost in the thickets and helps newcomers avoid being scarred by the brambles.

Interpersonal Skills

From the outset of the project we realized and accepted that teachers work not only with children but also with adults (Chapters 1 and 2). Our experience during fieldwork and the subsequent analysis of the case studies strengthened this conviction. Both processes revealed the interpersonal skills of the staff groups in the project schools (Chapter 5). Yet these were not simply the product of fortuitous selection. The school's culture shaped the behaviour of ancillary and teaching staff, including ourselves, by, for instance, making it normal to praise one's colleagues and welcome strangers. It also affected the attitudes and actions of heads and deputies.

Yet 'collaborative' ways of working together also created and helped to sustain relationships between staff which were characterized by both openness and a sense of security. These schools were not simply pleasant places in which people supported one another; they had also developed structures through and by means of which differences could be faced, frank speaking could take place and rows and arguments could happen. It would be simplistic to regard any of these schools as 'cosy'. The collaborative schools in particular were emotionally comfortable places, but they were also tough-minded. Their staffs could confront and attempt to resolve differences, not least because they were able to deal constructively with the personal and professional aftermath of any disagreements that might occur (Chapter 8).

It follows then that staff in other schools who wish to work together need also to be proficient in interpersonal skills and knowledgeable about group processes, such as communication, active membership and conflict resolution. They also need to be aware of the part that they play in developing and maintaining the cultures of their schools. Currently, opportunities to develop this knowledge or these skills are not widely available, although they may be increasing in frequency, judging by courses offered in the eastern region of England. Moreover, arrangements through LEATGS (Local Education Authority Training Grant Schemes) may provide schools with greater scope to organize such provision. The introduction of in-service days for complete schools creates opportunities for all the staff to undertake group and interpersonal activities and these in turn might enhance and accelerate their capacity to work together.

Staff Selection

In the project schools, the selection of staff clearly provided a key opportunity to develop and maintain the school's culture. Our evidence both here and elsewhere (Southworth, 1987c) suggests that the process of staff selection should be carefully planned and organized. Heads and other staff need to be skilled and therefore trained in selection procedures. The process itself needs ample time for meetings between candidates, head and staff. At the heart of the process lie perceptions by the selectors about individuals' personal qualities, beliefs and professional competences. Although the prediction of these is always uncertain, a hurried or shallow selection process increases the risk of mismatch between the appointed individual and the school.

A change of headteacher was shown to be the greatest single discontinuity in the life of a school. Consideration should be given to planning the succession of headteachers. Incoming heads should be provided with opportunities to see 'their' new school at work, in order to learn something about its habits and rituals and to learn, at first hand, from the outgoing head about his/her guiding beliefs. Although 'seeing' a school and finding out about its culture are lengthy processes this should not mean that newly appointed heads have no opportunity to acquaint themselves with their prospective school's culture. Moreover, since we advocate that all teachers and staff should be helped to understand the notion of culture and recognize symbols and rituals, it is only consistent and right that this opportunity is extended to heads. Given their central role in culture founding (see Chapter 6), it is of paramount importance that they are acquainted with every aspect of their new schools.

Recognizing the Significance of the Ordinary

Another aspect of perception is the need to recognize and appreciate the importance of the seemingly insignificant. Throughout, our evidence has often been concerned with modest affairs — eating and drinking, conversations, tales from the past. Yet although on the surface conversation and coffee arrangements might appear trivial matters, they are in fact manifestations of beliefs. Moreover, all the ordinary acts of, for instance, kindness, consideration or confrontation create the culture — the way we do things here. Therefore each meeting, staff get-together, argument, joke, tour of the school, quick conversational exchange, expression of annoyance or helping hand helps to found or maintain the culture. Ordinary, everyday actions drip-feed the culture, and, like the action of water dropping on a stone, shape preferred ways of working together. Perhaps greater prominence, and status, needs to be given to the mundane. Just as chat is a high-level activity (Chapter 5), so too are 'ordinary', 'everyday' acts and actions.

CHANGING SCHOOLS AND A CHANGING CONTEXT

The idea of the school as a mobile presents a picture only of the adults who work inside it. Principally, this is because our research focus was staff relationships so we have almost entirely filtered out references to governors and parents. This is a limitation, since both were important figures in the schools and do, indeed, from time to time, appear in the evidence (for example, at Greenfields where the returning head had first to defend one of his central educational policies to the governors and then, later, reassure governors and parents concerning the failing teacher). It should also be noted that in all of the schools there were, proportionate to the size of the staff, large numbers of parent and other voluntary helpers. Further, two effects of industrial action were to reduce the number of after-school activities which would normally have involved outsiders and, more importantly, to increase the staffs' negative feelings about their schools' environments. Certainly some staff in all the schools felt that many people outside their school (the public at large, politicians, central government, local government) were hostile towards teachers.

Yet notwithstanding our deliberate neglect of the other adults with whom the staff were involved, it would still be true to say that the schools were inward-looking. This characteristic cannot pass without further comment, not least because schools are at present placed in a context of considerable change, much of it initiated or mandated from outside the schools, particularly as a result of the Education Acts 1986 and 1988.

First, there is the issue of school development. Although it was not part of our brief to comment on classroom and curriculum matters it would be unfair to the schools to imply, as we may unwittingly have done from time to time, that they were inert or self-satisfied institutions. In one or more schools pedagogical or curricular development was taking place in: mathematics education; multicultural education; science education; language development; computers; team teaching. Furthermore, we have mentioned that staff attended in-service courses: one deputy was studying for a PhD; two teachers were working, part-time, on advanced diplomas in Education, whilst others had previously obtained such diplomas; many others regularly attended local, non-award-bearing courses. Three of the heads either had been, or still were, involved in planning in-service activities with their LEAs and, as our period of fieldwork was ending, two of the heads were invited on to regional management courses. We should also report that two schools were given Society of Education Officers' Curriculum Awards in the year after our research. In short, the schools were not complacent or lethargic.

Nevertheless, it is also true that the great majority of these developments came from within: either individual teachers felt the need for some kind of further study or the staff (or some section of them) identified an aspect of the curriculum they wanted to develop. Yet, to a far greater extent than ever before, the contemporary primary school is embedded in a changing social and administrative context which places increasing demands upon it. Second, therefore, we need to address the question of whether the project schools were impervious to external change.

One possible explanation for the schools' concentration on internal development may come from curriculum conventions in the 1980s. The school self-evaluation movement (McMahon *et al.*, 1984; ILEA, 1985), which influenced and was viewed favourably in some of the project schools, emphasized internal review and development. Moreover, it also stressed the importance of schools being 'healthy' organizations if they wished to manage change successfully (Holly, 1987). A healthy organization has been defined (Fordyce and Weil, 1971) as one that has a strong sense of its own identity; the capacity readily to adapt to change; and goals congruent with the demands of the environment; and in which problem solving is pragmatic; communications are open and free; leadership is flexible; and people have a genuine sense of growing and developing as persons and as professionals (see also Coulson, 1978). In our research, the collaborative schools have many of these characteristics, a finding which is consistent with those of writers such as Deal (1985) who have made connections between the existence of strong cultures and school development. Yet the project schools did not match up in one notable respect to descriptions of organizational health, that is, they were relatively unwilling to respond to the demands of their environments. One reason for this is perhaps that the schools, having strong cultures and resilient social organization, did not feel the need to respond to external change. Alternatively, it may be that an emphasis on internal review and development inhibits responsiveness to the demands of others outside the school.

A further explanation may lie in the recognition that these schools, particularly the three collaborative ones, were self-confident. Heads and staff were reasonably assured that what they were doing was, in their own terms, 'right'. This was partly because the leaders were convinced that their mission was appropriate to the school and the children in it and partly because it was shared by the majority of the staff group. Both factors were instrumental in creating strong, self-confident corporate cultures, a finding echoed in studies of successful businesses (Peters and Waterman, 1982; Deal and Kennedy, 1982; Goldsmith and Clutterbuck, 1985). Yet one by-product of this self-assurance may be a resistance to external change. We have shown that these schools were not resistant to changes initiated from within, perhaps because they had confidence in their own self-analysis and diagnosis. It appears, therefore, that the collaborative schools were more open to internal than external influence.

Another reason may be the extent of change which already existed in the schools, and its impact on the staff. In the project schools change was continual and endemic, was felt as well as experienced. Writers concerned with studying school development and change processes have long recognized that for successful innovation to occur there is a need for stable pre-conditions (Fullan, 1982; 1985). Yet the picture we have presented (Chapter 7) suggests that a school is rarely wholly stable. At best it is finely poised, which makes the introduction of any internally planned or externally imposed innovation problematic. It may disturb the balance of the school, causing a loss of stability and, in turn, a reduction in the conditions necessary for successful development. Furthermore, we know that too much change is counterproductive (Fullan, 1985). Because these schools were continually involved in self-adjustment their capacity to deal with external initiatives may have been limited. Given the long agenda of change which schools have faced in the 1980s and will encounter in the future (e.g., 'mainstreaming' of children with special educational needs; annual parents' meetings; LEATGS; new roles for governors; local management and devolved budgets; national curriculum; assessment and testing), policy-makers might be well advised to rethink their implementation schedules in order to avoid destabilizing schools by over-extending their capacity to adjust to these changes.

It is also possible that the staff in the project schools were so busy (e.g., maintaining equilibrium, adapting to change, developing some aspects of the school) that they were unreceptive to other changes. To be sure, in the collaborative schools staff had created, by mutual trust and co-operation, a certain amount of spare capacity or organizational 'slack'. However, being relatively small organizations, this reservoir was limited so, for example, the unexpected absence of a single teacher could create a disturbance, particularly for the head. The chances of these schools absorbing other changes without a commensurate increase in resources may be very low, as some of those outside the schools have appreciated (House of Commons Select Committee, 1986). It could be that the schools were not so much resistant to change as unable to take any more. If this is the case, those who prescribe change should prescribe a corresponding increase in resources.

To sum up, the project schools, as organizations, were densely populated, actively constructed, finely balanced and continuously changing. At the same time they were stable, subject to the authority of the head and the influence of the peer group, controlled by allegiance to shared beliefs and values. The key to this apparent contradiction is the notion of organizational culture. Those who wish to work effectively within or change such schools must be provided with opportunities to perceive and understand school cultures. Above all it is important for staff themselves to realize that they make and maintain these cultures. In the last resort, the manner in which heads, teaching and ancillary staff behave towards one another and the ways in which they work, or do not work, together are in their own hands. Whatever the pressures upon them from outside, primary schools have the capacity to become the kinds of organizations that the adults who work in them choose that they will. Cultures lie within the control of those who participate in them; leaders and members together make their own schools.

Bibliography

Abercrombie, M.J. (1969) *The Anatomy of Judgement: An Investigation into the Processes of Perception and Reason*. Harmondsworth: Penguin.

Abercrombie, M.J. (1981) 'Changing basic assumptions about teaching and learning', in Boud, D. (ed.), *Developing Student Autonomy in Learning*. London: Kogan Page.

Alexander, R. (1984) *Primary Teaching*. London: Cassell.

Ball, S. (1986) *The Micropolitics of the School*. London: Methuen.

Berlak, H. and Berlak, A. (1981) *The Dilemmas of Schooling*. London: Methuen.

Bernstein, B. (1971) *Class, Codes and Control*, Vol. I. London: Routledge and Kegan Paul.

Blake, R.R. and Mouton, J.S. (1978) *The New Managerial Grid*. Houston: Gulf Publishing Company.

Burgess, R. (1984) *In the Field: An Introduction to Field Research*. London: Allen and Unwin.

Campbell, R.J. (1985) *Developing the Primary School Curriculum*. London: Cassell.

Clark, B. (1983) 'The organizational saga in higher education', in Balridge, J. and Deal, T. (eds) *The Dynamics of Organizational Change in Education*. Berkeley, Calif.: McCutcheon.

Coulson, A.A. (1976) 'The role of the primary head', in Peters, R.S. (ed.) *The Role of the Head*. London: Routledge and Kegan Paul.

Coulson, A.A. (1978) 'Power and decision-making in the primary school', in Richards, C. (ed.) *Power and the Curriculum*. Driffield: Nafferton Books.

Coulson, A.A. (1986) *The Managerial Work of Primary School Head Teachers*, Sheffield Papers in Education Management, No.48, Dept. of Educational Management, Sheffield City Polytechnic.

Coulson, A.A. and Cox, M. (1975) 'What do deputies do?'. *Education 3–13*, **3** (2), 100–3.

Coulter, F. and Taft, R. (1973) 'Professional socialization of teachers as social assimilation'. *Human Relations*, **26**, 681–93.

Day, J. (1977) 'A review of the current state of negotiated order theory: an appreciation and a critique'. *Sociological Quarterly*, **18**, 126–42.

Day, C., Johnson, D. and Whitaker, P. (1985) *Managing Primary Schools*. London: Harper and Row.

Deal, T. (1985) 'The symbolism of effective schools'. *Elementary School Journal*, **85** (3), 601–20.

Deal, T. and Kennedy, A. (1982) *Corporate Cultures*. Reading, Mass.: Addison-Wesley.

Deal, T. and Kennedy, A. (1983) 'Culture and school performance'. *Educational Leadership*, **40** (5), 14–15.

Delamont, S. (1976) *Interaction in the Classroom*. London: Methuen.
DES: Department of Education and Science (1985) *The Curriculum from 5 to 16*. London: HMSO.
DES: Department of Education and Science (1986) *Education Statistics for the United Kingdom*. London: HMSO.
DES: Department of Education and Science (1987) *Primary Schools: Some Aspects of Good Practice; an HMI Publication*. London: HMSO.
Duignan, P. and Macpherson, I. (1987) 'The educative leadership project'. *Educational Management and Administration*, **15**, 49–62.

Elliott, J. (1981) 'The Cambridge accountability project', *Cambridge Journal of Education*, **11**, 146–66.
Elliott, J. *et al.* (1981) *School Accountability*. Oxford: Blackwell.
Etzioni, A. (1964) *Modern Organizations*. Englewood Cliffs, NJ: Prentice-Hall.

Fielder, G. (1968) 'Personality and situational determination of leadership effectiveness', in Cartwright, D. and Zander, A. (eds) *Group Dynamics*, 3rd edition. New York: Harper and Row.
Finch, J. (1986) *Research and Policy: The Uses of Qualitative Research Methods in Social and Educational Research*. Lewes: Falmer Press.
Fordyce, J. and Weil, R. (1971) *Managing with People*. London: Addison-Wesley.
Fullan, M. (1982) *The Meaning of Educational Change*. Columbia University, New York: Teachers College Press.
Fullan, M. (1985) 'Change processes and strategies at the local level'. *Elementary School Journal*, **85** (3), University of Chicago, 391–421.

Gerth, H. and Mills, C.W. (eds) (1946) *From Max Weber: Essays on Sociology*. New York: Oxford University Press.
Glaser, B. and Strauss, A. (1967) *The Discovery of Grounded Theory*. London: Weidenfeld and Nicolson.
Goldsmith, W. and Clutterbuck, D. (1985) *The Winning Streak*. Harmondsworth: Penguin.
Goodacre, E. (1984) 'Postholders and language assertiveness'. *Education 3–13*, **12** (1), 17–21.
Goodchild, S. and Holly, P.J. (1989) *Management for Change: The Garth Hall Experience*. Lewes: Falmer Press.
Goodlad, J. (1975) *The Dynamics of Educational Change: Towards Responsive Schools*. New York: McGraw-Hill.

Halpin, A. (1966) *Theory and Research in Administration*. New York: Macmillan.
Hammersley, M. and Atkinson, P. (1983) *Ethnography: Principles in Practice*. London: Methuen.
Handy, C. (1981) *Understanding Organizations*, 2nd edition. Harmondsworth: Penguin.
Handy, C. (1984) *Taken For Granted? Understanding Schools as Organizations*. York: Schools Council/Longman.
Handy, C. and Aitken, R. (1986) *Understanding Schools as Organizations*. Harmondsworth: Penguin.
Hargreaves, D. (1978) 'Whatever happened to symbolic interactionism?', in Barton, L. and Meighan, R. (eds) *Sociological Interpretations of Schooling and Classrooms*. Driffield: Nafferton Books.
Hargreaves, D. (1982) *The Challenge for the Comprehensive: Culture, Curriculum and Continuity*. London: Routledge and Kegan Paul.
Hartley, D. (1985) *Understanding the Primary School: A Sociological Analysis*. London: Croom Helm.
Heckman, P. (1987) 'Understanding school culture', in Goodlad, J. (ed.) *The Ecology of School Renewal*, 86th Yearbook for the National Society for the Study of Education, Chicago: NSSE.
Heckman, P., Oakes, J. and Sirotnik, K. (1983) 'Expanding the concepts of school renewal and change'. *Educational Leadership*, **40**, 26–32.

Holly, P.J. (1986) ' "Soaring like turkeys": the impossible dream?'. *School Organization*, **6** (3), 346–64.

Holly, P.J. (1987) 'Making it count: evaluation for the developing primary school', in Southworth, G.W. (ed.) *Readings in Primary School Management*. Lewes: Falmer Press.

House of Commons Select Committee (1986) *Achievement in Primary Schools*, Vol. I. London: HMSO.

Hoyle, E. (1986) *The Politics of School Management*. London: Hodder and Stoughton.

Hughes, M. (1985) 'Leadership in professionally staffed organizations', in Hughes, M. *et al.* (eds) *Managing Education: The System and the Institution*. London: Holt, Rinehart and Winston.

ILEA (1985) *Improving Primary Schools*, Report of the Committee on Primary Education. London: ILEA.

Jackson, B. (1964) *Streaming: An Education System in Miniature*. London: Routledge and Kegan Paul.

Jones, A. (1981) *Leadership for Tomorrow's Schools*. Oxford: Blackwell.

Kelman, H.C. (1961) 'Processes of opinion change'. *Public Opinion Quarterly*, **25**, 57–78.

King, R. (1978) *All Things Bright and Beautiful: A Sociological Study of Infant Schools*. Chichester: Wiley.

King, R. (1983) *The Sociology of School Organization*. London: Methuen.

Landau, M. (1969) 'Redundancy, rationality and the problems of duplication and overlap'. *Public Administration Review*, **29**, 346–58.

Lieberman, A. (ed.) (1988) *Building a Professional Culture in Schools*. New York: Teachers' College Press.

Little, J.W. (1982) 'Norms of collegiality and experimentation: workplace conditions of school success'. *American Educational Research Journal*, **19** (3), 325–40.

Little, J.W. (1987) 'Teachers as colleagues', in Koehler, V. (ed.) *Educators' Handbook: A Research Perspective*. New York: Longman.

Little, J.W. (1988) 'Assessing the prospects for teacher leadership', in Lieberman, A. (ed.) *Building a Professional Culture in Schools*. New York: Teachers' College Press.

Little, J.W. (1989) 'Conditions of professional development in secondary schools', in McLaughlin, M. (ed.) *Working Conditions in Secondary Schools*. New York: Teachers' College Press.

Lloyd, K. (1985) 'Management and leadership in the primary school', in Hughes, M. *et al. Managing Education: The System and the Institution*. London: Holt, Rinehart and Winston.

Lortie, D. (1975) *Schoolteacher: A Sociological Study*. Chicago: University of Chicago Press.

McCall, G. and Simmons, J. (eds) (1969) *Issues in Participant Observation*. London: Addison Wesley.

McLaughlin, M. and Yee, S. (1988) 'School as a place to have a career', in Lieberman, A. (ed.) *Building a Professional Culture in Schools*. New York: Teachers' College Press.

McMahon, A., Bolam, R., Abbott, R. and Holly, P.J. (1984) *Guidelines for Review and Internal Development in Schools: Primary School Handbook*. York: Longman/Schools Council.

Manasse, A. (1985) 'Improving conditions for principal effectiveness: policy implications of research'. *Elementary School Journal* **85** (3), 439–63.

Mintzberg, H. (1973) *The Nature of Managerial Work*. New York: Harper and Row.

Miskel, C. and Cosgrove, D. (1985) 'Leadership succession in school settings', *Review of Educational Research*, **55** (1), 87–105.

Mortimore, P., Sammons, P., Stoll, L., Lewis, D. and Ecob, R. (1988) *School Matters: The Junior Years*. Wells: Open Books.

Myer, J. (1987) 'The first year of primary headship', unpublished report for Cambridgeshire LEA.

Nias, J. (1980) 'Leadership styles and job satisfaction in primary schools', in Bush, T. *et al.* (eds) *Approaches to School Management*. London: Harper and Row.

Nias, J. (1981) 'The nature of trust', in Elliott, J. *et al. School Accountability*. Oxford: Blackwell.

Nias, J. (1984) 'The definition and maintenance of self in primary teaching'. *British Journal of Sociology of Education*, **5**, 167–80.

Nias, J. (1986) 'Lowmeadow Nursery and Infant School: a case study of co-operation'. Cambridge: Cambridge Institute of Education, mimeo.

Nias, J. (1987a) 'Learning from difference: a collegial approach to change', in Smyth, W.J. (ed.) *Changing the Nature of Pedagogical Knowledge*. Lewes: Falmer Press.

Nias, J. (1987b) 'One finger, one thumb: a case study of the deputy head's part in the leadership of a nursery/infant school', in Southworth, G.W. (ed.) *Readings in Primary School Management*. Lewes: Falmer Press.

Nias, J. (1987c) 'The Primary School Staff Relationships Project: origins, aims and methods'. *Cambridge Journal of Education*, **17** (2), 83–5.

Nias, J. (1989a) Refining the 'cultural perspective', *Cambridge Journal of Education*, **19**, 2.

Nias, J. (1989b) *Primary Teachers Talking: A Study of Teaching as Work*. London: Routledge.

Nias, J. (1989c) 'Meeting together: the symbolic and pedagogic importance of school assemblies within a collaborative culture', Paper presented to Annual Conference of the American Educational Research Association, San Francisco.

Open University (1981) 'Policy making, organization and leadership in schools', Block 4, *Management and the School*, Course E324. Milton Keynes: Open University Press.

Open University (1988) 'Leadership and decision-making in schools', Block 2, E325, *Managing Schools*; (Part 2 Management Roles and Responsibilities: the Primary School). Milton Keynes: Open University Press.

Parlett, M. and Hamilton, D. (1977) 'Evaluation as illumination: a new approach and the study of innovatory programmes', in Hamilton, D. (ed.) *Beyond the Numbers Game*. London: Macmillan.

Peters, T. and Austin, N. (1985) *A Passion for Excellence: The Leadership Difference*. London: Collins.

Peters, T. and Waterman, R. (1982) *In Search of Excellence: Lessons from America's Best-Run Companies*. New York: Harper and Row.

Pollard, A. (1985) *The Social World of the Primary School*. London: Cassell.

Pollard, A. (1987) 'Primary school teachers and their colleagues', in Delamont, S. (ed.) *The Primary School Teacher*. Lewes: Falmer Press.

Reid, K., Hopkins, D. and Holly, P. (1987) *Towards the Effective School*. Oxford: Blackwell.

Richards, C. (1986) 'The curriculum from 5 to 16'. *Education 3–13*, **14**, 3–8.

Riches, C. (1984) 'The management of nonteaching staff in a school: a methodological exploration', in Goulding, S. *et al.* (eds) *Case Studies in Educational Management*. London: Harper and Row.

Rosenholtz, S. (1985) 'Effective schools: interpreting the evidence'. *American Journal of Education*, May, 352–88.

Sarason, S. (1971; 2nd edition 1982) *The Culture of the School and the Problem of Change*. Boston: Allyn and Bacon.

Schatzman, L. and Strauss, A. (1973) *Field Research: Strategies for a Naturalistic Sociology*. Englewood Cliffs: Prentice-Hall.

Schein, E.H. (1985) *Organizational Culture and Leadership*. San Francisco: Jossey-Bass.

Selznick, P. (1957) *Leadership in Administration: A Sociological Interpretation*. New York: Harper and Row.

Sergiovanni, T.J. and Corbally, J.E. (eds) (1984) *Leadership and Organizational Culture*. Chicago: University of Illinois Press.

Sharp, R. and Green, A. (1975) *Education and Social Control: A Study in Progressive Primary Education*. London: Routledge and Kegan Paul.

Silverman, D. (1970) *The Theory of Organizations*. London: Heinemann.

Smith, L. and Keith, P. (1971) *Anatomy of Educational Innovation: An Organizational Analysis of an Elementary School*. New York: Wiley.

Southworth, G.W. (1986) 'A community called Greenfields: a case study of a primary school'. Cambridge: Cambridge Institute of Education, mimeo.

Southworth, G.W. (1987a) 'Primary school headteachers and collegiality', in Southworth, G.W. (ed.) *Readings in Primary School Management*. Lewes: Falmer Press.

Southworth, G.W. (1987b) 'Staff selection or by appointment? A case study of the appointment of a teacher to a primary school', in Southworth, G.W. (ed.) *Readings in Primary School Management*. Lewes: Falmer Press.

Southworth, G. (1987c) 'The experience of fieldwork: or insider dealings, who profits?'. *Cambridge Journal of Education*, **17** (2), 86–8.

Southworth, G.W. and Myer, J. (1988) 'Follow my leader'. *Education*, **171** (9), 186.

Stenhouse, L. (1975) *An Introduction to Curriculum Research and Development*. London: Heinemann.

Stenhouse, L. (1983) *Authority, Emancipation and Education*. London: Heinemann.

Taylor, P. (1986) *Expertise and the Primary Teacher*. Slough: NFER-Nelson.

Thomas, N. (1987) 'Team spirit'. *Child Education*, **January**, 10–11.

Tomlinson, J. (1986) 'Primary education: the way ahead'. *Primary Education Review*, **24**, 2–3.

Walker, R. (1986) *Doing Research: A Handbook for Teachers*. London: Methuen.

Waller, W. (1932; 1961 edn) *The Sociology of the School*. New York: Russell and Russell.

Waters, D. (1987) 'Deputy as trainee head', in Craig, I. (ed.) *Primary School Management in Action*. London: Longman.

Whitaker, P. (1983) *The Primary Head*. London: Heinemann.

Woods, P. (1981) 'Strategies, commitment and identity: making and breaking the teacher role', in Barton, L. and Walker, S. (eds) *Schools, Teachers and Teaching*. Lewes: Falmer Press.

Woods, P. (1983) *Sociology and the School: An Interactionist Viewpoint*. London: Routledge and Kegan Paul.

Yeomans, R. (1985) 'Are primary teachers primarily people?'. *Education 3–13*, **13** (2), 6–11.

Yeomans, R. (1986a) 'A different way of dancing'. *Cambridge Journal of Education*, **16**, 216–20.

Yeomans, R. (1986b) 'Hearing secret harmonies', paper presented to Annual Conference of British Educational Research Association. Bristol.

Yeomans, R. (1986c) 'The Sedgemoor way: a case study of inter-adult relationships at Sedgemoor Primary School'. Cambridge: Cambridge Institute of Education, mimeo.

Yeomans, R. (1987a) 'Becoming a good school: a case study of Hutton Junior School'. Cambridge: Cambridge Institute of Education, mimeo.

Yeomans, R. (1987b) 'Checking and adjusting the lens: case study clearance'. *Cambridge Journal of Education*, **17** (2), 88–9.

Yeomans, R. (1987c) 'Getting to know you: a case study of Lavender Way First School'. Cambridge: Cambridge Institute of Education, mimeo.

Yukl, G. (1975) 'Towards a behavioural theory of leadership', in Houghton, V. *et al. The Management of Organization and Individuals*. London: Ward Lock Educational.

Name Index

Subject Index